PRAISE FOl
TO RAISING ⌐NS

"Douglas Haddad delivers parents a no fail app. ⌐ raising children. If you could read only one book to help children become successful and reach their unlimited potential, *The Ultimate Guide to Raising Teens and Tweens* has everything you need and is the one to get!" —**Jack Canfield**, multiple #1 *New York Times* and *USA Today* best-selling coauthor of *Chicken Soup for the Soul* ® series; success coach; and human potential thought leader

"Dr. Doug's tools for the 3 S's are a MUST for all parents! There are so many challenges that children deal with these days, and Dr. Doug truly gets it! His advice will help you gain the confidence you need to handle problems effectively and make the right choices so you can help your child succeed in every way." —**Marci Shimoff**, #1 *New York Times* best-selling author of *Happy For No Reason, Love for No Reason, Chicken Soup for the Woman's Soul*

"This book is a window into Dr. Haddad's world of practical insights, methods, and tools that have made him a highly effective teacher. As Simsbury's 2016 Teacher of the Year, Dr. Haddad's passion for science, his fun and engaging teaching style, and his results in the classroom make him stand out among the best." —**Matthew Curtis**, superintendent of Simsbury Public Schools in Connecticut

"If creating a more fulfilling relationship with your children and seeing them grow into inspired and empowered individuals where they are living a productive and meaningful life in highest accordance with their highest values are your goals, then applying the tools found within *The Ultimate Guide to Raising Teens and Tweens* can certainly bring you those results." —**John Demartini**, DC, international best-selling author of *The Values Factor*; educator and human behavioral specialist

"Dr. Haddad's generous, highly readable new book *The Ultimate Guide to Raising Teens and Tweens* could not be more appropriately titled. Through anecdotes and research, Doug thoroughly walks parents through the importance of empathy and strength in parenting in order to foster a 'smart, successful, self-disciplined' child. He then comprehensively takes on each of the critical challenges and pitfalls faced by today's teens and tweens from drug use to sexuality and beyond. I cannot recommend the book enough. You will find it to be an invaluable and urgent read today, as well as an important reference for many years to come." —**John Duffy**, PhD, #1 best-selling author of *The Available Parent* as featured on Steve Harvey

"Dr. Haddad has been an instrumental contributor to *Parenting Special Needs* Magazine for more than six years. He is an exceptional writer who never fails to deliver positive, extremely well-written articles that contain information, knowledge, and experience that benefit parents and their children. He is a valued and valuable member of this special needs community." — **Chantai Snellgrove**, founder/ editorial director, *Parenting Special Needs* Magazine

"Thanks to Dr. Haddad's vision, advice, and knowledge in educational technology and understanding the market, our company has been able to successfully introduce and market the Forbrain product at a global level. Dr. Haddad has been a great education ambassador for us and has been instrumental in helping our company grow." —**Gregoire Tomatis**, cofounder of Sound for Life, Ltd.; director at Tomatis Développement S.A.

"Today's parents have a good idea of the challenges they face in trying to guide their children through the hazardous tween-teen years. From cyberspace to drugs, from sexuality to motivation, from eating disorders to depression—successfully negotiating these years so as to emerge a physically, emotionally, and psychologically healthy adult is a daunting task for these children and their parents. Dr. Haddad provides parents with a road map for facing those tasks. Practical advice is what these parents seek, and practical advice is what they will find here. In a veritable tour of these crucial years, parents learn valuable information, presented concisely in plain language, as well as crucial advice—the do's and don'ts that can make the difference between success and failure." —**Joseph Nowinski**, PhD, author of *The Divorced Child: Strengthening Your Family through the First Three Years of Separation*

"A thoughtful, authoritative, and practical guide that will help parents guide their children through the tween and teenage years." —**Carl Honoré**, author of *Under Pressure: Putting the Child Back in Childhood*

"Douglas Haddad has written a comprehensive 'how-to' for parents—specifically for those whose children are in or nearing the 'tweens and teens.' Because these are such formative and potentially difficult years for parents, Dr. Haddad presents very practical and workable solutions to the parenting issues of our day in a manner that can be assimilated into virtually any family scenario. This is a 'manual' that can soften some of the harsh blows of these ages when families are committed to developing successful and contributing adults to America's future." —**Tom Ziglar**, CEO, Ziglar, Inc.

"Douglas Haddad, PhD, affectionately known as Dr. Doug, brings his years of experience to one of the most critical challenges facing parents: how to raise smart, successful, and self-disciplined children. Our children's worlds are full of amazing opportunity and daunting dangers. Hazards like drugs or bullying, violence or despair, may cause a premature exit on this path to a fulfilling and productive life for our children. Helping to navigate this developmental highway is the privilege of the parent. Focusing on tweens and teens, Dr. Doug provides concise and practical strategies and exercises that engage parents and their children, building relationships, and paving the path to a productive future." —**Joseph Shrand**, MD, Chief of Adolescent Psychiatry, High Point Treatment Centers; medical director, CASTLE

"In *The Ultimate Guide to Raising Teens and Tweens*, Dr. Haddad asks the important questions that we need to be asking both ourselves as parents, as well as ourselves as a society in how we raise the next generation. Navigating parenthood without a manual is a mix of trial and error, underscored by our own fears and patterning. *The Ultimate Guide to Raising Teens and Tweens* acts as that guide, with sound research, questions that get us to challenge our current ways of raising kids, and straightforward steps and solutions. I highly, highly recommend all parents read this. This is my new parenting handbook." —**Kate O'Brien**, Voice for Empowered Feminine Leadership; creator of GameChanger and founder of GameChanger Global Summit

"I've seen Dr. Doug on television discussing different educational tools to engage learning, motivation, and keeping a child's mind active. He understands the child and realizes how important interactive technology is both at home and in the classroom." —**Stephanie Jimenez**, senior account executive, SSPR Public Relations Agency

The Ultimate Guide to Raising Teens and Tweens

Strategies for Unlocking Your Child's Full Potential

Douglas Haddad

ROWMAN & LITTLEFIELD
Lanham · Boulder · New York · London

Published by Rowman & Littlefield
A wholly owned subsidiary of The Rowman & Littlefield Publishing Group, Inc.
4501 Forbes Boulevard, Suite 200, Lanham, Maryland 20706
www.rowman.com

Unit A, Whitacre Mews, 26-34 Stannary Street, London SE11 4AB

Distributed by NATIONAL BOOK NETWORK

British Library Cataloguing in Publication Information Available

Library of Congress Cataloguing-in-Publication Data

Names: Haddad, Douglas, 1976– author.
Title: The Ultimate Guide to Raising Teens and Tweens : Strategies for Unlocking Your Child's Full Potential / Douglas Haddad.
Description: Lanham : Rowman & Littlefield, [2017] | Includes bibliographical references and index.
Identifiers: LCCN 2016025359 | ISBN 9781442256958 (cloth : alk. paper)
Subjects: LCSH: Home and school. | Parent and teenager. | Parent and child. | Education—Parent participation. | Parenting.
Classification: LCC LC225 .H23 2017 | DDC 373.236—dc23 LC record available at https://lccn.loc.gov/2016025359

♾️™ The paper used in this publication meets the minimum requirements of American National Standard for Information Sciences—Permanence of Paper for Printed Library Materials, ANSI/NISO Z39.48-1992.

Printed in the United States of America

This book is dedicated to Mary Glendening and Patty-Lou Peters, who demonstrated unwavering passion and dedication for the success of all children.

Contents

Disclaimer

The Ultimate Guide to Raising Teens and Tweens: Strategies for Unlocking Your Child's Full Potential is intended to provide helpful and informative material for parents to understand the major issues and challenges that school-aged children may encounter and provide solutions for parents to help guide their child to achieve overall wellness. This book does not provide medical advice. One must consult a medical or health professional before engaging in any new exercise, nutrition, supplementation, or wellness program. The author specifically disclaims all responsibility for any liability or losses, personal or otherwise, that occur as a consequence, directly or indirectly, of the use and application of any of the information that is provided in this book. Names in the book that are italicized have been changed to protect confidentiality.

Acknowledgments

This book is the culmination of a team effort of individuals who in their own special way supported me along this journey. I extend my deepest gratitude and thanks to the following:

The Lord, Jesus Christ. Your love is patient. Your love is kind. Thank you for being the example that love goes beyond words or tongue and speaks volumes in actions and in truth. Thank you for always being there and guiding me through the mysteries of life.

Laura Haddad, my wife. Thank you for providing incredible support for this project and working with me from conception of this book, through countless edits, and contributing to the overall evolution of this book. Thank you for all of your patience and support throughout this project and throughout all of my endeavors.

Michael and Donna Haddad, my parents. Joseph and Clare Petrucelli, my grandparents. Joseph J. Petrucelli, my uncle and godfather. In writing this book, I thought about how grateful and appreciative I am for all the unconditional love and support you provided me while growing up and how that has shaped and impacted me throughout my life. Your genuine love and caring nature, along with the appropriate *limits* that you set for me while growing up, has allowed me to reach *unlimited* heights in anything I choose to pursue in life. Thank you for being with me every step of the way throughout my life and allowing me to have dreams and fulfill them!

Linda Konner, my literary agent for this project. Thank you for your belief in me and this book and all of your editorial revisions to help polish the proposal. I appreciate and admire your professionalism, encouragement, and patience throughout this entire process. It is because of your unrelenting determination, after we encountered some unexpected bumps in the road along the way, that this book ultimately found a home.

Suzanne Staszak-Silva, the executive editor, Kathryn Knigge, the associate editor, Rae-Ann Goodwin, the copyeditor at Rowman & Littlefield, and the entire editing and marketing team. Thank you for your professionalism, your concentrated efforts and sincere desire to make a difference in a child's life, and for deciding to work with me on this project and publish this book.

Joseph Schrank, my department supervisor, mentor, and good friend. Thank you for your belief in me and being more than just my boss at work for the past fifteen years. Your constant emotional support, enthusiastic encouragement, wisdom, guidance, friendship, and leadership, by example, with parents, colleagues, and students have inspired me and allowed me to grow in my work with children all these years.

All of the middle school students that I taught at Henry James Memorial School in Simsbury, Connecticut. Thank you for allowing me to be a part of your lives as more than just a teacher and opening up to me about your concerns and expressing what matters most to you in life. Thank you for putting up with the dances of joy and the different science songs and music videos that I made you listen to, watch, and sometimes sing. It was all to unleash and expand into realms beyond what you may have thought to be possible. Thank you for teaching me how to "get out of the way" and let you grow, while still being there to help guide and support you along your life journeys.

My colleagues at work—past and present. Thank you for being the best group of educators on the planet and leading by example, starting at the top with highly supportive administration and teachers who provide environments conducive to help children reach their unlimited potential day in and day out.

Parents of the students that I taught. Thank you for your support over the years and allowing me to connect with your children. I greatly appreciate your willingness and open mindedness to allow me to impart my philosophies of life onto your child. How children first learn to be successful is through your guidance. The goal of this book is rooted in helping you form a lasting, loving connection with your children and to help guide them toward achieving self-mastery and ultimate fulfillment in life.

A portion of the proceeds from this book will go to Educated Canines Assisting with Disabilities, a nonprofit organization that provides service dogs to individuals with disabilities.

Introduction

Forget the Three R's! Why
You Must Instill the Three S's in Your Child

It was 6:30 a.m., the usual time I arrived at school each day. I turned on my computer and went through my morning routine of posting the day's homework assignment on our school's homework page and updating the online grading portal so the parents and students could see the grades. I also scanned a handout for that day's lesson into my Elmo document camera for parents and students to have available for download in my Google Classroom. To boot, I opened up the SMART Board and created a review game for an upcoming unit test.

I thought to myself how lucky kids are today, with all the technology available and the dynamic, interactive lessons they receive on pretty much a daily basis. While certainly an advocate for technology as a resource for learning, I stopped and questioned how technology has affected today's generation of kids.

Before the students arrived in my classroom that morning, I also checked my e-mail. Ironically, I noticed the subject line of an e-mail sent to me by one of my colleagues was titled "To Those of Us Born 1930–1979." As I was reading through it, I couldn't believe how quickly things have changed in our society within a relatively short time span.

Growing up, we didn't have Playstation, Wii, or Xbox. There wasn't any Instagram, Facebook, Twitter, YouTube, or even Internet for that matter. No tablets or "smart" gadgets were around to occupy our attention. We went out and made friends and played outside for hours at a time and no one was able to reach us with a text or a phone call.

We made tree houses, fell out of trees, got cut, broke bones, and chipped teeth. There weren't any lawsuits from those accidents. If I got into trouble at school, my parents would find out and I would also be punished at home—twice as bad.

We ate all kinds of food and didn't have problems with being overweight or obese. We rode bicycles or walked to a friend's house and knocked on the door or rang the doorbell. Sometimes, we just walked inside if the door was left open.

My friend and I shot BB guns in his backyard when we were little and didn't hurt anyone or turn into deranged killers. Not everyone made a sports team. Those who were cut had to learn to deal with disappointment. The statement at the end of the e-mail summed it all up by saying, "If YOU are one of them, CONGRATULATIONS!"

It is undeniable that the character of American schoolchildren, as a whole, has changed dramatically over the decades. Back in the 1950s, the biggest discipline problems involved talking in class and chewing gum. In the 1970s, it was rather common for kids to have pocket knives in high school without anyone raising an eyebrow, concerned that someone was going to be stabbed. During hunting season, some kids would even walk into school with their rifles, some from hunting that morning, some who were going hunting right after school. No one back then considered that a student could possibly stab or open fire and shoot, if not kill, fellow classmates and teachers. If you got caught showing off or playing with a weapon in public, the extent to your punishment was a stern lecture from the principal, but that's about it.

Because of the highly publicized events of the last couple of decades, spurred in large part by the Sandy Hook tragedy and other school shootings that followed, many school districts around the country are reinforcing zero-tolerance policies on the possession of weapons on school grounds. A kindergartener in Pennsylvania was suspended for referring to "shooting" a friend with a Hello Kitty bubble-making gun. A second grader in Maryland was suspended for biting a Pop-Tart into a gun shape. So, why have school rules become bizarrely strict where unintentional or minor offenses have ended in severe punishments? You would think that school administrators would have more discretion in these cases.

It's not all that simple. Because of the highly litigious society in which we live today, teachers and administrators have to take all matters seriously. As a middle school teacher, I am used to hearing all kinds of silly comments spewing from kids. Certain comments cannot be ignored or brushed off as simply "kids just being kids" anymore.

Discipline at school had always been handled by principals and teachers. But today, we see more school resource officers as permanent fixtures roaming the hallways in schools. Students are being arrested for incidents involving cursing, bad attitudes, and defiant behavior. There are even parents across the United States who receive fines or jail time over their child's unexcused truancies.

Between the years of 2000 and 2013, the Berks County school district in Pennsylvania had over 1,600 people, mainly mothers, imprisoned for failing to pay truancy fines.[1] Tragically, a woman died while serving jail time for her children's unexcused absences. How have we gotten to this point of paranoia where our public schools are being run like prisons? And not only children but parents are paying a heavy price. We must ask ourselves, "Are these tactics solving today's problems and helping prevent these kinds of issues from taking place?"

We are also witnessing today that kids are capable of violence to themselves and to others in a way that didn't happen to children of previous generations. Why are some kids stabbing and shooting their classmates and teachers? When did kids begin considering making bombs? When did teenagers start "cutting" themselves?

It may seem harsh to proclaim this cohort of children as the "generation without restraint," but the coalescence of all of society's influences has driven this group of kids to become *unlimited* in the sense that they can see anything and everything, whenever they want, and they are getting what they want right away! They have been coined "over the top" in just about all meanings of the phrase. We see them taking it to the extremes in terms of what and where they text, send pictures, and share videos on social media.

Keeping up with the latest trends in pop culture and all that is going on within the different social networking websites is no easy feat and takes on double duty for today's parent. Today's tweens and teens are not only concerned about face-to-face interactions with their peers but also worried about embarrassing photos, mean information, or rumors being spread about them and seen by "everyone" online. Many are in constant "follow wars" and compete against their peers to see who can get more followers on Instagram, without taking into consideration the dangers in sharing their personal information with strangers who may be posing as someone they really aren't. And that's just for starters!

We often hear the all too familiar narrative that "kids today aren't what they used to be." I find that every generation of kids is criticized for something or other. If we go back to examine the press reports in the 1930s, the interpretation of "The Greatest Generation" isn't so great after all:

"This is a generation, numbering in the millions, that has gone so far in decay that it acts without thought of social responsibility."

"They are youth gone loco: Villain is marijuana."

"Drug-crazed teens have murdered entire families!"

"High-school kids are armed and dangerous. Watch out for what they can get."

"This generation of kids is rotting before our eyes."[2]

According to many journalists at the time, the kids of the 1990s were considered the "worst generation appearing apathetic, asocial and coldly murderous."[3] At the time, Governor Gray Davis of California proposed a mandatory community service for college students, so they could regain their sense of the future and get back to the ethics earlier in the century.

We can't deny the fact that today we are faced with challenges that didn't exist in past generations of children. First off, more kids these days are growing up in single-parent households than ever before. Many single parents struggle to provide basic necessities for their children and themselves. They are constantly trying to make ends meet, which requires more time working and less time supervising and raising their children. This, in turn, translates into an elevated risk of their child partaking in unsafe behaviors.

Children today are also living a less-active lifestyle and spending an excessive amount of time playing video games, texting with their friends, sitting around and surfing the Internet, listening to music on their "iThis" or "iThat," and watching television from channels 1 to 5,000 for hours at a time. As we've seen, this sedentary lifestyle has caused an increase in more overweight and obese kids than ever before in history. It's gone beyond just physical ramifications from too much technology. This pandemic has resulted in some far-reaching social, emotional, and physical concerns that didn't exist even a decade ago.

Over the past seventeen years as a middle school teacher, I have also noticed that handwriting, spelling, math, and overall problem-solving skills have gotten far worse. Despite the increased rigor and testing aligned with the Common Core State Standards given to many students these days, most states don't require children to learn cursive writing anymore. Instead, many kids are learning keyboarding skills starting in kindergarten. Yes, I realize that we live in a fast-paced, ever-changing, technology-driven society, but even though many children use computers to write papers at home, most writing done within the confines of the classroom is still by hand.

Among all the problems that exist today, parents fear for their child's safety at school more than ever. According to research conducted by Everytown for Gun Safety Support Fund, following in the wake of the Sandy Hook Elementary School tragedy, there has been a dramatic increase in school violence resulting in injuries and death from over 150 school shootings, whereas the number of school shootings that took place over the entire first decade of the twenty-first century was less than a third of that figure.[4]

Is it fair to blame this generation of children for all these emerging problems and point our fingers at them for their mal-intended behaviors? Instead, we should work to come up with solutions to these issues by looking outside at the world around us to see what factors are triggering these kinds of behaviors.

Taking the time to recognize that we are in the midst of a kid crisis is an important first step in making a change. Children nowadays are exposed to sexualization, especially of younger and younger girls, and dramatized violence in the media, obscene language during online video gaming, and cyberbullying on multiple social media outlets.

I have also noticed how children today are losing out on opportunities to develop *resiliency skills* in learning how to handle adversity face-to-face. I've asked myself the question, "Are tweens and teens nowadays more *illiterate* than *e-literate*?" Has technology come so far and so fast as to significantly decrease a child's social skills, attention span, problem-solving ability, and overall well-being?

Presuming that children will navigate their way through the tween and teen years on their own, unscathed, with limited or no parental guidance to successfully overcome adversity with constant distractions always looming is naive, wishful thinking, and downright unfair to a child. You may have heard the popular adage "It takes a village to raise a child." Each person a child encounters, while growing up, certainly has some degree of influence on a child's life. However, it is the *parents/guardians* who are the most important, influential, and responsible people in a child's life. They impact a child's safety, feelings, overall well-being, and the decisions a child makes throughout the formative years.

Although the journey through the tween and teen years can be smooth at times, it is throughout these years that many changes take place in your child's life—for good and bad. New friendships are developed and decisions are made that shape and impact the rest of their lives.

At some point or another, your child will seek your help and ask you for advice on how to cope with a crisis and how to make important decisions. You can't solve all of your child's problems for them, and quite frankly, you shouldn't! There are certain things that are in your control and other things that will never be. But how you help foster your child's emotions, encourage communication, and handle the inevitable adolescent crisis when it hits—and it will hit—will shape your child's ability to handle adversity, react to difficult situations as they arise, and gain healthy lifestyle habits that become internalized over the long run.

Not every child will overtly tell you what's on his or her mind. For that matter, at times it may seem like your child is avoiding you like the plague when it comes to having a discussion about anything. Wise parents help successfully foster a child's emotions and encourage communication and self-expression through patience and understanding. They help children gain healthy lifestyle habits that become internalized to their identities.

I've written this book to provide you with the essential tools you will need to help you make that transition from sole decision maker and manager to a supportive facilitator in helping to successfully guide your child through turbulent waters and to set appropriate *limits* as they grow to become *unlimited* in their potential as smart, successful, and self-disciplined individuals.

In order to successfully support and guide your child as they encounter adversity, defeat, failure, and peer pressure, it is important that you possess specific strategies to fall back on when things get rough. Be confident in the knowledge that your children will not merely survive their adolescent years but also thrive during them and use the skills they are taught when faced with different challenges throughout their lives.

I've worked with children from a wide variety of socioeconomic and ethnic backgrounds, coming from a vast array of family dynamics. The chapters in this book are formulated with a specific vision in mind—to help strengthen the connection with your children and build confidence in them to overcome challenges through this critical developmental phase that they will carry with them into adulthood.

During the tween and teen years, I personally encountered challenges that at the time seemed insurmountable and never-ending. I didn't understand why many of my peers would attempt to bring down my confidence and make me feel less valued. I used to ask myself, "What did I do to deserve having awful pictures drawn of me and placed all over the school?" Thank goodness there weren't any social media networks back then to share those pictures with the masses. But the reality is that there is some child out there right now who is experiencing these kinds of challenges and having to cope with a crisis of this nature each and every day.

I used to worry about making friends so I didn't have to sit by myself eating lunch. I also wondered how I could stand up for myself so kids would stop calling me names or beating me up. Until children are taught the tools to become unlimited in their potential through developing a sense of purpose and forming a positive identity, these kinds of issues will continue to exist.

Have you ever thought about your role as parent and how much influence and impact you have on your child's life path? While there are conflicting educational theories about who ultimately has the biggest influence on a child—parents, teachers, peers, or other influential figures in the media—I will say that I had some unforgettable teachers growing up who made a remarkable difference in shaping my life. I also had a couple of close friends growing up who I enjoyed spending time with, sharing secrets with, playing with on a regular basis, and who were there to listen and be supportive during difficult times with other peers.

As for my parents and grandparents, their roles were monumental in how I was able to survive and navigate through childhood and adolescence and successfully into adulthood. They have been the one consistent and outstanding source of support for me during the milestone achievements of my life, as well as throughout the tumultuous transitions from childhood all the way to adulthood.

In elementary school, I learned how to handle verbal and physical assault from kids in the neighborhood and daily interactions with bullying on the school bus. During the middle school years, I was trying to find ways to stop being the butt of what seemed like everyone's jokes and being excluded from social groups. In high school, I endured being an outcast by most of the players on the basketball team that I played on, including the coach. Through it all, my parents were there to provide me with the proper guidance and stability to flourish and rise above any and all adversity as I encountered challenges throughout childhood and adolescence.

Parents, like no one else, can ingrain certain intangible qualities into their children. Through their emotional support, love, acceptance, understanding, wisdom, patience, and regular involvement in my life, my parents have greatly shaped who I have become today and who I will be as I continue to evolve as a person throughout my life.

The main reason I chose to write this book is to honor your neverending, exhausting, sometimes thankless and ultimately rewarding job as a parent. My goal is to help make your life easier and your relationship with your child a stronger one by providing a set of practical, empowering tools to help guide you through weathering the "sensational storm" that is adolescence and unlock your child's full potential. There may be times when you are faced with situations that feel out of control. Your child may be attempting to overtake the power in the household, talk back to you, not do their homework, fail to follow the rules, make poor choices with peers, and/or display risky behaviors, which could be the start of bigger problems down the road.

The topics throughout this book relate to helping you best handle these situations and raise your child during one of the most turbulent phases of his or her life. In part 1 of the book, you are provided with ten "Child Unlimited" strategies needed to simplify parenting in this fast-paced, technology-driven, complex world. The specific strategies will help you handle frustrating situations and gain a lasting connection with your child, while helping prepare him or her for an adulthood filled with unlimited possibilities.

In part 2, you will learn about the top ten "Child Limiting" issues that your child is exposed to today, including the perils of escalated violence at schools, increased exposure to sexualization and dramatized violence in the media, cyberbullying, misuse of social media, body-image issues, depression leading to higher suicide rates among today's youth, and traditional addictive behaviors that continue to persist such as gambling, sex, alcohol, smoking, and drugs, and what you can do to prevent these issues from limiting your child's future.

The information provided in this book is the result of scientific research and firsthand practical experience incorporating successful solutions that I have implemented for over seventeen years while working as an educator to customize specific academic, behavioral, and health plans for children from a variety of backgrounds.

Throughout each chapter, specific prevention and intervention strategies are provided: *preventatives*—used before situations turn ugly; and *interventions*—used when a problem has already taken hold of you and/or your child.

In order to effectively encourage desirable behavior from your child, practice what you preach on a regular basis. The basic rule of thumb is to live a lifestyle as if your child were watching your every move, because that is, in fact, what is happening. *Your child is always on the lookout* and taking what they see and hear and applying it to the decisions they make in life.

While working with tween and teen children all these years, I've noticed three common skills that adolescents must possess to become adults who are *SMART, SUCCESSFUL, and SELF-DISCIPLINED*: the three S's.

1. Young people must be good *problem solvers*. They need to learn how to set meaningful goals, map out a plan to achieve their goals, and develop resiliency skills to persevere through adversity.
2. Young people must be able to effectively *communicate* their emotions and talk about their problems with trusting adults.
3. Young people must learn and practice *coping mechanisms* that are non-destructive and emphasize self-responsibility.

One fact is for certain: your children will experience many different things throughout tween and teenhood. But how they react to different situations and the choices they make can be largely influenced through three powerful parenting practices:

1. sagacious decisions made via your parenting techniques,
2. quality time you spend with your child, and
3. genuine care, interest, patience, and support exhibited toward your child throughout his or her life.

You are the captain of this ship steering you and your child through calm and stormy seas, helping to build your child's self-esteem, and feeling genuinely happy throughout the course of the exploration. Let's begin our voyage and set sail into uncharted waters. The most effective ways to parent are from a position of strength, making this a pleasant, unforgettable experience that will be equally fulfilling for you and your child for a lifetime.

"In a hundred years, it will not matter what my bank account was, the type of house I lived in, or the kinds of clothes I wore, but the world may be much different because I was important in the life of a child."

—ANONYMOUS

I

TEN "CHILD UNLIMITED" TOOLS FOR UNLOCKING YOUR CHILD'S FULL POTENTIAL

• 1 •

Use Empathy and Consequences

"You can accomplish by kindness what you cannot by force."

—Publilius Syrus (Latin writer)

It was about ten minutes before the bell was going to ring for lunch. The students in my seventh grade science class were quietly copying down notes from the SMART Board™ into their notebook. I was explaining to them the differences between carbohydrates, lipids, and proteins. It was right before lunch time and I asked a few of the students what they were going to eat to see how much energy, in calories, they were about to consume.

One student's reply was, "I don't know. Whatever my Mom gave me today for lunch."

Another student said, "Whatever they serve up in the cafe."

And yet another student just shrugged his shoulders at me, without a clue.

Then I asked, "Does anyone know what they are eating today or is it all a big mystery?"

All of a sudden from nowhere I heard "*POP!*" It was the sound of a student blowing a gigantic-sized bubble from a piece of gum. The bell rang and the students were dismissed to have lunch. I asked the girl who had made the loud-sounding pop to see me before she left for lunch.

Chewing gum was against the school rules and this was not the first time that I had caught her doing this in class. I had told her to spit out the gum a number of times before and threatened to give her a detention, but never actually followed through on it. I quickly learned that my repeated warnings and lectures had no meaning to her whatsoever. Each time I made those empty threats, my power was being stripped away from me. At that point, I came to the realization that when I say "no," it should mean "no" if I were to

3

see a change in her behavior. It was time for the girl to learn a lesson from the poor choices that she was repeatedly making in class.

At that moment, I issued her an office detention that she was required to serve for an hour and a half after school later in the week. When I handed her the slip, she immediately shouted at me, "Are you kidding me? This rule is so stupid!" She continued by saying, "Why are you giving me a detention for something so dumb like this? My parents aren't going to sign this. I'm not serving it!"

The following morning I received an e-mail from her mother mentioning how she couldn't believe that I had given her daughter a detention for something "so stupid." The mother did not support my decision to give her daughter a detention. She believed that not letting her child chew gum in the classroom was a "stupid rule" that she hated when she was in school. She stated curtly that my decision was wrong and told me that she refused to sign the detention slip.

She fought the consequence tooth and nail with me for the next several days, demanding me to retract the detention. When I finally told her that the consequence was the natural result of her child choosing to break a school rule and the decision would stand, she went on to take matters to administration to get the detention revoked. Her incessant persistence got her what she wanted, or so she thought, at the moment. The detention was, in fact, rescinded.

What appeared to be a victory at that moment for the mother and her daughter was actually the start of much bigger problems to come. The mother's decision to abandon responsibility of her child's blatant disregard for school rules caused her to lose out on a golden opportunity to teach her child a valuable lesson for this infraction, albeit a minor one.

A few weeks after the gum incident, our team of teachers noticed some significant negative academic and behavior changes in the student and decided to request a meeting with her mother. At the meeting, Mom candidly expressed her frustrations in which she was losing control of her daughter and becoming increasingly upset with her behaviors. She expressed how she tried so many tactics, each one harsher than the other, and still was unable to get her daughter to listen to and follow the rules.

The mother's decision to take the side of her daughter for breaking the rules provoked a cascade of graver problems to come that I'm sure was not something she expected would happen. As time passed, the girl was getting herself into bigger trouble at school with other teachers, hanging out with the wrong group of peers, and letting her grades slip. Ultimately, Mom's actions gave her daughter the green light to keep making poor choices and preventing the girl from learning from her mistakes.

What had happened was the daughter resented her mother's "authority" and problems continued to arise between the two of them. A vicious circle had developed at this point when the parent became increasingly angry and delivered harsher consequences, out of desperation for control, which triggered further disobedient behavior by her child.

With all the teachers and the mother at that meeting, we called the girl in to sit down with all of us to hear what we had discussed. We provided her with an opportunity to reflect on her actions and come up with a personal solution on how she would improve her grades and make better choices.

The important point to that meeting wasn't so much to fix the problem at that moment, but rather for Mom to make sure that her child was *responsible for her own choices* and that consequences would be given and followed through for *choosing* to break the rules.

Mom's change in her own behavior, to support the teachers, was a major step toward obtaining the behavior she desired in her child. Instead of the mother being upset with a teacher for a bad grade or a detention that her daughter received, she became *empowered* by speaking highly of teachers, empathizing with her child, yet sticking to the consequences.

The takeaway message from this scenario is that it is important to let your child experience natural consequences for poor decisions made, such as getting a detention, missing recess, or getting a bad grade. If you attempt to bail your children out of trouble and undermine authority, they receive the message that they don't have to listen to teachers, or for that matter any form of authority, which could result in worse behavior exhibited later on at home, at school, with peers, and in the community.

For that reason, a child misses out on an opportunity to learn from his or her mistakes and fails to make wise choices in the future when faced with more serious issues. A child, for that matter, may ultimately grow to become rebellious and defiant, and to resent a parent, which could result in even greater conflict.

In situations like this, it is important for parents to remain empathetic with their children, while still holding them accountable for their actions by saying something to the effect of "*I really disliked that rule, too. However, I had to follow the rules like everyone else.*" This functional response not only helps parents better relate with their child but also empowers them.

In *Parenting with Love and Logic,* Charles Fay, Jim Fay, and Foster Cline discuss the power that lies in *empathy* and *consequence. Empowerment* comes from empathy and consequence, which allow children to reflect on the decisions they have made. And as soon as a child is able to suffer the consequences, he or she can make better decisions in the future.[1]

Empathy is the ability to understand and share the feelings of another person. It strengthens the relationship you have with your child and restores *your power*. It stimulates thinking and in tandem with consequences, allows children *to own* the choices they make and learn to make better ones next time.

Showing empathy and letting your children experience the natural consequences for the choices they make allow them to grow as they learn from their mistakes. Empathetic parenting gains a child's respect, strengthens a close bond with a child, and helps build *emotional intelligence*. Learning how to support the development of this type of intelligence is not easy, but is one of the most important skills you can teach your child.

Communication problems between a parent and a child lie in a lack of "listening to understand" and being more in a mode of "listening to reprimand." The following exercises will help you be more present in a conversation with your child and actively listen to his or her feelings.

EXERCISE: REFLECTIVE LISTENING AND RESPONDING

Being empathetic with your child requires *active listening*. When one person speaks, another listens and reflects what was said to them. This form of communication demonstrates respect and lets the other person know that you were genuinely interested in, and truly listening to, what he or she had to say.

If your child gets upset over something that happened, he wants to know that he is being listened to and understood. It is important to accept and value whatever feelings of anger, frustration, and sadness are being expressed. You can let your child know that you understand how he feels by reflecting his feelings back to him by saying,

> "What I hear you saying is . . ." (follow that by restating what the child just said without any interpretation or spin put on it)
> "From what you said, I can imagine you feel pretty _____ (upset, disappointed, sad, etc.)."
> "If I get what you're saying . . ." (follow that by repeating what the child just said to the best of your ability)

After you've repeated a child's words back to him, you want to ensure that you have accurately reflected what he expressed to you. To do this, ask, "Is that correct?" This solidifies a mutual understanding between you and your child and invites you to proceed further into the conversation.

EXERCISE: PUTTING YOURSELF IN YOUR CHILD'S SHOES

Once a child openly expresses his or her feelings and a parent actively listens by providing reflective responses, it is important to then validate the child's feelings. Validation is not about agreeing with the other person, but rather about understanding and accepting the other person and their situation. Here are some examples:

> "If I were in your shoes, I can understand why you would feel that way."
> "Looking at it from your point of view, I can see why you would feel that way."
> "I can only imagine how that must have made you feel."
> "Those kinds of things happen, and I understand how you must feel."
> "I see what you're saying."
> "This is a lesson that we all learn at some point in our life and next time I'm sure you will make the right decision."

When children express their feelings, they desire validation, appreciation, and acknowledgment, especially from a parent. This form of communicating will produce a safe, open means for your child to express thoughts freely, experience empathy, take responsibility for his or her own choices, and accept consequences for his or her actions.

When beginning to learn from mistakes, the younger the child, the smaller the price to pay. If you are looking to "REV" up the communication lines between you and your child, think:

R—Reflective listening and responding
E—Empathy
V—Validation

Don't be afraid to include *empathy* as part of discipline. By sharing what a child may be feeling or going through, and showing how every choice made has consequences associated with it, helps reinforce the development of a child's empathy toward others.

Children who are allowed to learn from small mistakes early in life are far less likely to make more serious mistakes later on. If you demonstrate love and empathy, instead of anger and frustration, and allow your children to learn from their mistakes by experiencing natural consequences, you are likely to raise respectful and responsible individuals.

———◦◉◦———

Allow a child to make mistakes and let consequences do the teaching.

———◦◉◦———

Be Cool and See the Child in You

"Every child is an artist. The problem is how to remain an artist once we grow up."

—Pablo Picasso (Spanish artist)

$\mathcal{W}$hen the weather is warm outside, I enjoy going to the local park down the road shooting hoops with kids half my age. All the while, I notice some parents sitting on a bench watching their children play, as they climb up the jungle gym, pass through tunnels, and rock back and forth on the spring horses, while other parents actively push their kids on swings or cheer as they land at the bottom of a slide.

Play is where children exhibit their true feelings and emotions. It is the bridge for parents and children to make a deeper connection by sharing laughs, joy, encouragement, and enthusiasm. Studies show that play is critical to a child's cognitive, physical, social, and emotional well-being.[1]

The relationship that you have with your child will strengthen over time by doing the so-called little things that involve play on a consistent basis. Having a catch, shooting some hoops, or playing a board game together helps to develop your child's imagination and dexterity, and contributes to healthy brain development.

The important thing to realize as a parent is that relating to your child doesn't necessarily mean you must have a bunch of things in common with them. If you enjoy the outdoors, but your child prefers to watch a movie, learning to compromise and embrace your child's hobbies will help to build a long-lasting bond. This shows your child that you are not only physically there, but also emotionally present and spending quality time together.

I will admit it. I tried to show off in front of my students a time or two. A few years back, I wanted to show them that Korean pop sensation Psy had nothing on me, despite having over 2 billion views on YouTube at the time and worldwide fame. I was determined to do the "Gangnam Style" like nobody's business. I was stepping to the left, then right, then left, and left again quickly. I was swinging my arms and bending my wrists up and down and then sliding to the right.

Could you picture this scene going on in the classroom for about thirty seconds or so? "Embarrassing?" you ask. An understatement to say the least! But, hey, I received some laughs, cheers, strange faces, and fist pumps. The point is that I got their attention and showed them that I knew "what was up." I also wanted to seem cool by rattling off the names of the current R&B, rock, rap, and pop artists, while even throwing in some lyrics of popular songs.

Could you get away with that with your child? Trying to communicate and relate to your child by speaking their language, with trendy words and phrases like *swag, yolo, that's the bomb, off the chain, totes, epic, lit, noob, fam, don't be hatin', you got owned, roasted, that's boss,* and *that's sick* can be a challenge. When you speak with your child, it can sometimes appear as though they are speaking another language, but this is their way to developing self-esteem, confidence, and a sense of belonging that helps carve their personal identity.

Your children may feel embarrassed by you "trying to be cool," especially in front of their friends. Regardless, you may or may not feel comfortable showing off your dance moves in front of your children or throwing out slang terms that died out with MC Hammer pants. In any case, do you have to try and be cool to relate to your child or can it be accomplished another way?

As children grow, they will be discovering new ways to define their personality and seek out independence. This is a normal part of the growth and development phase of adolescence. However, this doesn't mean you shouldn't get regularly involved in what's going on in your child's life.

ASKING QUESTIONS

The question "How was school today?" may very well be the most frequently asked and least answered question by you and your child, respectively. As your children get older, the description of their day may become less and less detailed. What you are really trying to find out from them, especially as they get older, is not just how school was, but rather "How is your life going?" Oftentimes, the response shrinks down to "Fine," which could allude to a bunch of things that your child may be thinking or feeling:

"I hate school! It is so freaking boring!"
"I have a crush on one of my classmates, but I'm not going to tell you!"
"This kid keeps picking on me, but there's nothing you can do about it!"
"My life sucks and everyone hates me!"

I have spoken with and witnessed many parents out of touch with their children's lives and far removed from their own educational experiences. They focus heavily on their child's grades and place less emphasis on psychological health, which has such a profound influence on a child's overall well-being. The feeling of being back in school may or may not be a distant memory for you, and recalling exact emotions that you once experienced may be a challenge.

However, there are plenty of questions that you can ask your child that will help prompt a meaningful conversation. Asking "How was your day today?" seems to be a bit of a loaded question for a child to answer. Instead, you can help spark conversation with your child and discover what is really going on in their life by asking pointed questions such as these:

"Did you do anything special today in school?"
"What was your favorite part of the day? Tell me all about it."
"What was your least favorite part of the day? Why so?"

The importance of listening to your child to best understand him or her starts with reliving your own days as a student and evoking more than just selective, warm, fuzzy, and dreamy memories. It also includes recalling the day-to-day pressures that affected the decisions you made choosing your peer group, activities you took part in, and effort you put forth in school. These all contributed to your perceptions on life and how they have accumulated to impact you, positively and/or negatively.

EXERCISE: REAWAKEN YOUR YOUTH

Take a few minutes to answer the following set of questions to help reawaken your adolescence. Make note of any associated feelings that come to mind for each question. Ask yourself,

- Are these memories fond or would you like to forget about the past? Why so?
- Were there moments of inspiration that you experienced that sparked a change in the course of your life? A friend standing up for you? A teacher believing in you?

- Did you look forward to going to school each morning?
- How did you feel when the bus arrived to pick you up each day?
- How did you feel riding the bus in the morning? in the afternoon?
- How did you feel at the bus waiting area near home? at school?
- Do you remember walking into class and seeing your worst enemy staring at you?
- Do you remember the difference a teacher you liked or hated had on you and how they made you feel?
- Do you remember the first day of elementary school? middle school? high school?
- Did you look forward to going to gym class? math class? science class? art class? social studies class? English class? foreign language class?
- How did it feel to sit in those hard chairs all day?
- Did you look forward to eating lunch with your peers?
- How did you feel when you had to change your clothes in front of others in gym class?
- Were you afraid of being picked last for games?
- Did you ever write notes to or text message friends in school? To whom and in what classes did you write/text them?
- How did you feel when your parents saw your report card?
- Were you proud of your efforts?
- Do you wish that your parents understood you better growing up?
- Do you wish that your parents imposed more limits on you or gave you more freedom?
- Do you wish that your parents pushed you harder in some areas of your life?
- Did you feel loved and cared for by others?
- Why did you choose the friends that you had growing up?
- Was there someone you were afraid to face in school and tried to avoid?
- Did you worry about dressing to impress others?
- How did you feel right before going to sports practice after school?
- How did you feel when you first asked that special someone out on a date or to the prom? had your first kiss? had your first serious relationship?
- How did you feel when you were being laughed at or made fun of by a select person or group of people?
- Were you anxious walking in the halls from class to class? Did you feel safe?
- Did your parents care about how your days were at school? How did it make you feel?

- Did you feel embarrassed to be around your parents in public places? with your friends?
- How did you feel when you were in a situation with someone or a group of people and you were asked to try or do something that you didn't want to?
- Do you have any regrets while growing up? How would you have changed events if you could go back in time?
- Do you wish that you had done something differently in previous relationships with friends—including boy/girlfriends, bullies, parents, siblings, teachers, coaches, or sports teammates?

Hopefully by asking yourself all of these questions you were able to rekindle specific feelings of your past school days. Despite this exercise falling somewhere between painful and pleasant, it serves as a necessary and useful launching pad for you to better understand your child's needs and what he or she experiences on a daily basis.

I wear many hats throughout the day teaching children from all different backgrounds, and it is my job to relate with each and every one of them to the best of my ability and influence their lives in a positive manner. I am able to do this, in large part, by conjuring up my own past experiences and putting myself back in school and reliving how I felt in different circumstances while growing up. Fortunately, I still remember the smells and textures of the classrooms, locker rooms, restrooms, libraries, and gymnasiums and recall my inner feelings, fears, joys, and dreams as if it were yesterday.

Even if you were unable to evoke the exact feelings from being back in school, asking yourself pointed questions from your adolescence is one of the first and crucial steps to help you *connect with your child*, *understand their point of view better*, and *build a trusting line of communication* with them for the rest of their lives.

As your children grow, they experience various highs and lows and are looking to you to understand what they are going through, whether they admit that to you or not. They are seeking guidance and answers through the changes they experience throughout their formative years. Being able to make a difference in your child's life requires you to relate to and best understand their experiences.

Apply these strategies to stay connected and build a strong, long-lasting bond with your child:

- Parents who are giving, kind, empathetic, listen, and make time for their children will stay better connected with them and have a strong influence on raising caring, positive, secure, and loving people.

- Playing pretend games like "doctor," "house," or "school" with your children is a great forum for them to learn role play, leadership, effective communication, and problem-solving skills.
- Taking your children to different places, such as parks, museums, libraries, movies, and stores, can spark curiosity and help inspire them to keep active, explore, ask questions, and learn.
- Finding ways to demonstrate that you are sincerely interested in your children's lives reassures them that they are heard, understood, and important. Consequently, open and effective communication lines will begin to form naturally between you and your children.

Make it a point to relate to your children by listening to them, playing with them, and taking a genuine interest in their lives. Share stories of your own life to help enlighten what might be going on in theirs.

• 3 •

"Monkey See, Monkey Do," It's Up to You

"Even though fathers, grandparents, siblings, memories of ancestors are important agents of socialization, our society focuses on the attributes and characteristics of mothers and teachers and gives them the ultimate responsibility for the child's life chances."[1]

—Sara Lawrence-Lightfoot (American sociologist and author)

I had to laugh! The other day, I went over to my parents' house to visit them and my mother was eager to show me what she had discovered when going through and cleaning the drawers in the dining room. She had found a faded manila envelope with my name written on it. Out of it she pulled my second-grade report card!

When I looked at it, I was pleased to see that all of my grades, work habits, and attitude scores were in good standing. But then I glanced to the right column and noticed what my teacher had written for the yearly progress comment. It said, "Doug seems to have trouble staying in his seat and getting back there when told to."

With a wry smile plastered on her face, my mother pulled out another manila envelope and out came my third-grade report card. This time I was a bit apprehensive as to what had been written for the end-of-year comment. My teacher wrote, "A big improvement in behavior, however, Doug is still talkative."

All the memories growing up when my mother told me, "You're not here to socialize! You're here to learn and listen to the teacher," are quite ironic statements now, considering the fact that social skills have given me the ability to lead a classroom of children, conduct parent meetings, provide instruction, and guide children toward effectively handling an array of problems. These skills continue to be utilized during my public speaking appearances on different television programs and in front of large crowds.

15

Growing up, I used to be enthralled when I watched people give a speech, interview others, or be interviewed on television. One of the first speeches I vividly remember, which had a profound impact on me, was Martin Luther King Jr.'s famous "I have a dream" speech. I recall Dr. King's rhetoric and how it left a lasting impact on me and the rest of his audience. What I perceived in watching Dr. King's speech was an individual who had an electrifying, fearless, unifying, and sincere delivery of words that could inspire others with a universal message: all people are created equal.

Wrestling icon Hulk Hogan had been a big part of my life while growing up in the 1980s and 1990s. He was a figure that appeared larger than life in the wrestling world to many kids of my generation. But for kids who experienced being bullied, he was something of a demigod. It was his contagious charisma, his positivity, and the steadfast conviction in his voice during interviews with Mean Gene Okerlund before and after wrestling matches that rendered a lasting impression on so many of us "Hulkamaniacs," who were greatly moved and empowered by his words:[2]

> "I fear no man, no beast or evil, brother."
> "Train, say your prayers, take your vitamins and you will never go wrong."
> "Negativity and Hulkamania—two things that don't go together."

I was fascinated by public figures, both real and animated, who portrayed images that represented inexorable justice and stood up to the bad guy. The likes of Dr. King, Hulk Hogan, Rocky Balboa, the Karate Kid, Michael Jordan, He-Man, and Popeye exuded a superhuman strength that never gave up hope and demonstrated that with hard work and determination, you can overcome all obstacles and achieve anything that you put your mind to—and one day become the "champion."

The fact that people could make a living by talking to other people on television excited and mesmerized me. When I was in seventh grade, my parents purchased our first video camera for the family, and I immediately fell in love with being able to reenact my passions for being a television host or commentator, and being interviewed as a heroic character of some sort. The unencumbered commentary about basically anything from wrestling matches to video-game play to outdoor adventure games excited me and became one of my greatest passions. This relationship with human communication became one of the highest values that I carried with me throughout my childhood and into adulthood, as I began to appear on television as a regular guest expert, host different live events, and speak at seminars, conferences, and events on a variety of topics.

Sociologist, psychologist, and philosopher George Herbert Mead understood the "self" as the basis of humanity that develops through social experience. He said that humans begin the understanding of their world through play. The child takes on different roles that he observes in the "adult society" and gains an understanding of general, acceptable norms within that group or setting.[3]

Childhood experiences at home and at school play a large role in the socialization and development of an individual. Going back to second grade, playing the bean bag game helped to spark my creativity for storytelling. In third grade, playing the "Where in the World" map game exposed me to different cultures and helped hone my abilities to locate different geographical points.

In fourth grade, I enjoyed the friendly competition of playing strategy games such as Tic-Tac-Toe and checkers with other classmates. In fifth grade, it was the waste basket game of shooting crumpled-up paper to see how long I could last without missing a shot in a sudden-death elimination-style format against my other classmates, which in turn helped my hand-eye coordination and focus.

All of these social games exposed me to a diversity of experiences that were invaluable for setting the framework for maximizing my learning potential and strengthening my various multiple intelligences as I went through my middle and high school years.

Many kids enjoy playing sports and look up to their favorite college and professional athletes. However, today we are seeing many of these individuals lose their tempers on and off the field. Television cameras are showing close-ups of athletes and coaches mouthing profanities in reaction to an official's call. Parts of post-game interviews are being censored due to a showering of colorful expletives and obscene comments being made by these sports figures. When it comes to athletics, however, they aren't the only people engaging in these kinds of off-putting behaviors. How have these actions at the "professional" level funneled down to affect parents, coaches, and youth athletes?

After attending my twenty-year high school reunion, I was inspired to see how times have changed at my old school and decided that season to watch a varsity basketball game. I sat in the bleachers and looked around to see if I noticed anyone that I knew from twenty-plus years ago. Faces were unfamiliar, and as the game went on, clapping and cheering turned into contemptuous roars from spectators.

As both teams battled back and forth throughout the game, the home-team coach would give an earful to the referees for a call that went against his team, while the away-team coach yelled profusely at his players when a turnover was made. At one point in the game, a mother stood up in the stands right in front of me, screaming obscene comments at the referee for supposed "bad or missed calls." A father in the stands berated the coach yelling, "Coach, call a timeout. Oh, come on. You suck, coach!" Another spectator shouted, "This is bulls**t!" Another person from the crowd followed by dropping an F-bomb. Soon thereafter, a technical foul was called on a player for throwing his hands up in the air and swearing at the referee.

The point is that cursing, shouting, and disrespectful behavior seem to have found their way into youth sports. Angry parents and coaches verbally assaulting officials is only a portion of the problem. Adults have been found to cross boundaries and physically attack young athletes and officials. These unnecessary and uncalled for behaviors have a significant impact on a child's perception of sports. Research conducted by the National Alliance for Sports showed that nearly 70 percent of kids drop out of youth sports by the age of thirteen, attributing the top three reasons as adults, coaches, and parents.[4]

What can you do to make your child's athletic experience a fun and rewarding one?

- Don't engage in behaviors that you wouldn't want to see from your child (e.g., lying, cursing, being rude, shouting, hitting, etc.).
- Encourage your child to play the sport for the love of the game.
- Regularly attend your child's sporting activities.
- Cheer for your child and reiterate how much you love to watch him or her play.

HOMESCHOOLING

There is a popular misconception that home-schooled children are isolated at home all day and lose opportunities to socialize with others, thus adversely affecting their academic success. Dr. Brian Ray of the National Home Education Research Institute conducted the most recent and comprehensive study of homeschool academic achievement to date, "Homeschool Progress Report 2009," surveying more than 11,000 home-schooled students and their families from fifty states. The results showed that the average homeschooler outperformed their public school peers by 37 percentile points on standardized achievement tests.[5]

A few years ago, I taught a student named *Jack*, who had been homeschooled up until the seventh grade. He entered my homeroom on the first day of school with his emo eye-covering haircut, appearing withdrawn and shy. Jack's mother was concerned about his transition to middle school after seven years of being homeschooled and wondered if he would be able to adjust and fit in with the other students.

Jack's mother was a dedicated, busy, single mother who was responsible for running a daycare business from home while simultaneously homeschooling her son. Jack observed his surrounding environment, witnessed his mother's tireless work ethic, and saw the examples she had set for him.

Contrary to what critics of homeschooling believe, Jack was off the charts scoring among the highest in his grade at the 90th percentile for all standardized scores in all subjects. Opponents of homeschooling have long insisted that parents who decide to homeschool their child should obtain a teacher certification. Research has shown that high scores on standardized academic tests were not impacted by whether a parent was teacher certified or not.[6]

If you are considering homeschooling your child, studies have shown that a child will have as many friends and activities as they so choose and are allowed by a parent. Research shows that they are typically above average on measures of social, emotional, and psychological development.[7] By running a daycare facility out of her home, Jack's mother had the opportunity to strengthen her son's social skills by educating him on how to behave appropriately in different settings around adults and peers.

Jack adjusted quickly to middle school life and was well liked by his peers. He and a group of friends stayed afterschool in my classroom a few days a week to write original songs and play music. Jack was a respectful, easygoing, and engaging individual to be around. He was a precocious young man that would find a way to readily engage in meaningful conversation.

Jack particularly loved talking about philosophy and music. He spent many hours practicing on his bass guitar and taught himself how to play many songs by ear. By the end of eighth grade, he was telling me how he and his friends were regularly playing out in public doing gigs and open mic nights.

COMMUNICATING WITH OTHERS

No matter how you decide to provide an education for your child, through public, private, or homeschooling, he or she first learns how to communicate with *you and other people in the household.* Your own values, attitudes, and prejudices can be implicitly or explicitly passed on to your child. Prejudice is still a problem in most societies, along with discrimination and racism. Children are like sponges and can easily pick up on any prejudice imparted and hatred displayed.

In the movie *Akeelah and the Bee,* a Chinese American boy named Dylan Chu, who had been runner up at the past two national spelling bees, was acting contemptuously toward an eleven-year-old African American girl from South Los Angeles named Akeelah Anderson. In the film, Dylan's father showed disdain toward Akeelah by reprimanding his son for nearly losing in a game of Scrabble to "a little black girl."

At one point in the film, Akeelah attempted to convince Dylan's father to have his son take a break from studying for the tournament and join the other contestants in a pre–spelling bee party. Akeelah was chided for her behavior and told by Mr. Chu that *"they didn't study that way."*

Family socialization practices differ around the world. For instance, American families view storytelling as more entertaining and lesson learning. On the other hand, Chinese families use personal storytelling as a medium of socialization. This culture is deeply rooted in the Confucian tradition, which places an emphasis on proper moral and social standards. They see shame as a virtue and, from an early age, place a high order on strict discipline and fulfilling social obligations. This explains, in large part, how Dylan's harsh and cutthroat persona displayed throughout the movie came about as a result of the constant pressure to achieve that his father placed on him.

SOCIAL RELATIONS AT HOME

For many children today, the social relations within the family that ensure a smooth process of socialization are collapsing. One of the biggest shifts in family dynamics is the percentage of children today living with an unmarried parent. According to the U.S. Census Bureau, 34 percent of children today are residing in a single-parent home. This is a marked increase from 9 percent in 1960 and 19 percent in 1980.[8]

Many parents are working long hours, consumed with their own day-to-day concerns; children often experience erratic or poor parental discipline, low or no parental involvement, or no supervision. Furthermore, conflict between parents often results in backlash onto the child. In the bestselling book *Cry Silent Tears*, author Joe Peters relives his past experience of survival from a childhood filled with violence and sexual abuse by his schizophrenic mother, Leslie, and two of his older brothers who spent years beating him, locking him in the cellar in the family house, and feeding him scraps that he was forced to lick from the floor. At times he was left naked in the dark for days on end, without human contact.[9]

Joe's father, William, tried to protect his son from the horror and abuse by bringing him every day to the garage where he worked fixing cars. When an unexpected accident occurred and Joe witnessed his father burn to death before his eyes, it left him dumbstruck, wretched, and at the mercy of his abusive mother. Unable to speak for four and a half years after seeing his father die and being unable to read or write, Joe could not communicate his pain or ask for help—his world turned into a real life hell.

At fourteen years old, Joe finally found the courage to run away; he hid in a hut by a railway line and ate scraps anywhere he could find them. After overcoming nearly impossible odds and circumstances, Joe now has five children, is a spokesperson on behalf of all children, and has set up a service to assist children who have suffered from similar experiences.

The story of Joe is a truly exceptional, compelling inspiration, a heartbreaking story of triumph, and one that should have never happened in the first place. But the one thing that Joe credits to his survival during his childhood, and what provided him a source of love and how to truly care for someone, was his one and only friend from school and one of his older brothers who did not beat him.

There are two major groups that have been characterized as integral to a child's socialization. The *primary group*—typified by close, long-lasting, loving, and nurturing relationships—is necessary for young individuals to be happy, healthy, and secure. Family and close friends comprise this group, which functions as the strongest working unit in a child's life.

The *secondary group* is characterized by impersonal and short-term relationships in which people work together on common tasks or activities. These are individuals that also affect the socialization of a child. Members of this group have less, if any, emotional ties to the individual. They include classmates (except for close friends), most teachers, professors, mass media outlets, and other people who will inevitably come and go in a child's life.

This group will usually listen politely to conversations, but they will not have a vested interest in the whole child. These people will not typically care to hear all of the details of a child's life and will not be available in the case of an emergency. The socialization of your child, however, takes place through contributions from both the primary and secondary groups.

Parental interaction has a strong impact on a child's overall well-being. Some researchers state that children as young as six months old display distress when their parents fight. They exhibit signs that include anger, anxiety, and sadness.[10] Children who are exposed to chronic aggressive conflict have an increased risk of a variety of health-related problems, disturbed sleep, and trouble focusing and succeeding academically at school.[11] Kids pay close attention to their parents' actions and reactions, which in turn teaches them how to deal with their own stresses and solve problems throughout their lives.

Conflict is a normal part of everyday life. However, it's not about whether parents fight that is of prime importance, but rather the kind of conflict that is taking place. Children who live in a high-conflict home where parents use verbal aggression such as derogatory name calling, shouting, profanity, criticism, sarcasm, and threats of abandonment and/or display physical aggression toward each other, such as hitting and pushing, experience *destructive conflict*. These children, throughout their lifetimes, are more likely to have poor interpersonal skills, be socially incompetent, suffer from physical health and emotional problems, and lack problem-solving skills.

Another form of destructive conflict is *parental emotional withdrawal*. Kids understand conflict and expect it to be worked out, coming to some sort of resolution. Withdrawal makes the situation not only harder on children, but also on the marital relationship. When a parent refuses to communicate or to give in, or demonstrates nonverbal anger, the child is not learning an effective strategy to resolve the conflict in a healthy manner.

When parents have conflict that involves both parties equally expressing their feelings in a calm manner, using positive emotions and language, and working together to compromise in solving a problem or making a decision, children experience *constructive conflict*. These children develop social competency and a positive self-esteem, enjoy emotional security, and learn conflict-resolution and problem-solving skills that they can apply to their own relationships throughout their lives.

EXERCISE: RESOLVE CONFLICT SO EVERYONE WINS

Apply the following five-step strategy to maintain a positive relationship with the other parent (spouse or not) and demonstrate effective conflict resolution and problem-solving skills for your child:

1. Express empathy by showing that you are paying attention to the feelings as well as the spoken words of the other parent.
   "I know that you work very hard and that you are very busy . . ."
   "I know that you want what is best for our child as do I . . ."
   "I understand where you are coming from . . ."
2. Give your full attention to the other parent. Allow him or her to speak without interruption and assume positive intentions.
3. Manage your tone and volume during the conversation. Avoid raising your voice and using disrespectful words and actions.
4. Be willing to end the conflict if it doesn't come to a resolution and come back to it at another point, if need be. Remain calm and agree to disagree respectfully.
5. Forgive and forget. Resolving conflict may not be easy depending on the magnitude of the problem, but it is impossible if one or both

parties are unwilling to forgive the other person or express their own wrongdoings in the situation.

Your child will have different experiences in relation to family, school, sports, and peer relationships. Modeling a good relationship with your child's other parent is one thing, but what about specific behaviors that you wish to pass on to your kids? Start by identifying specific goals and outcomes that you are looking for with your child and how you might model them.

Suggestions for ways to model desired behavior with your children include the following:

- saying sorry to your children or to others when you're wrong;
- telling the truth to your child, even if it's painful;
- taking responsibility for shortcomings, failures, or other "bad behaviors";
- working hard at your job and getting things done (explain that sometimes some other "business matters" come first—whether for your job or something around the house—so that they might take schoolwork to be more important than going out with friends or playing sports); and
- honoring commitments, even those you no longer feel you want to pursue (e.g., not quitting a team or an activity until it's seen through to the end).

Raising your children takes a great amount of time, effort, and patience in teaching them how to become responsible citizens, to have self-control, to live up to societal and cultural expectations and to exhibit the proper values in life, all while expressing and fulfilling their deepest desires. It is important for you and all members of your child's primary group to be aware of all factors that contribute to your child's understanding of the world in order to best help him or her become a happy, responsible, respected, and contributing member of society.

The lexicon of messages that you send to your children forthrightly, subtly, and through interactions with family members, friends, and strangers has a direct impact on their behavior. Modeling is paramount.

· 4 ·

Be the Boss by
Sharing Power with Your Child

"Caring for children is a dance between setting appropriate limits as caretakers and avoiding unnecessary power struggles that result in unhappiness."[1]

—Charlotte Sophia Kasl, PhD
(American psychotherapist and author)

It was all happening before my eyes, while eating dinner at a local restaurant with my family, one Sunday afternoon. There were complaints from the family sitting across from us that the food was too spicy and that their two daughters hadn't received their meals yet. The waiter apologized profusely and explained to them that they were short-staffed and the kitchen manager called out sick, but he would get things taken care of right away.

By the end of the meal, we could clearly hear the fiasco going on between the waiter and the father in regard to being overcharged on the bill. I heard the waiter explain to him that the salad bar didn't come with the meal. The father renounced his statement and insisted that it be taken off the check. The waiter replied to the father by telling him that the menu clearly stated the salad bar was not a side dish with the meal he had chosen. The father remained persistent and stoically said, "You didn't tell me this before. I want it removed from the check right now."

The waiter, becoming increasingly frustrated, gave in to the verbal clash and said, "I apologize, sir, I know I should have told you this earlier. I will take care of it."

Did the waiter ever have a chance of winning this argument? Now mind you, the two daughters who appeared to be around eight or nine years old were sitting as astute observers noting and recording the entire transaction of events taking place. What was happening here? They were forming beliefs about cause-and-effect relationships. In other words, they were learning that if they fuss over something long enough like their father did with the waiter, then they would eventually get their way.

Ironically, when the waiter left to adjust the bill, the two daughters became impatient and started insisting to leave. The father fell into the argument trap, as did the waiter with him. He started "moving his lips" and got into a war of words with his daughters. Each time that one of his daughters would argue back, he would rebut.

This behavior continued on for a few minutes until the father looked at the mother and asked, "When is this guy coming back with the check?" As the daughters continued to complain, the father, not wanting to deal with the situation any longer, told the mother to bring the girls to the car.

When a parent falls into the trap of arguing with a child to inevitably succumb to their demands, it is teaching the child a sad lesson: "If you persist long enough with me and continue to argue, I will eventually submit and give in to your wishes. All that you have to do is keep arguing and you will get what you want."

Alfred Adler, one of the founders of psychoanalytic thinking, who later developed his own method called individual psychology, was one of the first individuals to coin the term *inferiority complex*. He noted that every child experiences feelings of inferiority as the result of being surrounded by stronger, more capable adults. Interestingly, Adler mentioned that the healthy child will strive to overcome his or her feelings of inferiority by developing compensation methods as a means of survival and a need for superiority.

Adler went on to identify four destructive behavior patterns that children display in order to bring those perceived disadvantages to an end:[2]

1. **Power-struggling**—involves a child attempting to gain control and seize authority over adults. Children who seek power don't like to be told what to do. They like to create the rules.
2. **Revenge**—involves retaliating back at perceived abuse or injustice. Children can say hurtful statements to their parents such as "I hate you!" or "You don't love me!" They can even damage something belonging to an authority figure.
3. **Attention-getting**—involves arguing or distractive behavior usually rooted in deeper issues. If a child is not receiving positive attention, then he or she will likely seek negative attention (e.g., upsetting others, being defiant or unruly, clowning around, or bullying others). Sometimes, they can even injure a sibling, oftentimes a baby or toddler.

4. **Feigning incompetence**—involves a child pretending to be incapable of doing a task or chore with the intent to avoid doing it, such as "I don't understand my homework" or "I can't vacuum the entire house." Saying they "can't do it because it's too hard" relieves them from the responsibility, thus freeing up valuable time for doing what interests them.

These exhibited self-centered behavior patterns can be a nightmare for parents, but it is important to realize that they are merely survival instincts that a child uses to accomplish a major goal of theirs, which is *gaining power over authority*. Developmental psychologist Jean Piaget said that it all begins with an egocentric behavior during early childhood where the child is preoccupied with their own world in which everything revolves around their needs.[3] Adolescents display these behavior patterns primarily out of a desire for independence.

POWER STRUGGLES

It is *impossible* to win a power struggle with your children. Trying to "make your child react or behave a certain way" will likely backfire in the long run with additional problems that may ensue. If you win, or so you may think, then your children learn a lesson that your power is what caused the victory and "defeated them." Therefore, the next time, they will strike back with a vengeance using stronger tactics. If you lose a power struggle with your children, this also reassures them that they have defeated you and they, once again, believe that "power" was the cause of their victory.

Power-seeking children understand that you are the adult and are expected to behave in a responsible, moral manner as a trusted, loving, forgiving, honest, and helpful figure. As well, they may believe that throwing temper tantrums, crying, arguing, screaming, yelling, contradicting, rebelling, and being disobedient are socially acceptable for their age.

How then do you get your child to behave appropriately without all the power struggles? Children desire to be like adults in many ways. They see adults as being self-reliant, all grown up, having power, and doing whatever they want to do. Hence, they seek the same things but lack full cognitive development. You must detach yourself from the power struggle and provide your child with *options to choose from*. This, in turn, gives your child the feeling or thought that he has the *power of choice* and has some control over the situation.

Let's consider twelve-year-old *Trevor* who used to frequently get out of his chair, lean on the desk, and do his classwork from a half-standing position in my classroom. I was having difficulty getting him seated until one day I asked him if he would rather stand or sit while doing his work in class. Trevor said to me that he would rather stand. I also explained to him that the teacher across the hall was in need of a seat for her class. Trevor insisted on standing anyway. Trevor's chair was immediately taken away from him and placed into the other classroom. As a result, Trevor had no choice but to stand up for the remainder of the period.

At the beginning of the next day, Trevor was given the option as to whether he wanted to stand or sit for the entire period. This time, he made a different choice. He *chose* to sit. His seat was given back and no longer did he get up from it or do his homework from a half-standing position.

I have spoken with parents at countless meetings who felt discouraged by their children's unwillingness to oblige to their demands. These parents had the best of intentions in wanting their children to be cooperative and to do their very best, but they had become frustrated and discouraged by the children's defiance or rebellious misbehavior at home.

TEACHING CHILDREN ABOUT CONSEQUENCES

Many parents tell me that they have a consequence system put into place if their child misbehaves. Some parents provide harsh reprimands and lectures, whereas others punish their children by taking away toys, games, or a weekly allowance. On the other hand, some parents don't believe in using punishment but rather use bribery, constant reminders, and persuasion to achieve desired behavior.

Ask yourself the following:

- "What specific system do you have in place if your child doesn't comply with rules or expectations that you set forth?"
- "Is your child aware of the specific consequences for his or her actions if the rules are not followed?"
- "Do you follow through consistently or cave in on these consequences when the rules are broken?"

Being a teacher, parents often seek my advice about a variety of issues concerning their children. One of my students' parents came to me concerned about their thirteen-year-old son spending too much time playing video games and not enough time doing his homework.

When his grades weren't up to par, his parents would punish him by taking away his video games. However, when their son would throw a fit threatening that he wouldn't do any of his homework if he couldn't play his games, the parents would renege on their consequences and give in to their son's ranting and raving. They were caring parents who had good intentions in wanting their son to complete homework and get good grades. However, they were in need of an effective method and approach for handling this situation.

SETTING BOUNDARIES

The problem in this case was that the parents provided broad boundaries by allowing their child to play as much as he wanted just as long as he finished his homework. The messages that the boy received included "I will rush through my homework just to get it done and then play video games as much as I want," and "If I put up a fight long enough and tell them that I won't do any homework unless I am able to play video games, then I will get my way and play as much as I want."

These parents were having difficulty with *setting limits* on the video game play and allowing their son to experience the consequences of his poor decisions. I spoke with their son personally and told him that his parents and I had met and discussed a personal success plan. I thanked him for completing most of his homework assignments and valuing the importance of education. I also mentioned that he was missing a couple of assignments and that I would like him to keep working hard to complete and improve the quality of all of them. I stated that this would translate into higher grades for him which would, in turn, make everyone happy and give him a greater sense of satisfaction. From there, I presented him with clear and consistent limits followed by the consequences for his actions if he had not met the goal each week:

- "Each week, you will have the privilege to play video games for an hour on both Saturday and Sunday, if the completion and quality of your homework improves throughout the week. You will not be rewarded with video game play if this goal is not accomplished each week."
- "You will be allowed to play video games for an hour on both Saturday and Sunday and then for an extra hour on one of those days if the completion and quality of your homework improves and your grades continue to get better. You will not be rewarded with video game play if this goal is not accomplished each week."

Later that afternoon, I received an e-mail from his mother stating that her son clearly understood the expectations and consequences and was in compliance with them. Children need direction and rules that are clearly and firmly stated with *enforceable limits set*. When limits are unclear, inconsistent, and not enforced, it is easy for a child to veer off track and develop bad habits, behaviorally or academically, that they will carry with them for a long time.

The power of enforceable limits works with children of all ages. Over the years as a teacher, I've noticed how some children tend to interrupt conversations with their peers and adults. One of my students *Brian* would frequently try to interrupt me when I was talking with other students.

Each time that Brian tried to butt into a conversation that I was having with another student, I respectfully reminded him that it was not okay to speak over another person and he should wait for a pause in the conversation, say "Excuse me," and then wait patiently to be acknowledged before he speaks. It didn't take long for Brian to wait because he was not getting my attention when he chose to interrupt a conversation.

Let's consider what would happen if I decided to stop what I was saying with another student and provide Brian my full attention. Doing that would reinforce the message "Each time I interrupt someone, it is okay. They will listen to me." Do you think Brian would repeat this kind of behavior with me, his parents, other adults, or future conversations with his classmates? You bet.

Don't assume that this kind of behavior is something that a child will likely outgrow as they get older if they are not taught otherwise. If you let your child constantly interrupt you, he or she will likely grow up to be an adult that behaves in a similar, if not worse, manner. Over the years, I've met people who display this kind of interrupting behavior and it becomes draining and difficult to have a two-way conversation with them.

The message that Brian received from me was clear: "Interrupting is not okay and here is a clear solution for an appropriate, respectful way to get someone's attention when they are speaking with someone else in a conversation." Therefore, the sooner we teach children this valuable social skill, the better it will be for them and others they encounter.

Older children require the same clear boundaries to understand what is expected of them. Consider sixteen-year-old *Lauren* who asks to go out to the mall with her friends for a few hours. Her mother clearly tells her that she needs the car back by 4:00 p.m., at the latest, because she has an appointment that she cannot miss. Lauren returns at 5:00 p.m., an hour later than what was expected. When Lauren returns, her mother scolds her for being irresponsible and having to miss the appointment. She lectures about her lack of consideration for others. In the end, no consequences were given to Lauren.

Did her daughter learn a valuable lesson about the importance of returning the car on time? What she gathered from this experience was "I don't have to be on time with my mother's requests. It is optional." Do you think Lauren and her mother will have this conversation again in the near future? Most likely, they will.

On the other hand, what would have happened if Lauren's mother provided an upfront clear consequence saying, "Lauren, I will need to have the car by 4:00 p.m. because I have an important appointment at 4:30 p.m. that I cannot miss. If you are home early, that's great, but please be home by 4:00 p.m., otherwise you will not have the privilege to drive the car for a week." No lectures, no excuses, no screaming, no ifs, ands, or buts about it. What lesson would Lauren learn in this case if she were late in returning the car? The message would be "I know that what my mother says, she means."

EXERCISE: PRACTICE COMPROMISE OVER CONTROL

There are many benefits of sharing power with your children. By sharing appropriate amounts of power with your children, you teach them how to communicate effectively about their needs and fears and help them resolve issues in an appropriate manner.

When children are small, parents hold a large amount of the power and control. As children get older, the balance shifts. They begin to gain a significant amount of power. They may be out with friends and driving a car where they are forced to make choices and solve problems on their own. Through choice giving, compromises, and open communication early on in their lives, children develop a strong foundation for making wise decisions that will serve them well as they grow older.

There is a vast difference between a child asking for a compromise and a parent considering that request and a parent and a child getting into a squabble or a wrangle. Here is an example of a *power sharing* situation and how you can apply compromise the next time your child asks for something that you really want to say "no" to, but don't want to get into a *power struggle* with them.

Let's assume your child wants to stay up fifteen minutes past his bedtime and watch the rest of a television show. You see that he has to go to bed and you need to say "no." This is a prime opportunity to compromise your power to share it with your child.

Child: "Can I please stay up and watch the rest of this show? Please!"

Parent: "Not tonight. You need to go to bed now, but maybe we can do that compromise another night."

Wrapping this statement with possibility for the future respects your child's request, yet affirms your decision. If your child continues to ask in a pleading voice, "Please, oh please, can I stay up to watch the rest of this show," simply reaffirm that tonight he needs to go to bed on time and that request will be considered another night because you would like to say "yes" when you can.

Imagine you are at the mall with your teenage daughter for two or three hours and you want to leave, but she insists on going to yet another store. You are tired and have other things to do, but she wants to try on some clothes. How do you compromise with her to satisfy her desires and also have her respect your wishes?

> **Child**: "I want to go to this store and check out what they have."
>
> **Parent**: "We've been here for a while now, dear. I'm getting tired and have quite a few things to do when we get home. But if you'd like to go to one more store, we can do that. Would you like me to come inside with you or could I sit down and wait here for a few minutes while you look?"

Power *sharing* is about offering choices, making compromises, and negotiating shared decisions. Power *struggling* is about both parties trying to gain control and dominate the situation. A child who will be competent with decision making as a sixteen-year-old needs to learn how to share power appropriately from a young age. If you say "yes" appropriately to your child, he or she will learn to trust your "no" and take it seriously.

How do children know how much power and control they should have in their relationship with adults? Oftentimes, they don't know. Through pushing buttons and pushing to the limits, they discover their power and control. It is necessary for children to learn appropriate conduct and the expectations for proper behavior toward family members, strangers, teachers, and classmates. It is important to realize that it is not only the words spoken by parents, but also their actions that children regularly follow as their examples.

End power struggles with your child by not arguing. Set clear and consistent enforceable limits, provide your child with choices within those limits, and stick to the consequences if your child pushes beyond the limits.

"Kick Your Kid's Butt" Effectively

"Some people regard discipline as a chore. For me, it is a kind of order that sets me free to fly."

—Julie Andrews (award-winning actress, singer, and author)

How my grandfather described the discipline his generation experienced while growing up was completely different from how punishment is implemented at schools today. My grandfather had grown up during the Great Depression, and he said that kids who disobeyed at school would await their punishment by lining up outside the principal's office. The sound of the principal's belt smacking a child's bottom was their soon-to-be fate. One kid would come out from the room with tears welled up in his eyes, while another would anxiously enter through the door anticipating the painful spanking.

According to Grandpa, the Ping-Pong paddle was the most feared object, probably due to the large surface area available for striking human skin. He recalled the time that he got punished in class for not doing his homework. The teacher walked up to him in public view, at least sparing his writing hand, and smacked him with a ruler that was twice as wide as a regular yard stick, leaving my grandfather with a reverberating stinging sensation.

The principal would use a paddle, a ruler, his hands, or anything that he could find to inflict pain in order to "teach a lesson." Other students would hold a couple of books above their heads until their arms hurt so badly that they cried. Using that form of discipline in schools today is not an acceptable method for punishment and is strictly prohibited by law.

DISCIPLINING YOUR CHILD

Discipline comes from the Latin word "disciplinare," which means to *teach*. This term, interestingly, is often associated with *punishment*, which is only a small piece of the discipline puzzle. In this chapter, we will focus on using discipline as a teaching tool for moral and social standards. You will learn how to effectively call upon different techniques with your children as they progress into and through adolescence.

Disciplining your child may be the single hardest task that you undertake as a parent due to the great deal of time, effort, and energy that it takes to effectively implement it. The frenetic pace of today's society can certainly be an obstacle to regularly using these discipline methods. Applying them on a consistent basis, however, will render the outcomes that you are seeking.

You may find that these techniques don't come naturally at first and may be discomforting and something you want to avoid enforcing with your child altogether. But after you understand the reasons why discipline is necessary, you will be able to easily apply these tools—with great confidence. You will happily experience a great reduction in stress levels and not have to worry about being "the bad guy" and having to take things away from your child when he or she doesn't abide by the rules.

Parents often rely on discipline styles that were used on them while growing up. Some of those methods might still be acceptable; others might be outmoded or flat-out wrong. For the sake of you and your child, keep in mind that a major principle of parenting is to guide a child's *mental, physical, emotional, cognitive, and social development*. Hence, the main goal of effective discipline is to foster acceptable and appropriate behavior in your child. This leads to a child growing up and becoming an emotionally mature adult with a healthy conscience and an internal sense of control and responsibility, and ultimately developing his or her own self-discipline.

Effective discipline occurs in three different forms:[1]

1. in a loving, positive, supportive way that strengthens the parent–child relationship:
2. using positive reinforcement to encourage desired behaviors; and
3. using punishment (only when necessary) to decrease the frequency or eliminate undesired behaviors.

It's important to first understand that young children have trouble regulating their behavior based on verbal prohibitions and directions. As a child gets older, removing valued privileges by delayed extinction becomes a useful technique for eliminating undesirable behavior.

Over the years, there have been students in my classroom that despite consequences given would continue to display a variety of problem behaviors. They disrupted class repeatedly by shouting out abruptly, swearing, whining, displaying a temper tantrum, falling out of their seat, blowing their noses loudly, poking other students with a pencil, calling them names, hitting the backs of other students' heads or necks, messing up their hair, flinging something across the classroom, and getting up out of their seat to throw a piece of paper into the trash can from a far distance. These students desired attention and were acting out to get it.

Amid these problem behaviors, I used an extinction method to decrease the occurrence of them. In using this strategy, it is important to give attention to students when they are exemplifying positive behaviors rather than to immediately respond when they are displaying unconstructive ones.

If you decide to implement an extinction plan to reduce or get rid of an unwanted behavior with your child, you may see the behavior escalate before it gets better. When you decide to ignore the behavior, you must completely commit to it because your child may increase the intensity of the behavior seeing that you are ignoring him. Be aware that if you give in and eventually provide attention to your child, the behavior will likely persist at that new heightened level of intensity.

It takes practice to truly ignore problem behavior. It helps if you have something else to deflect attention toward or attend to someone who is behaving desirably and focus your complete attention on that person or situation. Before you decide to use this method, it is important to ask the following questions:

- Can the behavior that you are trying to reduce or eliminate be ignored or tolerated temporarily, even if it gets worse, or does the behavior compromise the safety and well-being of that individual or other people?
- Will others mimic this behavior?
- Have the specific individuals or activities that are producing reinforcement of the problem behavior and increasing its frequency been identified and can they be controlled?
- Have you identified alternative behaviors that would receive positive reinforcement?

A parent of one of my former students reached out to me for help saying that her eleven-year-old was going on two years of age. She said that he was extremely argumentative and would throw temper tantrums in public. She was concerned about his upcoming birthday party and how he would behave in front of his friends and their parents and how she should handle any public outbursts.

A few days prior, her family was about to celebrate her younger nine-year-old son's birthday. Her older eleven-year-old son wanted to sit in the front passenger seat of the car, but his younger brother beat him to the spot and sat there instead. The older brother was furious about it and demanded that his younger brother get out of the front seat and move to the back. He started yelling at him and told him to get out before he dragged him out and beat him down. When he started to pull him out of the car, his mother corrected him on his behavior telling him to get his hands off of his brother and sit in the back.

The situation, however, was not so easily rectified. The older brother wouldn't let go of his emotions and proceeded to hit his little brother in the head while heading to the restaurant. The mother became fed up and turned the car around to go back home. She sent the older brother to his room. And after slamming the door, pounding on the floor, and about five minutes of crying, the mother ran upstairs to the rescue and spoke with him about how his actions prevented them from celebrating a birthday dinner for his little brother. She was quite disappointed because her son refused to take responsibility for his actions and blamed his little brother for his own actions.

So why did this all happen in the first place? Could these behaviors have been prevented or handled in a different way to shift the focus away from the older brother? In situations of this nature, having a bag of *proactive* behavior techniques up your sleeve would both extinguish undesirable behavior and also increase well-behaved, responsible behavior. Providing clear expectations on good car behavior and consequences if those standards were not met is an important structure that should be put into place.

The mother's reaction to her son's crying and pounding on the floor after being sent to his room—running upstairs to the rescue—taught her child a lesson that when he whines, pouts, and cries, he will get his way and *receive attention* from a parent. This also *initiates a power struggle* between parent and child down the road.

EXERCISE: PRACTICE C.A.L.M. TO REDUCE OR ELIMINATE PROBLEM BEHAVIOR

All children, but especially adolescents, should be held accountable for their behaviors by receiving natural consequences, which helps them develop problem-solving skills. Undesired behavior is not going to fix itself. Change is not going to happen on its own, especially if the behavior has been working for a child, and he or she has been getting away with it for some time. The reality is that when children repeat these behaviors and continue to get their way, they develop unhealthy behavior habits that may stay with them for a lifetime, unless they are held accountable for their actions somewhere along the way.

Apply the C.A.L.M. technique to create lasting change in your child's behavior:

C—**Communicate**: Be clear as to both the expectations that you set regarding your child's behaviors and the consequences if they aren't followed. Clear communication and commitment to upholding expectations is an essential component of effective parenting.

A—**Avoid**: If your child tries to engage in an argument with you or throw a temper tantrum because he didn't get his way, give him a verbal reprimand in the moment and then leave the room to avoid confrontation.

L—**Listen:** After your child has calmed down, actively listen to him by focusing your complete attention not only on what he says to you but also to his body language and what he isn't telling you. He may be angry, frustrated, sad, afraid, or feel misunderstood. Acknowledging his feelings and emotions lets him know that he is important to you. You can initiate conversation by saying something like "It seems like you were _____ (e.g., upset) about _____ (e.g., not being able to go over your friend's house this weekend)."

M—**Mend:** Have an open and honest conversation that helps your child mend and solve problems. Refrain from laying blame or using criticism when speaking with your child. No matter what the behavior was, work to mend and correct it by stating the desired behavior and following that with a brief explanation as to why you want them to do that next time.

THE DEMAND FOR MATERIAL GOODS

Ever wonder why your child may insist on you buying something for him or her when in a store? Many kids seem to be drawn to the hottest video games, most popular and expensive brands of clothes, and the latest pieces of technological gadgets on the market. Many parents can't afford to buy these things but do so anyways out of a sense of guilt, frustration, or exhaustion in an effort to keep children happy, and so they can complete their shopping. Other parents who don't spend a lot of time with their children due to work obligations may overcompensate and purchase one thing after another out of a feeling of guilt, to appease their own feelings of remorse. This often results in a child coming to expect these materialistic rewards on a regular basis.

We must also consider the persuading influence of the media on young children and adolescents nowadays. According to the American Academy of Pediatrics, advertisers spend between $15 billion and $17 billion per year targeting children in the United States, where the average child is exposed to more than 3,000 ads per day on television, the Internet, billboards, and in magazines.[2] When they see the actual toy or game in person at the store, they get excited and want what appears to be so much fun and enjoyment.

It is natural for you to want your child to have everything he or she needs from the basics of food, clothing, shelter, and love, to plenty of games, toys, and books. But at what point is providing too many things causing a disservice to your child?

Authors Kim Payne and Lisa Ross discuss how children need time to become themselves through play and interaction. In their book *Simplicity Parenting*, they mention that when you overwhelm children with all kinds of "stuff and choices," they will only want more. They point out that as you reduce the amount of toys and stuff, a child's attention span and capacity for deep play increases. Consequently, there are greater opportunities for kids to use their imagination and unleash their creativity.[3] Further, teaching children that they don't need material goods to be happy or healthy is a message that is more easily communicated with consistent denial of those material items in the moment.

EXERCISE: FEWER WORDS, MORE ACTION

How do all of these toys and games in your home affect your child's overall well-being? It is important to teach children that they don't need material goods to be happy or healthy. Ask your children to really consider why they want a certain item and what use they'll get from it before you consider buying it for them. For younger kids, it's as simple as saying, "No, we don't get things every time we go to the store. We're here for x, y, and z and if you see something you like, you can put it on your wish list." More times than not, they forget about what they wanted in the first place.

What if your children ask you to buy them something in the store and you don't want to get it because it's either junk, they don't need it, or you simply don't want to reward them for just coming to the store? Briefly state, "Just because you came to the store with me doesn't mean I'm going to buy something for you." Also, if you were planning on buying your child a video game, electronic device, or something he or she wanted, and it was out of your price range, you can say, "I was planning to spend $20 on a video game for you. If you can come up with the other $40 today, then you may get what you are asking for. It's your choice."

Start by setting expectations before entering a store or other establishments. You can say to your child, "We are at the store to buy new socks because your socks are worn out. If you want to go to the toys and games section while I shop, that is fine, but we will not be buying anything from there today." Setting the goals for the shopping trip ahead of time will help them understand that any effort to sway you will fail. And then stick to the plan.

Too many toys equal too many options. And too many options create undue anxiety. As it pertains to video games, a child's brain goes on overdrive and hyper-stimulates a part of the brain responsible for emotional behavior and motivation called the amygdala. This causes the brain to remain in a hyper-aroused state, which results in a heightened state of constant alertness, elevated levels of the stress hormone cortisol being released throughout the body, and an increased desire for stimulation.

If your child travels between you and the other parent's home regularly, it is important that you are on the same page regarding the number of toys and games at each parent's house. If not, the parent who has less toys and games will be asked for more and more of them—and on will go the battle, indefinitely. The other parent who has more toys will be doing their child a disservice by exacerbating the negative effects of excessive toys and games on their child.

PRAISING YOUR CHILD

No matter the situation, my advice is to avoid getting into a war of words with your children. When you struggle for power, you lose the power struggle with them and become increasingly frustrated all the while, thus paying the price. Take small steps starting now to incorporate genuine praise statements to encourage desired behavior.

Consider using what I call the P.R.I.C.E. technique for incorporating praise into your parenting style.

> P—**Personalize** the praise to your child ("What a great job you did cleaning your room today!")
>
> R—**Reason** for the praise ("You didn't need to be reminded to clean your room.")
>
> I—**Include** the child's specific desired behavior in your praise ("Cleaning the entire bedroom")

C—**Contribution** of the child's behavior ("Thank you for being a contributing member of this family and remembering to keep your bedroom clean and organized.")

E—**Encouragement** for future desired behavior ("I really appreciate your cleaning up and am glad that we can rely on you when we need help around the house.")

REWARDING YOUR CHILD

Every time nine-year-old *Bailey* sees her mother come to pick her up from the afterschool program, she suddenly turns on the Mr. Hyde persona and becomes very disrespectful and defiant toward her mother saying, "Stay away from me. Don't touch me." She then starts running around the daycare facility wildly, refusing to go home. The mother reacts by chasing after Bailey until she catches her. At that point, she whispers to her, "I will take you to get some ice cream today and maybe tomorrow you can get a toy or a game."

The daughter is a master of manipulation and the mother, unfortunately, falls prey to it each time. When the daughter is promised something, the switch flips back to obedient behavior and the tantrums suddenly discontinue.

The frequent use of material rewards such as money, candy, food, and toys to "control behavior" can result in your child coming to expect a reward for every accomplishment, and he or she will not carry out the desired task without receiving one. Social rewards such as verbal praise, play, or talk may pose a concern as well, if given for every good behavior incident. Depending on your child's personality, he or she may become more attached to the reward than to the behavior and consequently demand sociability in return for performance.

Although rewards work fine for B. F. Skinner's laboratory rats, they may not necessarily work for your child. Various studies suggest that children praised for doing well at something were less interested in pursuing it or did less well at later tasks. Dr. Joan Grusec, a University of Toronto psychology professor, found that children who were frequently praised by their mothers for displays of generosity tended to be less generous on an everyday basis than other children.[4]

Rewards can come in a variety of positive reinforcements that do not have to be announced to your child all the time:

- Immediate positive verbal feedback (e.g., a smile, high five, or quick verbal praise)
- Involvement in deciding on a special meal during the week

- Earning "special points" toward a toy, game, or book of some sort
- A choice of a television show or movie to watch
- Involvement in choosing a fun activity to play as a family

If things do not appear to be working and your child is not complying with the rules and expectations that are set forth, then should punishment be used as a last resort?

PUNISHING YOUR CHILD

The third form of effective discipline is *punishment*. This form should be used infrequently and only as needed. It should be employed as an opportunity for teaching by reinforcing what is expected. If you choose, however, to use this form of discipline with your child, you must be diligent in the examples you display.

Poor examples of punishment will confuse your child and adversely affect him or her. Rather than looking for a temporary solution for problems, it is best to demonstrate love, patience, understanding, fairness, and consistency in handling difficult situations.

Keep in mind that "discipline" and "punishment" are two different things.

> **Example**: A 14-year-old boy doesn't come home after school, but instead goes on his friend's bus and hangs out with him.
>
> **Ineffective Punishment**: Scream at him and tell him that he is grounded until further notice.
>
> **Effective Discipline**: Briefly explain that you were worried about his whereabouts and that he didn't call or text to ask if he could go over his friend's house. Remind him that he abused his freedom and was irresponsible in his decision to not come home right after school as he was supposed to. Follow that up with stating the specific consequence that results from the child's poor choice (e.g., not seeing any friends after school for the next week).

A great deal of evidence indicates that punishment is largely ineffective in changing behavior. When it does seem to work, the results are short-lived. Most importantly, punishment causes unnecessary and counterproductive anger and frustration in the parent–child relationship. Much to the chagrin of many parents, punishment contradicts the intended goal by rewarding a child with attention and a sense of control during inappropriate behavior, which increases the odds of recurring misbehavior.[5]

Spanking a child still remains a common, yet controversial, means to discipline a child, even an older one. Nowadays, spanking your child in public is the fastest way to get the Department of Children and Families knocking at your door. Beyond that, spanking teaches a child that hitting is an acceptable means of communication, which may beget more violence. It also teaches a child to avoid telling the truth out of fear that he or she will be punished in this manner. It is humiliating and degrading to a child, and in the long run, spanking teaches a child to fear that parent and not listen to or respect them. The child will most likely go on to develop poor self-esteem, develop resentment toward his or her parents, distrust adults, and become impulsive and aggressive with peers and adults.

For punishment to be effective, it must be paired with information and feedback about what is appropriate behavior, rather than what isn't.

- **Using time out**—Your child should be ignored when placed here. The general rule of thumb is one minute per age upward to twenty minutes for children who are fourteen years old. The place chosen should not have any built-in rewards such as a television or electronics. When time is up, briefly explain to your child the desired, acceptable way to behave next time. Then, shift the focus by offering to start a new activity. Time-outs may not necessarily eliminate the undesired behavior altogether, but it will decrease the frequency and is a good opportunity for a child to take a breath, calm down, and reset emotions.
- **Taking away privileges**—This is child specific, depending on their personality and what they like and dislike. Most tweens and teens respond best to having privileges taken away from them such as watching television, playing video games, using the computer, having their cell phone, hanging out with friends, and driving the car. Upon returning the privileges to your children, ask them about what decision they will make next time they encounter a similar situation.
- **Grounding**—This form of punishment involves restricting your child's activities for a certain time frame. Be clear and communicate with your child that he or she is not allowed to visit a friend this weekend because a certain rule has been violated. Don't budge on it no matter how hard your child pushes back at you!

Forms of physical and verbal punishment send mixed signals to a child about what is appropriate and expected conduct. As I mentioned before, a child being spanked or yelled at is not being taught a desired good behavior but rather experiencing an unwanted behavior. This physical punishment that my grandfather and many other children in his generation experienced had been widely accepted and used, at the time, to end bad behavior. Nowadays, any form of discipline that infringes on a child's basic rights, whether physical or psychological, indicates child abuse.

EFFECTIVE DISCIPLINE

When it comes down to it, effective discipline involves more than rewards and punishments. It is important for your child to feel loved and valued and have a positive perception of others in society in order to grow into a responsible, productive individual. Albert Einstein once said, "The most important decision we make is whether we believe we live in a friendly or hostile universe."

Apply these strategies for effective discipline with your child:

- Choose a designated area of the house that is safe, yet free of distraction, for a time-out.
- Address your child's *behavior* as bad, not your child.
- Discuss what your child has done wrong, what he or she should have done, and what he or she will do in the future.
- Refrain from granting special rewards that would have been given for doing the right thing.
- Take away privileges as a consequence for misbehavior or not following the given expectations.
- Pick your battles. One of the best ways to encourage good behavior from your child is to hold your standards high and expect good behavior. Impart a policy that clearly states the expectations that your child must follow as an active, contributing member of the family.
- Ignore bad behavior unless it poses a threat to your child's safety or someone else's. This method of managing children is particularly effective in reducing the number of tantrums. Spanking, admonishing, or giving attention to your child while he or she is having an outburst may unintentionally reward the undesired behavior.
- Provide attention to your child only when he or she calms down. Be sure bad behavior does not get your child a material or social reward. Avoid statements like "If you stop screaming, I will take you to get some dinner" or "I will buy you ice cream if you calm down right now. It's your choice."

Helping your children internalize an understanding of right and wrong, while being taught effective strategies to solve problems independently, will help them develop a positive sense of the world around them and gain self-initiative, self-control, an acute sense of self-awareness, and a genuine concern for others.

———◦◉◦———

Effective and positive discipline is the foundation for the development of a child's self-discipline and good character.

———◦◉◦———

Use the Right Style to Shape Your Child

"An individual's self-concept is the core of his personality. It affects every aspect of human behavior: the ability to learn, the capacity to grow and change. A strong, positive self-image is the best possible preparation for success in life."

—Dr. Joyce Brothers (American psychologist, television personality, and advice columnist)

One day I decided to call a good friend of mine who has five children and quite a few interesting experiences among them. He told me about the time he brought his oldest daughter, then nine-year-old *Brianna*, to go roller skating. The girl had never roller skated, skied, or ice skated before she attended her friend's birthday party at a roller rink. The outer rink was designated for the more experienced roller skaters, while the inner rink was designed more for the smaller kids and beginners. Brianna laced up her skates and insisted on skating with the bigger, more skilled kids on the outer rink. She demanded, "I am not a baby and want to be with the older kids!"

The mother was nervously watching her daughter venture into the speed lane as the bigger kids whizzed by her. She couldn't convince her daughter to come back into the inside rink and would have to watch as Brianna floundered around, being bumped by kids passing by her, and falling on her behind time after time.

After three hours of circling around, Brianna had figured out how to skate around without falling. Through sheer determination, she learned how to move forward and side-to-side by moving her legs in and out. In the end as she left the rink, Brianna was very proud of her newfound accomplishments.

What makes one child so bold and courageous and another one unwilling to take risks? The great debate on which came first, the chicken or the egg, marches on in terms of the cause and effect relationship between parenting style and a child's personality. Is it that your child is born with a certain personality type that offers you a road map to the parenting style that would be most effective? Or is your child's personality mainly determined by your parenting style?

PERSONALITY TYPES

The Personality Type system was originally devised by Swiss psychotherapist and psychiatrist Carl Jung and was later expanded by the American mother-daughter team of Katharine Cook Briggs and her daughter, Isabel Briggs Myers, who extensively studied Jung's work and developed the Myers-Briggs Type Indicator (MBTI). This system categorized sixteen possible psychological types based on four opposite pairs:[1]

Extraversion vs. Introversion *(two opposing ways that show how children are interested in the world around them)*

The *extrovert* child is more outgoing, socially adept, appearing very confident and self-assured because they regularly speak their mind. These children tend to be doers and jump right into the action. They are more comfortable being the center of attention and are interested in the outer world of people.

The *introvert* child, on the other hand, is more of an observer who is concerned with the inner world of concepts. These children appear to be socially awkward, shy, withdrawn, aloof, or indifferent. They take information in and fully process it before speaking or acting. When these children do share their ideas or insights, they prefer to wait before speaking until the situation is comfortable and then share their story in its entirety, without people interrupting them.

Sensing vs. Intuition *(two opposing ways that show how children take in information about the world)*

The *sensing* child observes their surroundings by using their five senses and takes in the actuality or facts in the present moment ("a realist"). These children quickly become accustomed to the way things are and prefer stability in their world. Sensors enjoy playing games and sports that are more physically engaging. These children are described as "in their bodies."

The *intuitive* child is interested in things out of the ordinary and prefers to look at the meaning of things and the connections between different things—using the "sixth sense" ("a dreamer"). They tend to have futuristic thoughts of possibilities that could be. These children also enjoy playing games and sports, but in an intellectual way ("living more in their minds") studying the why and how and anticipating the different possibilities in a game.

Some sensing children can have difficulty with projects that are open-ended and become frustrated when they aren't able to see an example of how to use the materials and what the end product should look like.

One of my former students was very interested in building robots. His father told me a story about when his son wanted to put together a robot and was unable to locate the booklet with the building instructions and drawings of the different models. He mentioned how his son became very upset and didn't know where to begin. The father told his son to play around with it for a while and create something from his imagination. The boy became quite frustrated and insisted, "I can't do this anymore. I need to have the instructions and see the pictures." His father attempted to make some sketches, but they didn't contain enough detail for his son to understand how to build the robot.

Thinking vs. Feeling *(two opposing ways that show how children evaluate information and view the world)*

The *thinking* child tends to be detached and impersonal by using objective information to make logical decisions based on looking at the pros and cons of a situation. They tend to analyze a situation, considering the logical consequence of the action, before making a decision. If they are going to play by the rules, they desire them to be fair and logical. These children get easily confused and upset when rules and expectations are inconsistent or unexplained.

The *feeling* child draws upon their emotions and makes decisions in a more personal, subjective way. These children consider how the decision or choice they make will impact or make others feel. They are compelled to do what is right and make other people feel happy. They often desire to be liked and go to great lengths to establish and maintain peace and harmony in their relationships.

One day, I called my students over to my desk to receive their test scores. One boy received a higher score than one of his peers. The "thinking" boy, with the higher test score, looked at his score and was upset that his grade wasn't higher. He judged his performance based on his results; while the "feeling" boy, with a lower score, was pleased with his grade. He told me that he had put forth a great amount of time and effort into studying for the test and was genuinely content with his performance.

Judgment vs. Perception *(how children organize the world around them)*

The *judging* child prefers to have a plan in advance and likes predictability. These children prefer things to be organized, where decisions are already made and conclusions about the outcome have been drawn. They also enjoy making decisions and are comfortable and relieved when a situation is settled and they know what to expect. Most "judging" children don't like change at all. They need advance notice when significant transitions are about to take place.

In teaching at the middle school level, I notice the transition difficulties that many students face from elementary to middle school. Some kids spend the summer before entering middle school being anxious about everything from social interactions to opening up their lockers to academic challenges that lie ahead. The "judging" child would benefit from practicing their locker combination, visiting the school, seeing the classrooms, and meeting their teachers in advance.

The *perceiving* child takes life in stride and "goes with the flow." These children prefer flexibility, spontaneity, and ambiguity, and often procrastinate to do things or postpone decisions. They enjoy a variety of options, rather than being bound into having to make a particular decision.

I get concerned, however, about the "perceiving" child when I assign a class project. I've noticed these students struggle to get started on specific tasks related to the project. I advise them to work in a systematic fashion that breaks down each of the tasks that they need to complete in order to fulfill the requirements of the assignment. Having them work through the tasks in a linear, orderly fashion provides a much needed structure that these children tend to lack.

This system helps them move methodically through a specific process from start to finish. If your child tends to have difficulty breaking down large assignments, it would be beneficial to get them a wall calendar for their room and together plan out a schedule to help them stay organized in completing different assignments and projects.

According to Myers and Briggs, people "truly" possess either one or the other component in each of the four different categories. They can possess the opposing component as well, but the difference lies in the natural, innate preference for one trait from birth, while they can also possess the opposing component, which is an acquired, learned trait over time.

The MBTI doesn't take into account other factors that influence your children, including their relationships with family and friends, the way they are educated in school, the surrounding environment in which they grow up, and any traumatic life experiences that occurred in early childhood. These factors play an important role in how your child uses his or her inborn traits.

The MBTI system, nonetheless, is a good predictor of how your child will use these inborn traits to *view the world*, *deal with different life experiences*, and *react to various situations*. Recognizing these natural preferences in your children, early on, will help provide you with great insight into their thoughts. Young children may be small, but their personalities are already manifesting. Your child's unique personality profile started to show up years ago, typically by two or three years old, and became evident by five years old.

You could apply the knowledge of your child's personality during the adolescent years in two specific ways. First, you can take an introspective look at your own view of the world and identify your own specific strengths and weaknesses. Secondly, this knowledge can be used to formulate your parenting style and to shed light on dealing with your child's unique personality and the challenges that lie ahead.

To prevent power struggles and frustration with your child, it is important to understand the reasons behind personality clashes.

These include the following:[2]

- Opposite personalities conflict.
- Similar personalities aggravate/annoy one another.
- Behavior doesn't meet expectations or suit specific environments (e.g., a rigid classroom).
- An adult feels extra responsible for controlling a child.
- Stress exaggerates strong traits.

Then there are experts whose school of thought contradicts the common belief of these "inherited traits." They declare that genes have nothing to do with behavior, but rather it is the parenting style that determines the child's personality.

Throughout the history of the long-standing nature versus nurture debate, there has not been a clear, decisive conclusion to the dispute. With recent scientific breakthroughs in the human genome, as well as the enormous amount of human interaction with their environment, it would be fair to state that both genetic and social influences impact a child's personality.

ETJ (Extroverted, Thinking, Judging) boys and IFP (Introverted, Feeling, Perceiving) girls receive reinforced, positive messages from society supporting their "masculinity" and "femininity," respectively.

ETJ girls, on the other hand, often receive strong messages from society that they should be less assertive and gentler and tone down their self-confidence. If you have an ETJ girl, it is important to provide support and reframe her behavior as something positive. If someone labels her bossy, perhaps you could offer "assertive" as an alternative. Leadership qualities in girls are just as important as they are in boys. This will help your daughter retain her natural self-esteem in the face of society's expectations.

IFP boys often receive the message that their characteristics are not accepted within what is considered "masculine" in our society. They might be called "girlie," which cuts both boys and girls down. *Masculinity* is measured by power, success, wealth, and status. Masculine men are perceived as white, middle class, early to middle-aged, and heterosexual. This sociological phenomenon of "manhood" takes a step further to exclude and to devalue other groups of people that are not within that classification such as women, non-white men, non-native-born men, and homosexuals.[3]

Teaching children to identify and express their emotions openly and honestly is very important for their social-emotional development. Statements like "Boys don't cry," "You're acting like a baby," or "Stop being a wimp" should be avoided altogether because they prevent genuine emotions from being expressed.

According to the social learning theory model developed by psychologist Albert Bandura, children become *gendered*. They learn how to behave as boys or girls early on through *observation* and *imitation*. A boy's first role model of what it means to be a man comes from his father. A boy observes how his father behaves with his mother in various situations. Also, the tone of a father's voice used in reprimanding his son, versus his daughter, displays an early learned behavior of "being a man"—which is *aggression*.[4]

During the socialization process, a child learns what behavior is socially expected and appropriate for a certain gender. Gendering takes place consciously and unconsciously in all aspects of society where our perceptions and behaviors toward individuals are adjusted based on age, gender, race, ethnicity, sexuality, and other contributing factors. Examples include how parents and teachers behave with boys versus girls, friends in how they play games and socialize, the clothes kids wear, the competitive and aggressive nature of activities performed, and the images of celebrities portrayed in the media.

PARENTING STYLES

When it is all said and done, it is your *parenting style* that has the most influence on the development of your child's *personality*. It can further develop your child's personality by matching or opposing his or her innate characteristics. Parenting style has been found to predict a child's well-being in the domains of social competence, academic performance, psychosocial development, and problem behavior.[5]

Two important elements on parenting include *parental responsiveness* and *parental demandingness*. Parental responsiveness involves providing love, warmth, and support, and fostering a sense of individuality in your child; while parental demandingness involves the type of discipline that is used and the demands or expectations for responsible behavior.

There are four main parenting styles that are currently observed today:

- **Authoritarian**—high parental demandingness, low or no parental responsiveness; a highly controlling, strict form of parenting that expects children to adhere to rules and expectations; children have little or no input into family decisions
- **Permissive**—low or no parental demandingness, high parental responsiveness; doesn't exert much control, where parents are generally relaxed and accepting of their children's behavior, good or bad
- **Authoritative**—high parental demandingness, high parental responsiveness; equal level of providing strict discipline and expressing love, warmth, and affection; recommended as the most beneficial parental style
- **Unresponsive**—low or no parental demandingness, low or no parental responsiveness; the parent is uninvolved in disciplinary actions and detached emotionally, not expressing love and affection to the child; the least beneficial parenting style

Although specific differences are evident among each parenting style, studies have found the greatest disparities between children from authoritative homes and their peers whose parents are unresponsive. Based on child reports, parent observations, and parent interviews, the benefits of authoritative parenting—where there is an equal level of parental responsiveness and demandingness—have been demonstrated as early as preschool, continuing throughout adolescence and into early adulthood. Authoritative parenting predicts good psychosocial outcomes, higher academic achievement, and less problem behaviors.

Despite the extensive research conducted on the different parenting styles, when it comes to raising your kids, every child is different. Some are better self-starters, while others need a push to get going. Some kids are more active and love to run around, while others would prefer sitting down playing video games, watching television, or reading a book. Some children tend to comply with rules, while others may be inclined to rebel against authority.

When there are multiple siblings, birth order is another factor that has influence on a child's personality. In general, oldest children tend to enjoy taking charge of situations and are bursting with confidence. Parents for their first child can be overly protective and try to do everything right, while also being strict and demanding.[6] These children tend to be perfectionists, which can lead to unhappiness, and oftentimes depression, if things don't go as expected.

Whatever personality the first born child possesses, middle children tend to be the antithesis of that. They are more apt to be the opposite version of their older siblings. These children, however, are difficult to label because their personalities develop in response to how they perceive their older sibling. If they see the older sibling getting attention from Mom and Dad for obtaining high grades, they tend to gravitate toward something else, whether it is playing sports or breaking the rules to get attention.

The youngest born child in a family grows up with more experienced, laid back parents who tend to let more things slide. As the baby of the family, they tend to be a little spoiled, charming, easygoing, social, outgoing, and have fewer responsibilities. They have more freedom to do things they want, which makes them usually the most creative of the children.

It's not necessarily, or simply, the birth order that seals your child's "personality fate" but rather your parenting practices that shape your child's attitude and behavior. Whether your child is first, middle, last born, or an only child, a key component to shaping their personality is how you treat them.

There isn't a perfect "one size fits all" formula to raising and shaping your children. Many parents disagree over what is the "right way" to bring up kids in today's society. When one parent does one thing and the other parent does something else, young children see things in absolute terms as "right" or "wrong." Over time, this difference will only undermine the child's respect for the "wrong" parent. When a united front is not there, it is difficult for one parent to enforce rules when the other parent doesn't follow through or support them.

When children are little, it may not seem to warrant a major consequence, but they are learning behaviors that become their foundation as they get older and when issues become more serious. As children get older, they will eventually come to view one parent as strict and the other as lenient and learn to approach the lenient parent first when asking for permission to go somewhere or do something such as go to a party with friends.

Kids tend to push the boundaries set by parents and test what they can get away with. They learn how to manipulate and wear down their parents to get what they want. For this very reason, you and the other parent should support one another and communicate what is best for your son or daughter and not fall into a manipulation trap. It may, in fact, save your child's life.

When it comes down to it, your children desire love, a feeling of importance, respect, and acceptance for who they are. Their strengths and weaknesses become more identifiable as they get older, which ultimately fosters a greater understanding of themselves. Applying this knowledge of shaping your children based on their unique personalities will help guide them toward making good choices as the pressures mount and the stakes get higher throughout their lives.

———◉———

Tailoring your parenting methods to your child's unique personality will build self-esteem for all aspects of his or her life.

———◉———

· 7 ·

Be on a Positive
Wavelength with Your Child

"Watch your thoughts; they become words. Watch your words; they become actions. Watch your actions; they become habits. Watch your habits; they become character. Watch your character; it becomes your destiny."

—Lao Tzu (ancient Chinese philosopher)

$\mathcal{I}$ was playing in one of the biggest end of season varsity high school golf tournaments in the Naugatuck Valley League. The view was magnificent, but thoughts of potential dangers lurked omnipresent. Looking straight out, there were penalties so palpable. Red-staked hazards on the right, out of bounds to the left, and a pond staring us straight in the face. This was a hole that had not been friendly to others in the past and ranked as one of the more difficult holes on the golf course where driving accuracy was at a premium.

A player from an opposing team had honors because he had scored the best on the previous hole and took his swing first. His drive safely found the fescue grass in the fairway and now with the added pressure to hit a solid shot, the player from the other opposing team in the threesome stepped onto the tee box and placed his ball on top of his tee.

About ready to swing, I heard him mumble to himself the kiss of death phrase in golf: "Just don't put it in the water. Anywhere else would be fine, just not in the drink." He placed his energy into that single, predominant thought of avoiding the water. He took his swing and off went his tee shot. At such a crucial point in the match, his ball started low off the ground and headed straight toward the middle of the pond. And guess what? Kerplunk! He had gotten exactly what he didn't want—the ball landing right into the pond.

Now, it was my turn. I felt the weight of the match pressing on me and knew that I needed to hit a good shot. Considering the fact that I lost a few strokes on the previous two holes, was dripping with perspiration from the heavy humidity, and saw my opponent's shot sitting pretty down the center of the fairway, I had to take a breath, collect my thoughts, and focus my attention on hitting a shot that ended in a positive result.

Golfers who understand the game accept the circumstances and conditions as they are in the present moment and envision a positive outcome before any swing has taken place. I knew what had to be accomplished so I made sure not to be remiss at that moment. I remember taking dead aim at my opponent's ball. I had an exact focus—a specific intention, you could say.

First, I lined up my clubface square to the ball sitting in the fairway. Then, I aligned my stance and set my grip appropriately and had one thought in mind: "Hit that ball sitting in the middle of the fairway!" I took my swing and there was never a doubt as it left the clubface. It was traveling on my envisioned target line and parachuted with precision and accuracy, landing fifteen yards past my opponent's ball in the center of the fairway.

With a sense of relief and rejuvenation, I was back in business. The momentum had shifted in the match and I completed the remaining holes in grand fashion by capturing medalist honors—best score of the round—for the match and helping our team secure a bid to play for the state championship.

That experience taught me the power of the mind and how our thoughts—both positive and negative—determine our actions. By simply affirming "Don't go in the water," my opponent's mind really heard only one word: *water* and reacted to it positively. When that very thought got expressed aloud in words, it translated into an action that landed him misfortune.

POSITIVE COMMUNICATION

The same principle applies for how children best learn certain behaviors. By instructing them about what they *should do*, as opposed to what they shouldn't do, gives a child focus on a positive directive and ultimately a desired positive outcome.

- Saying, "Please speak quietly," is more effective than saying, "Stop yelling."
- Saying, "Please walk," is better than, "Don't run."
- Saying, "Please touch your brother gently," is more beneficial than "Stop hitting him."

As a child gets older, the mind first registers the *action* and most of the time understands what *not* to do. Although, the most important word and the one that is most understood by children is the *action word* in the sentence. If kids hear "don't," "stop," or "no," then their minds will register the actions that follow those words.

You may ask the question, "Will using positive communication with your child work right away and all the time?" Well, the answer is, not necessarily. Positive directions, however, are clearer and more effective than those that are framed in the "no" and should be used most of the time when communicating with your adolescent. If your child's safety is at risk, it makes logical sense to get their immediate attention in order to prevent them from getting seriously hurt. For instance, "Don't touch that" or "Don't go after that ball in the road," would be deemed appropriate.

As your child gets older, adding the "no" part to your positive statement helps to clarify *acceptable* versus *unacceptable* behavior such as "You need to walk, not run." When your child is able to listen and understand the "why" aspect to your command, you can add a brief explanatory statement describing the reason for your positive request. For example, "You need to walk, not run. You might run into someone or something and get hurt or hurt someone else."

Your child may be interested in playing a sport that you feel is too dangerous and may compromise his well-being. Speaking in the negative such as "Don't do this," or "Don't do that" may not get the desired reaction you are seeking from your child. Just saying, "I *don't* want you playing football. It's *too dangerous* and you could get *hurt*," may not be enough for your adolescent.

Try adding a positive spin to your statement by including a brief explanation such as "I know you expressed interest in playing football. However, the risk of getting a concussion, broken bones, or other serious issues is too high, and I want you to stay safe. You can choose to play either soccer or basketball instead. You can think about it and let me know. It is your choice."

Here are some examples of negative statements given by adolescents and positive responses given by their parents:

Child: "I can't do math."

Parent: "Take your time and go through the steps carefully and try again. I have confidence in you and know you can do it."

Child: "Jenna hates me. I have no friends."

Parent: "Sounds like you're feeling rejected by Jenna and that must hurt. I know you want her to like you. Remember that you're perfect just the way you are, no matter what she, or anyone else, says or does. And, you know, she may have her own problems that has nothing to do with you."

Child: "I'm just no good in social studies."

Parent: "You've brought up Cs before. I know you can do it again. Besides that, nobody is good at everything. And look at this B+ in math, you've always done well with numbers!"

Child: "I'm so clumsy. I'll never learn to skate!"

Parent: "It's tough learning something new. Every expert was once a beginner. Remember when you first tried to ski, how hard it was? But you stuck with it, and now you're really good at skiing."

Your children are at a stage where being self-conscious, having self-doubt and insecurities are commonplace. They are developing their own perceptions of the world around them and are experiencing various forms of pressures, both socially and academically. It is important for you to do everything you can to foster positive thinking in your child during these formative years.

Using pejorative words makes them feel less valued and less important. Parents who communicate positively and effectively with their children help influence their child's willingness to follow rules and expectations day in and day out. These children come to see their parents as trustworthy, helpful, and understanding and have less conflict in relationships and in the workplace as they get older.

SOCIAL MEDIA

Kids today are exposed to a massive amount of negative messages portrayed from different arenas including politics, film, television, music, video games, and on the Internet. These days, teens are visiting many different social media outlets and chat apps where they post, like, share, chat, and meet new people. This may sound like a management crisis waiting to happen and incredibly overwhelming to keep track of all the latest social media frenzy that your child is involved in such as Facebook, Twitter, Instagram, YouTube, Tumblr, Google+, Snapchat, WhatsApp, Kik, Whisper, Skout, Skype, and so on. But just as these social media outlets are simple for your child to use, there are ways for you to establish boundaries for these online activities.

A big concern for parents today is not only monitoring what their children see and do in the physical world, but also supervising their phone and online activities. In the United States, nearly 80 percent of teenagers own a mobile phone and half of them are smartphones—with access to the Internet, social media, cameras, and games.[1] When it comes to your child's phone use, you want to be able to trust them with the decisions they make and respect their privacy, but you also want to ensure their safety and overall well-being. Knowing all that your children are exposed to, you may consider purchasing tracking apps and monitoring software to keep up with their phone and online activity.

TeenSafe is an application designed to help parents monitor their children's text messages, call history, social network activity, and Internet use without them knowing. Apps of this nature, however, have their benefits and disadvantages. Being privy to the conversations kids are having with their friends and other people can alert parents to issues going on that their children may be reluctant to share, such as harassment, bullying, sexting, and sending seemingly innocent messages, photos, and videos. Giving parents full access and visibility into their children's world, however, may appear to violate their privacy and undermine their ability to make wise decisions.

Clearly, your children want you to grant them some level of independence and trust with the decisions they make with their phone and online activities. The Internet offers a world of undiscovered and uncharted territory that children are naturally curious about. Part of responsible parenting is open communication with children and educating them on these dangers.

If you decide to use a tracking app to monitor your child's phone and online activities, it should be used with your child's full knowledge and an explanation. Rather than the message coming off negatively as "I don't trust you and have installed an app to track your phone and online activity," you can have an open conversation with your child by positively stating, "There are so many people and things out there that are dangerous and can hurt you. I realize your privacy is important and I trust that you will make good decisions. However, it is my obligation and duty to make sure that your activities are safe and that is why a safety measure has been put into place with your phone for that reason."

Despite all the efforts that you put forth to protect your children from making bad choices on social media outlets or temptations to see things they shouldn't be viewing on the Internet, they may still make poor choices along the way. Tracking your kids' activities opens up an opportunity to have a discussion with them about the choices they are making and how to avoid making bad ones in the future. It also allows you to discuss issues in their lives when they are happening, rather than waiting to find out when it becomes too late.

FORMING POSITIVE BELIEFS

The effect of the mass media is quite pervasive throughout the world and is one of the most significant influences on shaping public perceptions through the choice of information shared and how it is disseminated. How media portrays or stereotypes various professions, genders, ethnicities, and other groups of people is widely evident throughout music, television, movies, articles, and pictures in newspapers, magazines, and especially on the Internet. This distorted perception can lead to misunderstandings that become part of your child's belief system, resulting in potential consequences in his or her interactions with other people.

Your child's beliefs, values, and traditions form in early childhood and by having the right attitude, kids can take the right actions to live a successful, fulfilling life. The messages that family members impart on children have a tremendous effect on how they view the world. It is critical that children receive positive messages about people from all backgrounds and communities, including how each person is instrumental in *helping our society* rather than *causing problems*. These empowering, positive messages help educate children and may possibly prevent acts of violence, racism, xenophobia, homophobia, elitism, and singling out a person based on their age, gender, sexuality, height, weight, or any other physical attributes or disabilities.

Your thoughts could be healing or sickening to your overall well-being. In addition to your beliefs and attitudes affecting your own relationships with people, they also become your basis for your mental, emotional, and physical health. There is a simple yet complex relationship between one's mind and body.

Many studies have shown a link between physical disorders and a negative state of mind. Attitudes associated with anger, fear, depression, and greed have been demonstrated to give rise to various health conditions such as heart disease, ulcers, digestive problems, asthma, and other specific organ complications.[2]

Positive statements are sources of *empowerment* that should be used regularly with your child. When your child is feeling down or upset about something, using positive statements can reinforce positive thoughts and feelings to help boost *self-confidence* and promote a *positive attitude*, thus encouraging desirable behavior. Here are some examples:

- "That's a great idea that you gave me. I love hearing your ideas."
- "You did a nice job taking care of the dog today. Thank you."
- "That's a great question you asked. I like how you think."
- "I love this drawing. You are such a talented artist."
- "Thank you for remembering to take out the garbage. You are so thoughtful."
- "You are such a smart kid. I am very proud of you."

You can also teach your children to make *positive affirmations* about themselves. Using words like "I will," "I can," or "I am," will help them generate self-confidence and a belief in their abilities. When your child is feeling down or upset, try to help alter the focus away from what he *does not* want and *can't do* and onto what he *desires, can,* and *will do.*

- "I will practice every day to make the basketball team."
- "I will learn how to play this song."
- "I am a good listener and a good friend."
- "I am capable of getting good grades when I put forth good effort."
- "I did it!"
- "I am smart!"
- "I can do this!"

Optimism and pessimism are learned behaviors and your personal outlook on life can largely affect your child's outlook. The messages given to us about who we are and the world that we live in start early in childhood and continue to change and evolve throughout the seasons of our lives. *Positive self-talk* can help in building confidence and in overcoming different obstacles. Just remember that your children's daily thoughts turn into self-fulfilling prophecies for them, either positively or negatively spoken, and largely determine the decisions they make throughout their lives.

Here are three self-evident truths that I would encourage you to print out, laminate, and post in your child's room:

1. *You get what you expect.*
2. *As you think, so shall you become.*
3. *Your attitude determines your destiny.*

Communicate positive messages and affirmations with your children to ignite in them self-love and love for others.

· 8 ·

Give Your Child the License to "Leadership and Problem Ownership"

"Leadership is solving problems."

—Colin Powell (former Secretary of State
and four-star U.S. army general)

It was another morning and yet another struggle for one of my students, twelve-year-old *Will*, who had already been tardy to school a dozen times and truant about ten or so days. Every morning, Will's mother knocked on the bedroom door to wake her son, but always to no response. And minutes later, she would go back into Will's room and remind him that it was time to get up and get ready for school. With each attempt more futile than the last, she reached a point where she went by his bedside and screamed at him to get him up.

Will would pull the covers over his head time and time again and refuse to obey her commands. From there, a yelling match would ensue between the two of them, each time resulting in Will missing the bus. Most of the time, Will got up thirty minutes to sometimes an hour late and his mother ended up driving him to school. It even got to a point where the mother went as far as calling the school resource officer to come and get him out of bed, and yet Will continued the same oppositional behavior pattern thereafter.

ACCOUNTABILITY

As long as the mother didn't make Will accountable for his behavior, he would continue this way and let his mother assume the burden. Will's unwillingness to get up on time to catch the bus, however, was his and not his mother's problem.

63

It was only the beginning of the school year and Will's mother already was struggling with this problem that wasn't truly hers, although she made it out to be something that *she* had to fix. Her son received a detention for his numerous unexcused tardies. But this consequence, however, didn't seem to change his recurring behavior, as he continued to arrive late to school each morning. Consequently, the mother was requested to come in for a conference to discuss a strategy to remedy the situation.

Our team had a long discussion with Will's mother about her son's inability to get himself out of bed and to school on time each morning. Will's teachers, guidance counselor, and social worker designed a plan that was presented to the mother. We started with restructuring Will's bedtime one hour earlier so he was able to obtain at least eight hours of sleep. We suggested that any electronic game or cell phone use cease a half hour before bedtime and during that time Will would pick out his clothes, organize his backpack, and help prepare his lunch for the next day. This would decrease the tasks that needed to be done each morning and would allow for extra sleep time as well. We also proposed to the mother to have the lights off and remove all electronics from his bedroom before he went to sleep.

The final piece of our plan was to call Will into the meeting and review the expectations and consequences with him. Presenting a plan during a time when everyone was calm, even-tempered, and in one room was an effective strategy to maximize the odds of a complete turnaround in Will's behavior. It was important that we were clear and up front with Will about the specific consequences that he would assume if he still didn't get himself out of bed when he was supposed to without any reminders. It was also necessary that all parties involved remain detached emotionally from the outcome—either good or bad.

The consequences that we stated to Will included removal of all electronic devices that day, having to make up any missed work after school hours, and losing weekend privileges. We asked Will if he understood why this plan was put into place and if he felt that he could do it. He didn't seem too cheerful about the plan, but it made sense to him and he clearly understood the repercussions. We asked for his input and he requested that his mother give him just one wakeup reminder in the morning. Mom agreed to that offer for one week and after that, he would need to find his own solution for waking up on time.

Will's mother left that meeting feeling sanguine about the prospects of her son getting out of bed and ready for school on time. What seemed like an overnight success was just a solid, well-structured plan with clear consequences put into place where problem ownership fell where it should—onto the child. Will was regularly getting to school on time and establishing a much improved routine, taking ownership for the choices he was making.

How do you know if a problem is going to affect you and your child or just your child? To accurately determine this, ask yourself objectively, "Will the problem directly affect me if it doesn't get resolved?"

> **Problem 1**: Your child refuses to eat dinner that you made.
> **Result**: Your child does not eat dinner and is hungry; you eat and feel satisfied.
> **Problem 2**: You get a call from the teacher that your child is in trouble for disrupting class.
> **Result**: The child gets an afterschool detention; you are not in trouble.

If you find yourself having difficulty getting your child out of bed, you must firmly lay the ground rules by saying, "I know that you have a hard time getting up in the morning and I've tried my best to help you. From now on, I am no longer going to wake you up to get ready for school. It is your responsibility to come up with your own plan to get up, get ready, and not miss the bus."

Provide your child an opportunity to come up with a *plan of his own*. If he truly can't think of a solution, you can suggest some choices for him. If your child still refuses to follow directions and doesn't come up with any solutions, make choices for him and reinforce the consequences.

The following consequences can apply to most situations in order for your children to learn how to *own* and *solve their problems*:

- **Pay back what was lost**—If you have to bring your children to school or call for a truant officer to pick them up because they missed the bus, determine how much money you or the officer spent on gas to get them to school and deduct that from their weekly allowance. If they don't have an allowance, set up chores for them to pay off the debt.
- **Walk to school**—Depending on the distance and how safe the environment is for your children to walk to school, this is a natural consequence that holds them accountable for their actions.
- **Removal of privileges**—This technique is best used when you are not satisfied with your child's behavior. Depending on their unique interests, not allowing your child to play a video game, use the computer, or have his phone for a specific time frame can be an effective way to curb unwanted behavior.
- **Providing a reward system**—This technique is best used when you are satisfied with your child's behavior. This may be useful when they earn back the privileges they lost and continue to demonstrate desirable behavior. Incorporate the "passes," "chips," or "tokens" system for

your child to earn different privileges such as computer time, video game play, phone use, a trip to the movie theater, a sleep over with a friend, a special meal or dessert, and so on. On the weekend, redeem the passes, chips, or tokens that were earned throughout the week.

When you have decided on the specific consequences for when your child breaks the rules, have him first remind you of the expected behavior, followed by the specific consequences associated with violating the expectations. You can say, "So, what is it that you should be doing? And how exactly will that work?" Then, have your child state the consequences in his own words as an agreement between you and him. From this point, you must be willing to allow your child to suffer the consequences if, and when, he goes against the expectations set forth.

There may be times where you feel the urge to want to "save your children" from their problems. But in actuality, you would be taking away a golden opportunity for them to learn from their choices and mistakes. The earlier children learn from their mistakes, such as forgetting to bring lunch to school, choosing not to do their homework, getting a bad grade on a test, or spending money on something frivolous, the less costly price they will have to pay for bigger problems in the future.

I've had many conversations over the years with parents about their children's grades. Recently, I had multiple e-mails going back and forth with the father of one of my students regarding his son's grade on a project. After stating the specific requirements for the project, which his son and partner did not satisfy, the father still could not understand why his son received a below satisfactory score on this project.

He wanted to dispute the grade and insisted on speaking with me over the phone about the concerns he had over the amount of work that his son had put forth on the project—as opposed to his son's project partner—and it not being reflected in his grade. He thought that the level of effort his son put forth on this project should have translated into a successful outcome. I realized that the father was *owning his son's problems* and that this would be a good talking point to have with his son.

The father expressed how this was a good learning experience not only for his son but also for him. He was pleased with the strategy we discussed— that he didn't have to micromanage his son's grades and could let the burden fall where it should—onto his son.

If children aren't held accountable for their actions and allowed to make mistakes and experience consequences when they are young, they will likely make poor decisions concerning more serious issues such as smoking, alcohol, substance abuse, gambling, sex, college acceptance, and career choices.

To achieve this momentous goal, it is important to realize that if your children see how concerned you are with their problems, they will no longer feel obligated to solve them on their own because "Mommy" and "Daddy" will come to the rescue all the time.

TAKING OWNERSHIP

You have a unique and challenging task to help guide your children in a positive direction, without controlling their every move. It is important, therefore, for your children to gain a sense of independence and responsibility, to take ownership of their actions and learn from their mistakes.

Taking ownership of problems tends to be an issue for a child of a *helicopter parent* who comes to the rescue at the first sign of difficulty or distress in their child's life. The term was first used in Dr. Haim Ginott's 1969 bestselling book *Between Parent and Teenager* by teens who said that their mothers hovered over them like helicopters.[1] It has become so widely used that it was added into the *Merriam-Webster* dictionary in 2011.

To the defense of these parents, I'm sure they have the best of intentions to protect their children from the dangers of the world and want what's best for them and don't see themselves in this role. However, this form of parenting often goes beyond just wanting to be involved in their child's life, but rather wanting to control much of what they do on a regular basis. They tend to assume too much responsibility for their children's lives: the choices they make, their success and failures included.

Many of these parents witness other parents being immersed into their children's activities and feel that it is their obligation to do the same; otherwise they are not fulfilling their duty as a "good parent." These overcontrolling and overprotective parental behaviors, however, could pose some major problems for a child's self-esteem and their ability to make good choices down the road.

A few years ago, our school district provided online access for student grades in each of the subject areas, broken down by homework assignments, projects, quizzes, and tests. The grading portal gives students an opportunity to become more aware of, and responsible for, their academic performance. It has also opened the door for parents to check up on their child's progress as often as they desire, which provides an opportunity for parents to send e-mails that question certain grades, request retakes for their child's poor quiz or test grade, and ask for late assignments to be accepted for credit.

There is a litany of psychological ramifications associated with this form of over-parenting. For one, if kids aren't given the opportunity to take responsibility for their actions and struggle through things on their own, they may have a hard time developing skills necessary for making good choices and solving their own problems. They tend to look for advice from someone else and rely on others to pick up the pieces for them when something goes wrong.

It's important for children to have an opportunity to make their own choices and organize their schedule. However, some children have their decisions and schedule already determined for them. I recall asking one of my students what she planned on doing when she got home from school; she had absolutely no idea. Her response to me was nonetheless surprising. "My mother has my schedule planned for me including the daily afterschool activities," she said. I asked her, "When do you do your homework?" She replied, "It depends. I'm not sure about today. My mother has it written down somewhere on a spreadsheet." Overplanning a child's schedule can lead to a *lack of self-confidence* in being able to achieve things and a dependency on others to make important choices throughout life.

LEADERSHIP

The greatest challenge of parenthood is to raise your children to become responsible adults. Former First Lady of the United States Eleanor Roosevelt once said, "You gain strength, courage and confidence by every experience in which you really stop to look fear in the face. You must do the thing you think you cannot do."[2]

In the book *Leading Minds: An Anatomy of Leadership*, Howard Gardner defines a leader as an individual or, rarely, a set of individuals who significantly affect the thoughts, feelings, and/or behaviors of a significant number of individuals.[3] Although some of today's leaders in society may not be seen in the most positive light, it is imperative for your child to witness the impact an individual can have as a good leader.

For instance, military leaders have organized groups of highly trained combatants to perform team-based leadership situations and make important decisions that they would carry out in wartime. These leaders have serious roles of establishing strategic plans of action and recreating battlefield scenarios.

In accordance with many political experts including the public, Abraham Lincoln, the sixteenth president of the United States, has often been considered America's greatest president for his leadership during the American Civil War and his eloquence as an orator in speeches such as the Gettysburg Address.

Lincoln was one of the greatest examples of perseverance, exemplifying someone who rose from poverty, endured countless failed political attempts, and eventually became an American president who worked tirelessly to end slavery. According to Russian novelist Leo Tolstoy, Lincoln's greatest trait consisted of the "integrity of his character and moral fiber of his being."[4]

Acts of leadership come in many different forms. Kids see it every day with teachers in running an effective classroom and the day-to-day choices you make as a head of household and caretaker. Some kids stand up for others being bullied, while others perform chores around the house without being asked.

I was truly amazed when I heard about the stories of some inspiring kids who demonstrated their leadership in extraordinary ways.[5] Twelve-year-old Abby Miller had stepped up to help collect donations for her younger four-year-old friend who suffers from neuroblastoma, a form of cancer affecting the nervous system. She raised thousands of dollars to help with her friend's medical expenses by singing songs in the street on a cold day, while passersby would graciously contribute to a donation bucket for her cause.

After seeing the BP oil spill in the Gulf of Mexico on television, eleven-year-old Olivia Bouler used her talents as an artist to raise money for cleanup costs. She had raised an incredible $200,000+ for the National Audubon Society and its wildlife recovery efforts.

Children who understand how to relate to other people through communicating and listening are viewed as leaders. They form positive relationships with others and refrain from attracting negative attention to themselves in various social encounters with their peers. They successfully interpret social situations and learn how to make judgments and decisions on their own about different circumstances.

Here are some techniques to help facilitate leadership behavior in your children:

- **Lead by example**—Being a role model by demonstrating respect to others presents a clear example of desirable behavior that you expect of your child. Communicate the message verbally that "Displaying respect for others shows respect for yourself." Also, when you see your children exhibit leadership behaviors, don't hesitate to praise them for their actions by saying, "I am very proud of you for _____ (e.g., helping your sister with her homework today)."
- **Include your children as part of the decision-making process**—Provide your children with regular opportunities to make decisions. This will help them feel empowered and not resent you for constantly making decisions for them. Allow them to make choices by asking, "What

would you like for dessert tonight, vanilla or chocolate ice cream?" or "Where would you like to go on Saturday, to the mall or to the movies?"

- **Encourage them to get involved in activities that promote leadership skills**—Offer your children different opportunities to become part of different afterschool clubs or activities such as Boy/Girl Scouts, student council, sports activities, stage shows, and authentic performances. If your children do not have an interest in joining an established activity, have them speak directly with an administrator at their school about starting a new club.
- **Expose them to leaders**—If you are able to bring your child to work with you, introduce them to your boss or someone you feel demonstrates the qualities of a good leader. When kids see firsthand how good leaders act, they are better able to emulate their behavior.
- **Help them set individual goals**—When your children learn how to set individualized goals, they tend to take ownership of them and desire to see them through to completion.

What makes leadership such an important skill today? The leadership skills are the backbone of your child's ability to handle different problems such as peer-related issues, school-related projects, group activities, and sports. As they grow older, their decisions become that much more important and the consequences of those decisions become graver. Emphasizing the motto "Great leaders are made, not born" will go a long way in helping develop leadership qualities in your child.

———————

The best leaders are problem solvers and the best solutions for your children's problems lie within your children. They must own them and resolve them.

———————

Get Your Kid "iMotivated"

"In essence, if we want to direct our lives, we must take control of our consistent actions. It's not what we do once in a while that shapes our lives, but what we do consistently."[1]

—Anthony Robbins (author and motivational speaker)

Christmas is supposed to be a festive time for many children around the world. This time of year in 2012, however, was a real-life nightmare for the Delhi 14 children. These young Indian boys became the victims of sheer inhumanity, exploitation, and neglect. They suffered while working long, continuous hours in harsh, inhospitable conditions.[2]

The moment eleven-year-old Rahim boarded a train to India's capital, he became enslaved as an indentured servant. The boy was taken to a dark and begrimed sweatshop in LNJP colony and was forced to work eighteen hours a day, every day. Allowed only two 10-minute breaks for eating, he was not permitted to leave the premises and had to cook food for both his employer and himself. He was not paid for his work either, despite being promised compensation. To make matters worse, Rahim would be scolded by his employer and even beaten with his shoe. Similar to Rahim, another boy, twelve-year-old Aslam was whisked away into the same unsanitary sweatshop and worked long, arduous hours without pay.

Unafraid of the violent reaction from the gangmasters, a courageous group called the Global March Against Child Labour prepared a rescue mission to save these boys. The police smashed the locks to the pitch-dark six-foot by six-foot cell where the fourteen boys were being kept. From that very moment, they were released from this imprisonment and saved from a life of child labor and bestial treatment.

The stories of trafficked, imprisoned, and exploited children, unfortunately, do not stop there. There are millions of children being sold by their families to child labor and forced into lives of despair and slavery. Although the worldwide number of children in child labor has declined by a third since 2000, child labor persists and denies millions of children the right to an education and often exposes them to downtrodden and violent environments. According to the International Labour Organisation, child labor persists for 168 million children worldwide aged five to seventeen, in which 120 million are below the age of fourteen and 85 million participate in hazardous work.[3]

Discussions are currently being made by the Indian Parliament to ban child labor under fourteen and restrict the minimum age to eighteen, ensuring that all children can attend school. Until all children are required to go to school in India, Southeast Asia, and Africa, this vicious circle will continue to spin and its depressing march from generation to generation will carry on.

In spite of all the long-standing adversity that these rescued children in India endured throughout their grueling work days, without any pay and sleeping in the same room where they worked, they possess an immense *motivation* to achieve great heights. One of the rescued children, eleven-year-old Abdul, shared his experiences on a film posted on EducationEnvoy.com. He said,

> A man approached my mother and asked her to send me with him to Delhi for earning money. She agreed and I came to Delhi along with that man. I was employed in a small workshop and used to work from 10 a.m. till midnight every day making gift items. It was extremely tiring to work for so long. My employer did not pay me anything. He used to scold me very often. I am very happy to be free and I would like to study and become a teacher when I grow up.[4]

Another boy said, "I want to study and become a soldier when I grow up." These stories are heart wrenching to read and unimaginable for us, but they are very real for children in third-world countries. However, even those children understand the importance of education and show desire and hope in making their lives better. This is a definite contrast from the mindset of the majority of adolescents today growing up in Western culture.

MOTIVATING CHILDREN

At one point or another, you may have experienced your child underachieving at something. Maybe it was a sudden drop in a grade or the desire to perform well at a certain task. There could be a myriad of explanations for why your child lacks motivation in certain things. Maybe there is a high level of difficulty in a subject matter or a low level of interest in a topic(s). Social interactions and relationships could be taking on a higher priority in their life.

Author Dr. David Goslin of *Engaging Minds: Motivation and Learning in America's Schools* discusses the variety of barriers that can impede a child's motivation. He says that children typically learn from their parents the value of *effort* as a key to success. They learn that a "good student" is one who works hard, puts forth good effort, and completes assignments on time.

When children reach puberty, they often become more concerned with peer opinion than academic success. At this age, they learn to compare themselves with their friends and greater effort becomes associated with lesser ability. Sometimes in class before a big test, I hear kids asking one another if they studied. The popular response is "No, I didn't study that much for the test" or "I didn't need to study. I understand it," when in fact, many of them associate effort with poor ability.

In Japan, children are groomed from early childhood on the importance of effort for success. This has been well documented on their hours worked per week. A stark contrast between American and Japanese test scores becomes apparent by fifth grade. This is the period when many American students begin to rely more on their ability than effort.

Insufficient student effort has been a major area of concern in American school reform initiatives. Dr. Goslin estimates that 25 percent of students are motivated to learn, 50 percent are engaged enough to get by to avoid both social stigma as a "nerd" or "geek" and negative consequences such as failing grades, while the remaining 25 percent are not motivated to achieve at all.[5]

So why are so many American children lacking *iMotivation*, an internal motivation, for high achievement? Let's take a look at this contemporary generation of American children—often called the "iGen kids"—and the unprecedented amount of materialistic goods they possess from clothes, toys, smartphones, cameras, computers, iPods and iPads, to all the video game systems and much more.

According to Jean Twenge and W. Keith Campbell, both professors of psychology and authors of *The Narcissism Epidemic*, American children of this generation possess a high amount of materialistic goods and have been granted "unprecedented authority" where they are no longer seeking their parents' approval, but rather parents are seeking their children's approval.[6]

Carolina Izquierdo, an anthropologist at the University of California, Los Angeles, spent several months with the Matsigenka tribe of about twelve thousand people who live in the Peruvian Amazon. One of her expeditions involved going on a leaf-gathering trip down the Urubamba River with a local family. A six-year-old girl named Yanira, who was from a different family, asked if she could come along on the trip. The girl's behavior during those five days made such an impression on Izquierdo.

Twice a day, Yanira swept the sand off the sleeping mats, and helped stack the kapashi leaves for transport back to the village. Then in the evening, she fished for crustaceans and cleaned, boiled, and served them to the others. Izquierdo recalled that the girl found ways to make herself useful to the family and asked for nothing in return.[7]

While Izquierdo was conducting research in the Peruvian Amazon, her colleague, Elinor Ochs, was studying social interactions among families in Los Angeles, California. She had arranged to have the families filmed as they ate, fought, made up, and did the dishes. In one instance, a father pleaded with his tween son five times to take a shower or a bath. After the fifth plea went ignored, the father picked up his son and carried him into the bathroom. A few minutes later, the child, still unwashed, went into another room to play a video game.

In another encounter, an eight-year-old girl sat down at the table ready to eat. Seeing that there wasn't any silverware laid out for her, she asked, "How am I supposed to eat?" Although the girl was clearly aware of the place the silverware was kept, her father got up and went into the kitchen and brought it to her anyway.

So, why did six-year-old Yanira gladly assist in these responsible tasks, while the children studied in the Los Angeles families would not willingly perform basic requested tasks? Both Izquierdo and Ochs wrote an article for *Ethos*, the journal of the Society of Psychological Anthropology, in recounting Yanira's behavior during the trip down the river and the behaviors in the Los Angeles families at home.

Although the study highlighted only two specific regions, it shed some light on our understanding of how American children differ in some key aspects of their values as compared to a foreign culture. It highlighted a major difference between how parents in different cultures rear young people to assume adult responsibilities. It is evident that the Los Angeles family members help their children at home like Matsigenka children help their families at home.

EXERCISE: MAKING AN *iMOTIVATION* SHIFT

So, what explains why today's kids often appear largely unmotivated to perform basic daily tasks and chores around the house while children from other cultures, like Yanira from the Matsigenka tribe, see this as a regular way of life? This exercise will help you to identify the expectations and responsibilities you have assigned to your children and how many of these you are actually taking on, consciously or not.

It may be easy to let things slide and less time consuming to complete the actual chore yourself, such as taking out the garbage, organizing your child's room, setting and cleaning the dinner table, or helping with homework, but these actions are not helping to develop your child's self-discipline.

Write down your responses to the following questions. This will help provide a focus to shift the onus onto your child for assuming day-to-day responsibilities.

- "What expectations do I have for my child?" – Write down at least five expectations that you have for your child and mention how they would be of value to him or her.
- "What specific responsibilities have I given my child? How will they best serve him or her and our family?" – If you have a hired hand come to your house for any service(s)—such as house cleaning, yardwork, landscaping, and so on—consider having your child take on that duty instead.
- "Do I come to the rescue at my child's beck and call?" – Write down ten to fifteen things that you have done for your child over the past week. Go through your list and check off the ones that can be easily and readily assumed by your child.
- "When have I said 'no' to my child and changed my mind?" – Write down the instances where you either said "no" and changed your mind, or you didn't want to frustrate or disappoint him or her and against better judgment said "yes." Check off those occasions and don't be afraid to say "no" the next go around and actually mean it.

Today's generation of kids may represent the most indulged young people in the history of the world. If children haven't been told "no" or aren't accustomed to having responsibility, they may have difficulty coping with stress, failure, adversity, and pain. If someone is there to always solve their problems for them, they may lack a realistic sense of their own strengths and weaknesses, and when the going gets tough, the *motivation* to succeed tends to disappear.

WHAT MOTIVATES YOUR CHILD

Each child, ultimately, differs in what makes him or her happy. Some children are motivated by academic success, while others find passion in art, music, dancing, and/or sports. For some, competition and winning a trophy or prize are great sources of achievement, while other children may value social popularity or getting money.

There are three major qualities associated with *high motivation* and ways to help your child develop them:[8]

- **Persistence**—This is the ability to continue with a task after the cause has been removed. Children who experience success at a challenging task tend to display a positive, engaged emotion and welcome another challenging task. It's a good idea to encourage your children whenever they hit an obstacle to keep going and not give up. You can also help structure the environment to be creative and exciting with books, paper, games, puzzles, and other materials for hands-on learning and discovery. Allowing your children ample time when doing a task so they are able to successfully complete it, without interruption, would greatly benefit them, too.
- **Low dependency on adults**—Children with high *iMotivation* do not seek adult approval or assistance in helping with tasks. Children who have a low level of *iMotivation*, or are extrinsically motivated, demand constant attention and approval from others, and have a difficult time achieving tasks independently. Be careful about using extrinsic rewards for increasing motivation, as this can interfere with your child's intrinsic desire to perform the task well. Consequently, your child may only do a task in order to receive a reward such as money, candy, a toy, and/or excessive praise. In such situations, children may develop a loss of self-worth and judge their own value through the number of rewards and/or the amount of praise they receive.
- **Positive display of emotion**—Children who show an optimistic, positive attitude toward a task get more enjoyment from it, as opposed to children who show a lack of motivation while doing a task, complain, are quiet, appear bored, or whine. You can introduce a different activity to your child to help spark interest, leading toward new discoveries and adventures.

Author, salesman, and motivational speaker Zig Ziglar said, "People often say that motivation doesn't last. Well, neither does bathing—that's why we recommend it daily."[9] His comedic message gives insight to the importance of continuously implementing strategies to help foster the three qualities—persistence, low dependency on others, and positive display of emotion—associated with highly motivated individuals.

Human behavior specialist and author Dr. John Demartini of *The Values Factor* indicates how motivation is derived from "awakening your genius."

When a child is labeled by his peers, parents, teachers, or coaches as something, such as ADHD, learning disabled, stupid, or clumsy, his confidence and motivation levels can drop and interest in that activity greatly dissipates.[10]

When parents, teachers, and counselors look at a "perceived disability" in terms of something that needs to be related back to a child's highest values, then motivation and achievement levels will greatly improve. Dr. Demartini says, "Children have an innate desire to learn whatever will help them fulfill their highest values or whatever is most meaningful to them."

WHAT YOU CAN DO

Take a minute to think about a topic that you have absolutely no interest in learning. Imagine that you were told that you were required to spend forty-five minutes a day for nine months straight in a classroom learning about this topic that you found completely boring. Would you agree that you may start to daydream, maybe even fall asleep in class, or not give your best effort—unless there was some tie in to what you find meaningful and of value in your life?

You probably would become frustrated and antsy to the point of finding any reason to leave the room or even finding excuses for not going to class at all. If you were to take tests, how well do you think you would retain the material? Would these assessments reflect your true intelligence?

If the subject matter doesn't suit a child, or for that matter any individual, the desire to learn about it is usually low. Finding a way to link boring or new content/activities to a child's highest values can be challenging. Here are some *iMotivating* strategies you can start using with your child on a regular basis:

Ignite your child's creativity.
- Introduce music, art, dance, and sports to your children and allow them to pick what they like, within your financial and time limits.

Expose your child to new things.
- When your children see something new or different, their natural curiosity and interest levels pique, which increases their motivation to learn.
- Presenting something already learned in a new way can increase interest levels, especially if they are struggling with understanding a concept.

Foster your child's academic interests.
- Showing interest in the topic yourself and asking your child questions about it can spark a newfound desire or passion.
- Have resources available at home for your child to explore topics in further depth.
- Taking your child on a trip to a museum, zoo, theatrical show, concert, or sporting event adds depth to their understanding and opens new worlds of interests.

Use a short-term reward as an incentive for achievement.
- Offer weekend game time, if homework is properly completed throughout the week.
- Play an educational game with your child after homework has been completed.

Ask your child to teach you about a topic.
- Ask questions such as these:
  "What did you learn today at school?"
  "Can you please explain that concept to me so I can better understand it?"
  "Can you tell me more about it?"
- Your child can teach, not only verbally, but also through other authentic expressions such as art, music, poetry, acting, and/or writing.

Turn a "boring/challenging concept" into a game or an activity.
- Encourage your children to create songs, skits, or games to help them learn and remember concepts better.

Discuss the importance of a topic as it relates to your child's life.
- Discuss cause and effect relationships. Say something to the effect of: "Putting in consistent effort by completing your homework, and taking the time to review and study the concepts, results in getting good grades and becoming smarter so one day you can have the dream job of your choice."

Challenge your child.
- Children who are not challenged may become disinterested and channel energies in a wasteful manner. If you notice the same activity repeated without variation, then that is a sign that your child is ready for a challenge.
- Provide your child with changes in resources, materials, experiences, and environment to help stimulate their mind and expand their learning.

- Have educational games, puzzles, and enrichment activities on hand, once your child has thoroughly completed the schoolwork.
- Allow your child the freedom to express their creativity and show off their skills to you and other family members on a regular basis.

Use the right kind of praise to encourage your child's efforts and successes.
- Not all praise is created equal. Studies have shown that praise centered on a child's traits such as "intelligent," "athletic," "good," and "bad" should be avoided, while praise that focuses on the behavior and efforts of a child actually improves motivation, develops a flexible mentality, and helps a child accept challenges head on.[11] Don't say, *"Good job at getting an A in math."* Instead say, *"Your hard work is really paying off in math class!"* Don't say, *"You're being a good boy for helping your little sister."* Instead say, *"Thank you for being so kind and sharing with your sister."*

Here are three main guidelines for determining the right kind of praise to use with your child:

- **Praise with a purpose.**—Be specific and sincere with your praise. Avoid praising low-challenge activities. This may convey the wrong kind of message to your child that completing tasks quickly and without mistakes is noteworthy of acknowledgment. Also, avoid giving praise after failures or mistakes as that can suggest pity and add to a child's belief that his or her mistakes are a result of something that is fixed—such as intelligence—and cannot be changed. The praise can lose its effectiveness and leave a child feeling helpless and hopeless when they make mistakes.
- **Praise the *efforts* of a child, rather than the *traits* of a child or *outcome* of an event.**—Children who are praised for their talents or abilities often associate success or failure with an outcome and compare themselves with others. They can give up easily when doing something new or challenging and are often afraid to make mistakes. If praise is used to compare a child with others or used on the sole basis of an outcome, a child can become externally motivated by competitive ranking, rather than mastery of a skill or goal.
- **Limit the amount of praise and make it meaningful.**—When children are praised for their every step, they become dependent on that reinforcement. They may lose their inherent interest and *iMotivation* for a particular activity and often become immune to the praise. If you

find yourself praising your child often to keep them interested in an activity or focused on accomplishing a goal, try adapting the goal to something more attainable or making the activity more to your child's liking to naturally increase motivation levels.

- **Include these encouraging statements of praise in conversations with your child**:
  "I see great improvement."
  "Keep going!"
  "You are giving great effort!"
  "I believe in you!"
  "You can do it!"
  "I care about you."
  "You are very special."
  "You can talk to me anytime about anything."
  "I am here to listen and help whenever you need me."
- **Avoid disparaging comments such as these**:
  "Can't you be more like your brother/sister?"
  "If you weren't so lazy, you would do better."
  "Do your homework, otherwise . . ."
  "This may be too difficult for you to understand."
  "You shouldn't . . ."
  "You can't . . ."
  "Don't . . ."

The key parental challenge that you have in *iMotivating* your kids is to recognize their unique genius and help them awaken it by connecting new skills and information to the things that already give them meaning in their lives. It is important that children experience success early on and don't have false labels attached to them.

Creating positive environments for your child to grow helps spark their *iMotivation*. The trick to sustaining this internal state of motivation for your child is to provide minimal direction in your child's play and activities, while allowing them to make choices suited to their interests. As your children continue to explore the things they enjoy, the momentum will shift where *iMotivation*—feelings of excitement, a sense of purpose, and satisfaction from the accomplishments made—will abound.

---

iMotivate your children by exposing them to a variety of activities and allowing them to discover their passions.

Have Your Child Achieve
the Goal by "Ready, Set, Grow"

"Goals are not only absolutely necessary to motivate us. They are essential to really keep us alive."[1]

—Robert H. Schuller (author, motivational speaker, pastor,
and former American televangelist)

The amazing power of goal setting is evident in the story of a twelve-year-old boy named Craig Kielburger who spent his childhood growing up in the comfortable suburbs of Toronto, Canada, raised by his parents who were both teachers. One day, Craig read a story about a boy named Iqbal Masih, who spent his childhood physically beaten, verbally abused, severely malnourished, and chained to his loom in a dingy carpet factory in Pakistan. Iqbal was "hired by his parents" at the age of four and paid less than a dollar a month in order to repay a $16 loan. He worked twelve to sixteen hours a day, seven days a week. For the next six years, Iqbal was a factory prisoner, until he was rescued at the age of ten.[2]

For the following two years, Iqbal was recognized as an international hero and a symbol of courage against the barbaric bondage that he underwent in Pakistan's carpet industry. Filled with excitement, the boy traveled for the first time on an airplane to the United States to receive a Reebok Human Rights Award. He had become an inspiration for change in child labor around the world. He visited other schoolchildren in Boston and dreamed that one day he might attend a university.

Brandeis University, just outside of Boston, had pledged to give Iqbal a four-year scholarship when he completed his studies in Pakistan. However, upon returning to his homeland from the United States, something tragic took place. Iqbal, at the tender age of twelve, was shot and killed by a gunman hired by factory owners.

After reading Iqbal's story, Craig knew exactly what he wanted to do and made it his *goal* to accomplish what Iqbal couldn't any longer. He made it his mission to help put an end to the exploitation of child workers. Craig woke up every morning asking his mother if he could travel to Southeast Asia and go backpacking on his own to meet these child laborers. It wasn't enough for him to just read about it, he wanted to see it firsthand and do something about this cruelty. His mother just laughed at him and said "no." Each day, Craig would wake up passionately asking his mother the same question over and over again until, one day, she relented and finally said "yes."

Craig, however, was too young to accomplish this goal on his own. Nonetheless, he was so determined to do so that he decided to sell some of his toys to help fund the trip and was able to obtain financial help from other relatives, matching the money that he had raised. With a backpack and video camera, Craig was chaperoned at each stop by local human rights activists.

He traveled from Bangladesh, Thailand, India, over to Nepal, and then to Pakistan visiting the pitch-black, windowless sweatshops and airless factories at each destination. He spoke with all the children subjected to this slavery, one by one, and witnessed the working and living conditions firsthand. Furthermore, he made a pilgrimage to visit the site of Iqbal's deplorable death.

Upon returning to Toronto, Craig had a *new goal* that would ultimately result in changing the lives of millions of children worldwide. After showing his classmates the shocking photos and sharing his horrifying stories, Craig rallied up a group of his twelve-year-old classmates and together they established a charity and youth movement called "Free the Children."

In two short years, the charity was comprised of thousands of individuals and expanded into an international movement. To date, the organization has worked in more than forty-five countries, built more than six hundred fifty schools and school rooms, provided education to more than fifty-five thousand children on a daily basis, shipped $16 million worth of medical supplies around the world, and supplied a million people with clean water, health care, and sanitation.[3]

As Craig amazingly displayed at such a precocious age, a child can accomplish many great feats never thought possible with the right mindset, passion, and determination. Craig's story also shows that it takes *consistent, positive daily habits* to make goals come to fruition.

SETTING GOALS

One of the most important habits necessary for developing a child's intrinsic motivation is *setting goals*. Goals provide a *clear focus* and help children make *better decisions.* When your child is about to make a decision to do something, ask them, "Is your decision going to get you closer or farther away from your goal?" Children are inherently excellent goal setters through their ability to envision what they "want to be when they grow up." They determine this, in large part, due to what they find meaningful and personal in their lives.

Children are constantly asked by adults, "What do you want to be when you grow up?" However, shifting the question from "*what* do you want to be" to "*who* do you want to be" puts an emphasis on character, values, identifying passions, and leaving a mark on the world, as opposed to being defined by a career.

The acquisition of skills and talents can be best understood by observing changes in an individual going through the developmental stages of life. For instance, a toddler must learn how to walk, talk, chew, and eat food. In young childhood, most individuals will learn to read, write, and do math. During adolescence and young adulthood, advanced talents develop in the form of speaking multiple languages, playing musical instruments, dancing, singing, drawing, painting, excelling at different sports, cooking specialty foods, writing different stories, building and designing various architectural structures, improving technology, and taking on leadership roles in the community and workforce.

All of these feats are attainable through setting achievable goals and staying dedicated to them. It's important to continue encouraging your children as they work toward achieving their goals. It becomes challenging when they compare themselves to their peers and see that other kids are getting higher grades, outperforming them in different sports, or getting the roles over them in the school play. They may get discouraged and lose faith when they don't see results happening quickly. Renowned motivational speaker Anthony Robbins said, "People who fail focus on what they will have to go through; people who succeed focus on what it will feel like at the end."[4]

It may be difficult for your children to look beyond present time. Remind them, however, that every expert at something was once a beginner who had to overcome obstacles to get to a high level. The most decorated Olympian in history, Michael Phelps, had somewhat of a complicated childhood as he faced major issues at a young age. His parents got divorced and shortly thereafter he was diagnosed with ADHD. That didn't stop him from shooting for the stars and achieving big heights. Phelps focused his attention on swimming as an outlet to burn off energy and make his two sisters, who were also swimmers, very proud.[5]

His legendary swimming success is the result of a combination of skill, physical ability, and years of hard work, which include practicing and working out hours a day, for years. His hard work paid off, literally and figuratively speaking. Phelps landed lucrative endorsement deals from major companies and received a million dollar bonus from Speedo for winning at least seven gold medals in one Olympic Games. He decided to use that money to start up his own foundation to help get kids involved in swimming.

Gary Ryan Blair, president of the GoalsGuy Learning Systems, describes the importance of goal setting in this way:[6]

> Learning how to set and achieve a goal is perhaps the single most important thing your child can learn to prepare for school, adulthood, and for future employment. The more adept your child is at understanding this important life skill, the more options he or she will have throughout their life!

When helping your child set goals, be as specific as possible with all facets of the goal so they can see a picture of it in their mind coming into reality. Also, it is important to take the process of goal setting slowly in the beginning. Small successful strides breed confidence and encouragement for attaining larger goals.

A goal is nothing more than a dream with a deadline. Jack Canfield, author of *The Success Principles* says that to bring your goal into reality, you need to quantify it and put a time limit on it. He calls it the "how much, by when."[7]

Let's say that your child really wants a game; lay out a plan that clearly outlines how they can work toward getting it. Prepare a piggybank and have your child calculate how much they will need to save, over the course of a chosen time frame, to achieve the goal. Stating the desire to get a game is merely an idea. Invoking measurable action steps, however, gives a focus and level of accountability for your child to follow through along each step to achieving that goal.

A way for your child to visualize the goal is to write it out with the action steps needed to achieve it, with time frames next to each step. According to a study conducted by Dr. Gail Matthews, a psychology professor at Dominican University, 56 percent of goals are likely to be achieved when written down on paper versus goals thought or spoken about. If you take the time to set up a weekly progress report with your child as a means to check in on meeting these time frames, the percentage of goals increases from 56 percent to 76 percent. Therefore, take time to sit down with your children and help them chart out a course for achieving their goals and have check-in dates to hold them accountable for following through along the way.

Here is an analogy that you can share with your child when introducing goal setting. Imagine that you are going on a family vacation and traveling to a place five hundred miles away. No matter how long the distance is, you know you will arrive at your destination at some point, earlier or later. How do you know? You have the course mapped out in some way that directs you on your intended place of arrival. Either you have it in your head from previous driving experience, on paper in the form of directions, or programmed into your GPS. There may be obstacles along the way in getting there—in the form of traffic delays or detours—but eventually your destination will be achieved.

The same principle applies for helping your child achieve any short- or long-term goals. First, help your child map out a clear idea of their intended direction, where they want to end up, and the path to take to get there—taking into consideration any potential obstacles along the way. It helps to make these goals *clear*, *specific*, and *attainable*. Challenging your child, but being realistic, allows them to maintain a sense of confidence in the face of difficulty and keeps the process moving forward. Dreaming is good, but be aware that lofty short-term goals can discourage your child and lead to failure.

A personal contract can be helpful in many cases. If your child has a difficult time committing to the steps needed to achieve a goal, involving a rewards system for achieving short-term goals along the way can help them remain on track. The reward can be a given certificate, a granted privilege, or a showcase of their work.

Goal setting can include any area of life, including personal relationships with family, friends, and/or classmates, self-confidence, obtaining good grades, mastering a particular skill, making a sports team, being healthy, helping around the house—and as they get older, making career choices and growing spiritually.

After working with tweens and teens in different capacities over the years, I have found the following practical method for helping them discover their passion and turning it into a focal point for goal setting to be highly successful:

1. Have a brainstorm session and decide on what your child's goal is by making two categories: *likes* and *dislikes* and writing down everything and anything that they enjoy doing in the like column and what they don't enjoy doing in the dislike column.
2. Disregard the "dislikes" category and focus on the "likes" category.
3. Branch the "likes" column into two categories: *realistic* and *unrealistic* based on current skill levels, opportunities for growth, and long-term desires. Assign number values (0–5) for how attainable the desire is (0 = very unrealistic; 5 = very realistic).
4. Disregard the "unrealistic" category and focus on the "realistic" category, those with scores of 3 or better. What is remaining on the list is a starting focal point for achieving goals.

5. Write down your child's ideal life and map out from start to finish how they plan on getting there. At various time intervals, evaluate where your child is at, with regard to continuing toward their ultimate goal(s). You may have to assist in making minor adjustments, refocusing the goal or possibly making major overhauls, but no matter what, your child will still be on course to achieving their goal(s).
6. Write down the big picture first and then work backwards, mapping out a course to success from longer-term to shorter-term goals.
7. Set yearly, monthly, and then weekly goals.

Examples of yearly goals:
- Make a sports team.
- Obtain good grades at school to get into the college of my choice.
- Play an instrument very well.
- Save money to purchase a bike.

Examples of monthly goals:
- Get stronger, run faster, and have more endurance.
- Take on leadership roles at school to make a difference.
- Obtain honor roll status.
- Play a song really well on a musical instrument.
- Save money for a bike from birthday, holidays, and regular weekly allowances.

Examples of weekly goals:
- Practice basketball drills five days a week.
- Stay organized and complete all homework assignments thoroughly.
- Get proper instruction and practice an instrument and song consistently one to two hours each day.
- Save money for a bike by doing extra chores around the house.

EIGHT SECRETS OF SUCCESS

The views on *success* can be summarized into eight success secrets. These "secrets" highlight the tools that successful people utilize to help them achieve their goals and keep them motivated throughout the process. It is invaluable for your children to understand different belief systems that coexist, levels of commitment necessary for achievement, and positive attitudes displayed in life.

Have your child write out each of these success secrets and make them visible as a constant reminder. From there, your child will be able to integrate these ways of thinking into their own belief system to best help them succeed at anything they put their mind to throughout the course of their life.

Provided are the eight success secrets from some of the top motivational experts in the field:[8]

1. Take 100 percent responsibility for your life.
2. Live your life "on purpose."
3. Be willing to pay the price for your dreams.
4. Stay focused.
5. Become an expert in your field.
6. Write out a plan for achieving your goals.
7. Never give up.
8. Don't delay.

A great way for your child to become a goal setter is by seeing that you are a goal setter. The daily practice of implementing goals is fundamental to fostering that "can-do" attitude and achieving success in any endeavor in life.

If you set high expectations for your child and have very clear goals that you explain, while discussing the importance of all of those expectations—such as doing homework, studying for tests, reading a book, writing an essay, eating healthy, doing chores around the house, making good decisions around friends—your child will see the personal value in goal setting. The focus will shift away from doing something to please someone else or to avoid punishment and toward making themselves better individuals, serving their highest values, and helping maximize their potential for their future.

In *Think and Grow Rich*, Napoleon Hill emphasizes, "When one writes down a goal, one feels committed and has made up his or her mind; this is one's 'definite major purpose.' The desire becomes intensified and one becomes driven to achieve the goal set forth."[9] Whether we realize it or not, we all have goals, but some are more potentially life transforming or life destroying than others. Ultimately, your child must learn how to set goals that are *inspiring* and allow for continuous *growth* and *expansion* throughout their life.

———◆———

Inspire and enable your children to set goals in order for them to become high achievers.

———◆———

II

"CHILD LIMITING" CHALLENGES TO BE AWARE OF AND HOW TO BEST HANDLE THEM

· *11* ·

Bullying

Take the "Bull" Out of Bullying

"It isn't enough to talk about peace. One must believe in it. And it isn't enough to believe in it. One must work at it."

—Eleanor Roosevelt (former First Lady of the United States)

From time-to-time, I hear kids shouting out phrases in my classroom that include the word *bully* such as "He's bullying me!" or "Stop being a bully!" Within seconds of making those statements, I watch as the accuser smiles or makes a jab back at the other person in a playful gesture.

TEASING VERSUS BULLYING

How can you tell if a child is actually being teased or bullied? It is not always easy to distinguish between the two as kids are quite good at hiding their actions and emotions. Both acts, teasing and bullying, involve poking fun at someone at the other person's expense. However, there are some key differences between the two that can help you know when a real issue is brewing with your child that you need to address.

First off, teasing is common and is done for many different reasons. It can be used to provoke a reaction in someone, as that person who is doing the teasing may desire attention back or wish to be reciprocated with being teased. Teasing can also be used as a means to show that person what behaviors are annoying or inappropriate by mocking them, in a non-confrontational way. If someone is making obnoxious noises or acting in a socially inappropriate manner, teasing can be a way to diffuse or eliminate that person's undesired behavior.

Teasing can also be a way to resolve conflict in a nonthreatening, perhaps even playful, manner. It can also be used as a means to reduce feeling socially awkward and fitting in when talking with peers. Teasing can be used to strengthen a relationship and is not meant to harm another person.

But when does teasing cross the line and turn into bullying? Most studies have defined bullying behavior as having all of the following characteristics:[1]

- A person feels as if they are being teased repeatedly and when asked to stop, the other person refuses.
- There is an imbalance of power and one person asserts more power over another person.
- There is an intention to make fun of, ridicule, embarrass, and/or exclude others in a hurtful manner.
- The person being "teased" is distressed, upset, or hurt from the words and/or actions of the other person.

A PERSONAL ACCOUNT

Growing up, like most children, I experienced my fair share of being teased, but the affectionate interaction of teasing was replaced by different acts of bullying. In the neighborhood, one boy in particular, *Carson*, was the ring leader of the pack of bullies who tormented me for years throughout elementary school.

Carson was popular, charismatic, and sported a flattop haircut. I remember him riding his bicycle or skateboarding with a group of the neighborhood boys who were just as intimidating in their looks and demeanors. Carson, however, had the ability to assemble a team of followers everywhere he went in the neighborhood.

I recall the times when Carson showed up with the gang on my doorstep asking my mother if I could play outside with them. All the while, I was upstairs listening from my bedroom window, as he left the front steps saying, "His Mommy never lets him take two steps outside of his yard. Do you think she knows that I just want to get him up the road so I can beat his ass?"

So many times, I wanted to go play with my good friend up the street, who lived a few houses past the bully, but I was always afraid of meeting Carson, face to face or with his pack of friends. For that matter, just the thought of walking up the road and possibly encountering him was enough to strike fear and put me into a panic-stricken state. There was one time in particular that I vividly recall trying to take the short cut through the field. I remember walking halfway through and hearing from afar, "There's Haddad, get him!"

And then it began, what felt like a run for my life. I felt as if I were stranded in the middle of the wilderness and being chased by a pack of hungry wolves. I darted across the field as the four of them were in hot pursuit after me. I ran through the woods and never looked back, with my heart feeling as if it were going to pound out of my chest.

"Come here, you chicken shit!" shouted Carson.

Fast approaching, two of the kids closed in on me from different angles. From my perspective, this was like being in the middle of a war zone, without anybody there to save me. They were sprinting toward me, quickly gaining ground. My clothes were getting ripped as I was weaving through the thick wiry branches of the ten-foot-high hemlocks, just praying that they wouldn't catch me.

Somehow I managed to barrel through those Canadian firs and made it to my next-door neighbor's yard. Then, from about fifty feet away, I saw Carson rushing toward me. With hostility written all over his face and tightly clenched teeth, I thought it was over for me. This may sound like something out of a movie, but it really wasn't.

This was a matter of my own survival, as I raced to the wooden fence in my backyard with everything that I had inside of me. Carson lunged toward me, as I jumped halfway up the fence and then catapulted the other half of my body laterally over the fence. Narrowly avoiding being caught, I hit the ground on the other side and tumbled a bit down the hill until I got to my feet and ran through my backyard and safely into my house as I heard, "You're dead next time, Haddad! You can run, but you can't hide!"

To this day, I remember feeling as if I were alone in a battle against the rest of the neighborhood. I had wished that I had one person who would stand united with me against Carson and his accomplices—to put an end to being bullied once and for all. But that wouldn't happen anytime soon. One day, I went over to my friend's house in the neighborhood and played basketball in his driveway, just days before entering fourth grade. As we were shooting hoops, we saw Carson walking up the street with an aluminum baseball bat in hand.

My friend, who I will refer to as *Patrick*, told me to ignore Carson and just keep playing as if we never saw him. My instinct, on the other hand, told me to make a run for it back home, as I had done once before. But I took Patrick's advice and just kept playing. However, I couldn't help looking over my shoulder to see where Carson was and what he was doing.

Patrick took a long range shot that hit the side of the rim, unluckily bouncing toward the end of the driveway where Carson was nearing. Carson walked up the driveway and kicked the basketball we were playing with into the neighbor's yard across the street. He then pointedly yelled to Patrick,

"Get inside unless you want a piece of this in your face," while referencing his bat.

Patrick stood there immobilized by fear and uncertainty, not knowing what to do, until Carson raised the bat toward him saying, "Get out of here, now, before I knock you out!"

I knew this wasn't going to be good at all. Patrick swiftly ran back into his house and peered through the large window, looking at me as I attempted to nonchalantly walk home to avoid confrontation.

"Where do you think you're going?" Carson asked, as I continued to walk down the street, ignoring him.

In the meanwhile, Carson blindsided me by throwing me to the ground and kicking me right in the ribcage. I tried to stand up to escape him and the situation. But then—*whack*—I felt a sharp, striking blow from the barrel of his bat come across my abdominal region, which took the wind right out of me.

While fighting back tears, I fell to the ground in extreme agony. I couldn't let him get the best of me and see me cry. He continued to add insult to injury while laughing at me and said, "Go ahead and cry, you little baby. Now go home and tell your Mommy what a loser you are. I bet you'll never want to leave your yard ever again."

Patrick saw the mistreatment taking place and chose to go to a safe location to observe what was happening rather than do something to stop it. I'm sure Patrick was scared and didn't want to be abused himself, which I never held against him. However, individuals who watch bullying events take place and do not do anything to remedy the situation are called *bystanders*. Many times, these people make the situation worse by perpetuating the vicious circle of bullying.

The lesson to be learned from my personal experience with bullying is that it is vital to encourage your child to stand up for others by becoming an *ally*—someone who supports the targeted person. This act has shown to significantly reduce bullying, and it is an essential step toward positively changing the climate and strengthening the voice of the targeted individual.

There were a number of kids who had many opportunities to intervene and end the torment for me, but instead chose to be either bystanders or accomplices to the bullying. Carson coerced others, even my supposed friends, to socially exclude me in class, at lunch, on the bus, and during recess. He would write messages about me or draw unflattering sketches of me and pass them around to kids in class or sneakily post them in the hallway to get a laugh at my expense.

Carson bullied me almost every single day for years in elementary school. He realized that he was successful at controlling me and developed more elaborate, entrenched bullying schemes to display his power and superior influence to intimidate me. It began with indirect acts of meanness; he would ignore me or call me derogatory names and continued to target me at school, in the lunchroom, at recess, in the bathroom, in the locker room, and in the neighborhood.

The majority of the bullying, however, took place on the school bus. Carson and his followers would trap me in the back of the bus and flick my ears until they turned beet red, give me noogies on top of my head, and sporadically punch me in my shoulders or thighs until they were black and blue.

On several occasions, I would tell the teacher about how I was being repeatedly picked on by this individual. Carson, however, was very charming with adults, and most teachers didn't witness any outright warning signs of bullying behavior in their classes, thus not taking the matter seriously. If any of them did see glimpses of harassment take place within the classroom, excuses would be made to justify his actions saying that he was going through a difficult time at home.

As the days became weeks, which turned into months and spawned into years, I learned to cope with the unrelenting verbal and physical tormenting. Many parents whose kids are bullied have no idea of the full extent of the suffering and tormenting until something bad happens.

My parents eventually realized that the situation had gotten out of control and that the bus driver, teachers, and the bully's parents were not handling matters appropriately. My parents tried their best to help me solve this problem by telling me to walk away from the bully, ignore him, and tell a teacher when I was being bullied. I even tried to get someone to stand up for me. At one point, my parents talked to his parents to try and resolve matters, but none of these tactics worked. It wasn't until the end of fifth grade that the tide would eventually turn in my favor and things would change forever.

One day, my best friend, who I will refer to as *Spencer*, and I went to the bathroom to wash our hands before lunch started. While we were at the sink, I looked back in the mirror and noticed someone coming out of the stall. Acting all smug, Carson approached Spencer at the sink with an intimidating glare and asked him, "Are you friends with Doug?" Spencer didn't want any trouble and just wanted to finish drying his hands.

Carson pushed him into the garbage can saying, "I asked you a question. Do you like Doug? Is he your friend?"

"Yes, Doug is my best friend!" Spencer confidently replied.

At that moment, I had an ally and felt that things were about to change. They certainly did, but not as I had expected. Without warning, Carson sucker punched Spencer in the midsection and took his head and rammed it into the soap dispenser. Soap went flying everywhere—against the mirror, wall, and all over the floor—as Spencer fell hard to the ground.

I couldn't believe what had happened. I felt so bad seeing my best friend holding his head and crying as he stumbled out of the bathroom—all because he stood up for me when I needed it the most.

Then Carson came for me and said, "You're next Haddad!"

He took a swing at me, but this time I grabbed his arm and threw him against the wall. I took his head with both my hands and slammed it into the wall, once, and then again, twice yelling out, "Bleed!"

A pouring of rage came from me and as he tried to half-heartedly fight back. I hurled him into the toilet stall and socked him a few more times until he fell down against the toilet bowl unable to get up. No longer was I afraid of Carson.

Looking back, I couldn't believe that it had to come to this kind of aggression to end this long-standing misery. But at that moment, I had finally turned a corner that was long overdue. I stood up for myself with the feeling that someone else stood up for me and had my back.

In looking back, I very well could have seriously injured Carson that day. I was a walking time bomb, built up with anger from years of being tormented, until it all came to a head and exploded in one fell swoop. Over the years, I had asked myself time and time again, as so many targets of bullying do, "Why is this all happening to me?"

"WHY IS THIS HAPPENING TO ME?"

If we take a peek inside the heads of bullies, we will find that there is one thing that they all have in common—*a feeling of insecurity*. Bullying is their attempt to gain power and control over others in order to fill a void and feel better about themselves. This is their way to feel important.

As I found out later, Carson grew up in a household with a verbally and physically abusive father who was a raging alcoholic. He was bullied himself, not by his peers, but by his own father. Growing up, he experienced watching his dad become angry and physically abuse him and his brother.

So, in turn, Carson struck fear in *everyone* he came across. He was socially competent using manipulation and aggression as a way to control others, and get them to join in his dirty work. Either you followed him, submitted to him, or got beaten up by him.

Perhaps things may have been different if I had established a foundation of coping skills early on and had someone who was strong enough to stand up against the bully and support me. I was left mostly by myself to endure the torment of being bullied and didn't know how to handle the situation effectively.

Although being bullied taught me how to introspect, persevere, and move past negative situations, many kids are unable to make it through these types of perilous situations unscathed. One of the stories that touched me involved a fifteen-year-old sophomore at a high school in Maryland who had been the victim of bullying since the sixth grade. His mother had to move him to another school due to students making fun of his clothes, projecting anti-gay slurs, and attacking him with repetitive, tormenting messages on social networking sites.[2]

While preparing for an interview with a local television station to discuss his experiences being bullied, a group of three boys suddenly appeared on the scene and pushed the reporter aside and sarcastically shouted, "What are you recording?" From nowhere, one of the boys lunged toward the boy and hit him square in the head. The reporter yelled at them to stop, but that didn't seem to thwart the three attackers from chasing after their victim who was desperately running across a busy street to avoid them. The reporter mentioned that the three aggressors had no shame about what they were doing and couldn't care less about the audience around the scene.

After that incident, the boy was targeted again in gym class when another boy tackled him to the ground. This time, he decided to fight back and consequently was suspended for three days from school, while the attacking student was not.

Having been the target of bullying for many years, along with the Maryland teen and many other kids, we don't understand why we are targeted and mistreated. The point is that bullied individuals desperately wish they had a Mr. Miyagi from *The Karate Kid* by their side to stand up against these insensitive people.

Bullies come in all different forms: tall, small, boy, girl, popular, smart, or jock. Some appear to have it all together, are well liked by kids and adults, and get good grades. They are all different, live with unique experiences, and have their own reasons for why they become bullies.

When it comes right down to it, bullies target others they think they can control and have power over. They pick on someone who may look different from the norm, be smarter than them, wear different clothes, or have something that they don't. Bullies, at some point, might have been abused by other kids or adults themselves.

Bullying happens everywhere and it can present itself in many forms:

- **Physical means**: poking, pushing, tripping, bumping, kicking, punching, and so on
- **Relationship**: exclusion from a group or activity, making someone do something they don't want to do, and so forth

- **Verbal**: name calling, teasing, yelling, threatening to hurt someone, spreading rumors, and the like
- **Property**: knocking books off the table or out of someone's hands, writing on someone's books/binders/clothes/body, closing a locker on someone, and so on
- **Cyberbullying**: posting rumors on social media, making fake profiles/ websites, sharing embarrassing pictures, posting negative comments, making derogatory text messages/e-mails, and so forth
- **Sexual**: inappropriate touching of another individual's body parts without consent

Peer pressure is a powerful thing that can overtake certain kids and make them do things they really would rather not do. A child may feel that if they don't conform and do what everyone else is doing, then they will not be accepted, will be picked on, and won't have friends. Why should something that makes a person feel miserable, alone, depressed, and/or hurt be a "part of growing up"? It doesn't need to be that way.

HOW TO HELP

Bullying and harassment should be taken seriously by listening to and talking with your child each day. It is against the law and should not be tolerated. Even though each state has its own official definition, bullying is generally defined as

> an intentional act that causes harm to others such as repeated verbal, written, stalking, or electronic expression or a physical act or gesture directed at a victim.[3]

It might be hard for your child to express that they are being bullied. Therefore, it is important to recognize the following warning signs:

- Change – this is the most significant sign of bullying, and potentially other issues that your child is struggling to resolve. Look for changes that are sudden and atypical for your child. These may include a change in grades in school, friends, and/or mood—such as feelings of depression, anxiety, anger, and or loneliness—change in appearance, behavior, eating, sleep, loss of interest in school and activities
- Physical injuries – such as cuts or bruises on your child's body

- Anxiety and nervousness displayed in physical ailments – such as headaches, stomach aches, or dizziness—or being reluctant to go to school or be out in public
- Violent thoughts or behaviors
- Suicidal thoughts

Bullying is a key factor in why many kids drop out of school, resort to violence at home and in the community, and/or commit suicide. The effects from long-term bullying can be quite pervasive on the victim throughout all aspects of their life, impacting social well-being along with self-confidence. A study published in the journal *Lancet Psychiatry* showed that individuals who were bullied by peers in childhood are 60 percent more likely to suffer from mental health problems than those who endured physical, emotional, or sexual abuse.[4]

IF YOUR CHILD IS A BULLY

The pain that bullies inflict on their victims can have a long-lasting effect. But the damage can be just as great, if not worse, on the bully himself. What should you do if you suspect that your child is a bully?

Not all bullying stems from family problems, but it is a sensible idea to observe the behavior and personal interactions your child witnesses at home from all family members. What may seem like innocent teasing at home may actually model bullying behaviors. Make your child aware that this kind of behavior is not acceptable by any means.

Children who become bullies may see it as a way to *control other children* they perceive as *weaker* or *more inferior* in some way. Teaching a child the importance of treating people from all walks of life with *respect* and *kindness* can make a big difference in how they interact with others.

Positive reinforcement is more effective than punishment; so praising appropriate behavior is more conducive for eliminating the undesired behavior. If the bullying keeps up, however, you can take away privileges, with the opportunity to regain them once your child has completed a meaningful task. You can require your child to partake in volunteer work to help less fortunate individuals. You can also have them watch a movie about bullying or do a research project about the effects of bullying on others and include strategies on how to reduce the behavior.

Over the years I've worked with many tweens and teens, and one of the top priorities at my job has been to make sure that children clearly understand the value of respect toward one another and know that they can turn to a trusting adult if they are being bullied. I don't tolerate bullying and if I see any form of it in my classroom, I squash it right away. Unfortunately, what I am unable to monitor is what goes on behind social networking doors. I have to say, what I overhear kids talking about in the halls sometimes throws me for a loop and makes me wonder, "Do their parents know what's going on?"

I often hear, "I was just kidding around" or "We're friends." However, a lot of "innocent teasing" can result in mean or hurtful posts, comments, pictures, videos, or rumors being spread online that can lead to more serious issues. I have met with parents who were shocked to hear that their child had been willingly participating in some form of online bullying. And sometimes all it takes is one mean thing said or picture posted that constitutes an act of bullying, due to the fact that it goes out to so many people at one time.

It may be hard for some parents to acknowledge the possibility that their child could be involved as a perpetrator of bullying. It is crucial for children to recognize the impact of their actions on others and that a cruel verbal or photo message is not acceptable behavior and can have serious ramifications.

BULLYING AND SOCIAL MEDIA

There have been many cases of young individuals who took their lives because they were being cyberbullied. Enduring nearly three months of routine torment by her fellow classmates via crude comments posted on Facebook and unrelenting text messages sent, fifteen-year-old Phoebe Prince tragically took her life.[5] This and other cases brought more international awareness of bullying as a major problem and the effects it can have on a single young person.

If you don't have one already, I encourage you to create your own personal profile(s) and go ahead and "friend request" and/or "follow" your child on the popular social networking websites. If your children give you any lip, saying that you are invading their privacy, mention to them that they already forfeited their privacy the moment their personal information went online.

It is tempting to intervene in mean online behavior aimed toward your child. It may feel natural to want to step in and take matters into your own hands to solve your child's problem. It's a wiser solution, however, to work together with your child to develop an appropriate plan to end the bullying.

Encourage your child to tell you when someone is not being treated with respect. Mention the difference between *snitching*—telling on someone to see them get in trouble; and *reporting*—telling an adult in order to help solve a problem.

IF YOUR CHILD IS A VICTIM OF BULLYING

What if you suspect your child is the victim of bullying? What steps should you take to effectively address the issue? First off, do not overreact. Begin by keeping your emotions in check before speaking with your child. Many kids who are bullied are afraid to tell their parents that they are bullied because they worry that their parents will take away their cell phone or contact the other kid's parents and make matters even worse.

I would advise to first sit down with your child and determine the severity of the bullying by asking what has happened, what strategies have been used to stop these actions from recurring, and from there, offer specific suggestions for handling future incidents. If things don't appear to be getting resolved, I would highly suggest contacting the school. Start by e-mailing or calling the teacher and/or guidance counselor and telling them the concerns you have by reporting what your child has told you, without calling it "bullying."

Stay positive and assume that this is the first time that an adult has been made aware of what has been going on and that the proper steps will be taken to fix the problem. From my experience as a teacher, I will tell you that the majority of bullying that goes on in school takes place in unstructured environments and where there are low levels of adult supervision such as in the hallways between class periods, in the lunch room, during recess, during gym class when kids are changing, waiting for the school bus, and while riding on the school bus.

You can suggest an increase in adult supervision in specific areas where the bullying is taking place. If you feel that a complete separation between the bully and your child is warranted, express that to the school official. You might also ask the teacher or counselor if there is another student who would be willing to spend time with your child, invite him or her to their lunch table, play together during recess, or befriend your child to prevent the social isolation that can result in bullying. If the teacher or counselor is unable or unwilling to solve the problem, I would suggest approaching the school principal next and working your way up to the superintendent until the problem gets resolved.

The most important thing you can do to help a child who is experiencing being bullied is to take action immediately. Contact the school right away when you see these problems. If you feel that the school is dismissing or not taking matters seriously, document every incident which involves your child being bullied and report it to the police.

The end of bullying begins with a unified commitment that takes parents, teachers, administrators, support staff, coaches, cafeteria workers, custodial staff, and students to practice *tolerance, acceptance, encouragement,* and *leadership* on a regular basis. Children must learn early in the elementary school years to use their voice and stand up for themselves and others—to do the right thing. Classroom and schoolwide activities should be continued throughout the middle and high school years to promote these themes and emphasize the importance of giving respect to people of all ages, genders, races, religions, ethnicities, sexual orientations, weights, economic classes, athletic abilities, popularities, and any physical or mental disabilities.

It is important to teach children to be assertive and to hold them accountable for standing up and doing the right thing. Ultimately, being a child's role model and demonstrating a positive attitude, excellent values, and sound morals are the most effective ways parents can influence their child to become a person of great character.

Teach a child to stand up to bullying.

Youth Violence

The Effects of the Media and Violent Video Gaming on Your Child

"When the power of love overcomes the love of power, the world will know peace."

—Sri Chinmoy (spiritual teacher and philosopher)

I called my childhood friend to wish him a Happy Birthday on December 4, 2012. That morning I attempted to write him a birthday message on Facebook, but surprisingly couldn't find him on there any longer. It was peculiar to me that he just disappeared as one of my "friends." On the telephone, I wished him a happy birthday and asked him if he was still on Facebook. He was quiet and oddly didn't have an answer for me. I was baffled by his silence and thought, "Could he have dropped me as a friend?" Due to our busy schedules, we hadn't talked much lately, but it wasn't like we were on unfriendly terms.

He worked long hours and was the father of two young boys, four and seven years old, at the time. I asked him flat out, "Did you block me or unfriend me for some reason?" With hesitation, he admitted, "I am tired of seeing all of your posts about why we need to save kids. I don't need to save my kids from anything. They will be fine and anyway, they need to save themselves!"

Ten days later on December 14, it was my birthday, and my students surprised me with birthday cards and well wishes written on my whiteboard. One class even sang happy birthday to me. It was a special day that was about to turn unforgettably tragic for parents, children, and so many people around the nation.

TRAGEDY AT SANDY HOOK ELEMENTARY

Before the start of my last class of the day around 1:30 p.m., a group of students ran into my classroom in stunned disbelief and informed me about a school shooting that had taken place earlier that morning at Sandy Hook Elementary School in Newtown, Connecticut, just twenty-five miles south of where I grew up.

Tears, fear, and a barrage of questions befell me in a blink of an eye. My twelve- and thirteen-year-old students asked, "How can something like this have happened? Why would somebody do this? Are we safe in our school? Who would save us if a killer came into this classroom with guns right now?"

There were no words to adequately describe the emotions that I was feeling at that moment. I was frankly overwhelmed, obfuscated, lacking information to what had just transpired, and not sure how to address the situation appropriately. Instinctively, I reassured my students that they were safe and reinforced the importance of our lockdown drill. I emphasized to them that they were loved and cared for and to always talk to a trusting adult about anything that was troubling them. For the remainder of the day, I was thinking about the helpless six- and seven-year-old children in that classroom who couldn't defend themselves against the attacker.

Why have these types of tragedies taken place in our schools? It is important, yet difficult, to confirm, to this day, the attacker Adam Lanza's specific motive(s) for this horrific event. Understanding the possible factors that led to this mass shooting, however, could help provide solutions to prevent other tragedies similar to this one from happening again.

If we could understand the impact of the attacker's mental disorder on the tragedy and the family dynamics over the years, we would be able to draw more verifiable conclusions to this tragedy. What makes it so frustrating for so many people is that there are many individuals who have mental illnesses, play violent video games, own guns, live with one parent, or use antidepressants, and don't go on to commit mass murder. We can't say for sure, but it is quite possible that this was the human equivalent to the "perfect storm" and that these incidents may be attributed to several psychological and social factors that resulted in a devastating outcome.

A couple of years prior to the shootings, the attacker disconnected himself from the rest of the world and spent his time in his bedroom playing violent video games for long hours and obsessing over mass murderers. The nearly three hundred postings he made on the now-defunct website "Shocked Beyond Belief," along with an audio recording, clues us into his tenuous relationship with others in society. He expressed that "society's pressure to conform to its immoral value system could make any living creature snap, and perhaps commit a mass shooting to express their rage."[1]

PREDICTING WHO WILL COMMIT A VIOLENT CRIME

Something of this nature and magnitude is an unpredictable, unfortunate eye-opener for parents around the world to be mindful of their children's behavior. We have little idea about what separates those who think about mass shootings from those individuals who actually carry it out.

Jack Levin, PhD, a professor of sociology and criminology at Northeastern University in Boston, Massachusetts, is considered an authority on mass murderers and has mentioned that it is hard to predict who will commit a violent crime of this nature. He mentions that "the overwhelming majority of mass killers are not psychotic, and they're quite methodical in the way they commit an execution of the people they feel are responsible for their problems."[2] They appear to develop a strategy, research about previous shootings online, interact with forums, and peruse websites to get ideas for planning their attack.

How can you recognize the warning signs of a child who might be harboring violent thoughts or struggling with depression or other mental disorders that don't typically show up until the later teen years? James Garbarino, professor of psychology at Loyola University Chicago and author of *Lost Boys: Why Our Sons Turn Violent and How We Can Save Them* mentions how many of the individuals who commit these kinds of crimes have some sort of mental health concern such as depression or anger, and have expressed feelings of rejection and exclusion. He says that many young Americans, and other young people around the world, develop "the war zone mentality" and have an obsession with guns and explosives. They develop a damaged, delusional sense of reality and view the world as a battle ground. They often believe they are victims and the people they are shooting are the enemies.[3]

This skewed perception of reality and moral damage are usually not enough to lead to killing, though. Garbarino says that the typical killer is emotionally damaged and suffers from a mental health problem. Factors such as being bullied, socially outcast by peers, or abused and neglected at home are possible contributing factors that can increase a person's risk for exhibiting these types of violent behaviors.[4]

A study was conducted to see if children who were born with minor neurological damage were more likely to end up as violent teenagers than biologically normal children. The results demonstrated that kids who had minor neurological damage and grew up in well-functioning families were no more likely than biologically normal children to end up as violent teenagers. However, if these neurologically impaired children grew up in abusive families, they were four times as likely to end up as violent teenagers as compared to biologically normal children growing up in similar abusive environments.[5]

There isn't one single risk factor to account for violence. A study conducted by University of Michigan psychologist Arnold Sameroff and his colleagues demonstrated the notion of risk accumulation. The Sameroff study showed that as risk factors increase—such as poverty, absence of a parent, drug abuse in a parent, mental illness in a parent, low education status in a parent, child abuse in the family, exposure to racism, and large family size—intellectual development becomes negatively affected, which plays a role in increased violence and aggression.[6]

Most school shooters had been bullied.[7] While some targets of bullying react in a withdrawn manner, others make bomb threats to blow up schools, bring guns to school, and engage in mass school shootings, thus claiming innocent lives.

In the mid 1990s, it appeared as if a "mass shooting epidemic" had hit American schools; it appeared there were more incidents of school shootings than in previous years. This began with the Richland High School shooting in 1995 and hit a peak with the infamous Columbine High School shootings in 1999. Eight years later, in 2007, the deadliest school shooting in U.S. history by a single gunman took place at Virginia Tech University. Two years after that, the Winnenden school mass shootings occurred in Germany, which was followed by the second deadliest school shooting in U.S. history at Sandy Hook Elementary School in 2012. Since then, there have been over 140 school shootings that have taken place.[8]

It is an oversimplification to identify these school shooters as "deranged monsters." We are always looking to blame these repugnant massacres on issues such as school safety protocol, gun control policies, and/or violence in the media. While undeniably important, these issues address the mere surface of a much deeper concern that we should bring to the forefront as a society—*tolerance and acceptance of people from all backgrounds, in all capacities.*

Mass murder of this nature is not about fame or recognition, but rather about a troubled individual who might have felt shamed, not accepted, excluded in some way, or felt wronged by others or society, in general.

The riveting words of these young individuals clue us into how these acts of violence may have been prompted in the first place:

> *"I am not insane, I am angry. I killed because people like me are mistreated every day. I did this to show society, push us and we will push back. All throughout my life, I was ridiculed, always beaten, always hated. Can you, society, truly blame me for what I do? Yes, you will.*

It was not a cry for attention. It was not a cry for help. It was a scream in sheer agony saying that if you can't pry your eyes open, if I can't do it through pacifism, if I can't show you through the displaying of intelligence, then I will do it with a bullet."

—Luke Woodham, student gunman at Pearl High School[9]

"You had a hundred billion chances and ways to have avoided today, but you decided to spill my blood. You forced me into a corner and gave me only one option. The decision was yours. Now you have blood on your hands that will never wash off."

—Seung-Hui Cho, twenty-three-year-old
Virginia Tech University gunman[10]

"They were tired of those who were insulting them, harassing them. They weren't going to take this anymore and they wanted to stop it. Unfortunately, that's exactly what they did."

—Eric Veik, friend of Eric Harris and Dylan Klebold,
the two shooters at Columbine High School[11]

"We knew he had difficulties with communication and social skills, which can lead to isolation and emotional problems." "He was a loner at school and hyper intelligent." "He was painfully shy and awkward." "He played violent video games in his basement all the time." "He used to hang with the freaks, guys who dressed in trench coats."

—Classmates of Adam Lanza, the twenty-year-old
shooter at Sandy Hook Elementary

RISK FACTORS ASSOCIATED WITH YOUTH VIOLENCE

Youth violence is the third leading cause of death for young people between the ages of fifteen and twenty-four. According to the Centers for Disease Control and Prevention, nearly five thousand young people aged ten to twenty-four are victims of homicide each year in America.[13] Violent tendencies begin early on in a child's life. There are many factors that may contribute to a person becoming violent: having violent parents; watching violent shows on television; playing violent video games with lewd or crude themes; listening to music with violent lyrics; demonstrating cruelty to animals; living in an impoverished violent neighborhood; being affiliated with a gang; associating with delinquent peers; using drugs, alcohol, or tobacco; getting poor grades in school; and being genetically predisposed from birth.

Having these factors does not guarantee that children will become juvenile delinquents and grow up to be aggressive people by any means, but the odds are largely against them. When triggers are added to the mix such as bullying, rejection, shame, or not being accepted, these individuals may make choices based in violence as an outlet to be heard.

The risk factors associated with violence have been frequently studied, but major questions still remain. Is violence more prevalent among people of a certain age, race, ethnicity, religion, gender, or socioeconomic background? Research has not demonstrated a single risk factor or set of risk factors to be a strong enough cause or predictor of youth violence. Violence is multi-factored and is a result of biological, social, and psychological actions.[14]

Certain variables can be shown to have the effect of increasing or decreasing the frequency and severity of violence, but it has been examined that *shame* is a necessary cause of violence. Dr. James Gilligan, an American psychiatrist and author, noted that individuals who have been exposed to poverty and/or discrimination of some sort for a prolonged period and who are subjected to feelings of shame and their perception that there is no escape from it, except through violent action, are at a higher risk of becoming violent.[15]

Most violent and hostile incidents commonly reflect the hatred that select people have toward other people who fall outside the boundaries that are deemed acceptable to them. This includes factors such as a person's socioeconomic background, sexuality, religion, race, ethnicity, and beliefs.

Most school attacks come from "loners" or "outcasts" who felt bullied or persecuted by others. Peers indicated that the two assailants in the Columbine High shootings, Harris and Klebold, felt that their peers were attacking their masculinity by calling them "gay" or "faggot."[16] What is also evident is that their perception of how their peers viewed them was of *disrespect*. Their mental reactions to the actions against them were of feeling shame, and they wanted to replace that feeling with one of respect. The only way they believed this could be achieved was through an act of rage and destruction.

> *"God I can't wait till I kill you people. I'll just go to some downtown area and blow up and shoot everything I can. Feel no remorse, no sense of shame. I don't care if I live or die in the shootout, all I want to do is kill and injure as many of you as possible."*
>
> —Eric Harris, Columbine shooter[17]

After years of abuse from his peers, dating back to middle school, Virginia Tech shooter Seung-Hui Cho had carried a feeling of anger and deep rage within him. When he gained the nerve to talk to girls he liked at the university, it resulted in him experiencing further rejection and being labeled as a stalker. From there, he turned his emotions into an outcry toward humanity. Quite possibly, his shame and frustration in seeing that nothing had changed in experiencing rejections, and being outcast and unable to fit in, caused him to be heard in a different light:[18]

> *"You have vandalized my heart, raped my soul, and torched my conscience. You thought it was one pathetic boy's life you were extinguishing. Thanks to you, I die like Jesus Christ, to inspire generations of the weak and the defenseless people."*
>
> —Seung-Hui Cho, Virginia Tech gunman[19]

When someone feels rejected, shamed, or does not feel accepted, there are choices the person has to make about how to handle the situation. Sometimes children resort to violence as an outlet to be heard and choose to hurt themselves or others. The situations that were described in this chapter denote the importance of teaching children to be *accepting* and *tolerant of all groups of people.* This is a key principle that can substantially reduce any shame-provoking inequities in social and economic status, and would subsequently improve the public health of today's society, serving as a protective factor against violent behavior.

Crises in a child's life can be triggered by a specific event that takes place during the day, at school or at home. Children can become easily upset by a variety of circumstances. Perhaps they get a bad grade, break their cell phone, can't watch their favorite show, or have to complete a chore around the house that they don't like. Children may also become violently upset to a major event such as the loss of a family member, chronic bullying, rejection, or disrespect from a peer group.

VIOLENT VIDEO GAMES

Many acts of violence, both real and portrayed, are displayed on television. Over the past thirty years, there has been extensive research conducted on the relationship between televised violence and aggressive behavior among youth. By the age of eighteen, the average American child will have watched over two hundred thousand acts of televised violence, including more than sixteen thousand depictions of murder, and that is not including what is viewed on the Internet.[20]

According to extensive psychological research, violence can have profound effects on youth:[21]

- Children may become desensitized to the pain and suffering of others and lose the ability to empathize with the victim and perpetrator.
- Children may be more fearful of the world around them.
- Children may be more likely to behave in aggressive ways toward others and view violence as a normal means to resolve conflict.
- Children may be less likely to succeed academically.

Retired U.S. Army Lieutenant Colonel Dave Grossman, author of the Pulitzer-nominated book *On Killing: The Psychological Cost of Learning to Kill in War and Society* stated,

> Violent video games are very similar to military combat simulators. You learn in the trainer, and then you go to the real thing and you're a lot better because of the trainer. But after you've done your transition fire, all that simulated training immediately translates into the real thing.[22]

According to the most recent comprehensive poll by the Kaiser Foundation, American children aged eight to eighteen play an average of eight hours of video games per week, an increase of over 400 percent from 1999.[23] When the release of a new video game entertainment system took place in November 2006, it caused pandemonium outside of stores throughout the United States. There were reports of attempted robberies where people were demanding money from others waiting in line.[24]

The types of video games vary, but the most popular and top-selling ones contain very strong violence. Many of these popular violent video games today, which include the *Call of Duty*, *Grand Theft Auto*, and *Halo* series, are so visually graphic and quite realistic that a person can go on a virtual killing spree and actually experience feelings of violence. There are reward systems involved where players hear reinforcing statements like "good shot" or "move on to the next level" for accomplishing their mission.

The effect that these video games can have on the psyche of a young person is sadly evident in fourteen-year-old Callum Green, who had been a regular player of violent video games and was found hung by his school tie from his bunk bed.[25] Another case involved 2011 Norway mass murderer Anders Breivik who claimed that he had "trained himself" to kill his seventy-seven victims by playing *Call of Duty*. Furthermore, the former wife of terrorist Mohammed Merah admitted that they played violent video games together, including *Call of Duty*, before he gunned down seven people in the 2012 Toulouse and Montauban mass shootings in France.[26]

It is important to note that there is a significant difference between violence in video games and violence on television or in the movies. The person playing these types of violent video games takes on the first-person role of assailant and tends to embody that character. On the other hand, someone watching a violent act on television or in the movies may or may not identify with that person and may actually empathize with the victim.

It may be unrealistic to try to eliminate a child's exposure to violence in all of its forms by banning video game play, use of the Internet, and television viewing. However, the following strategies can help you effectively monitor your child's activities:

- Position the video game system and the computer in a centrally located area of the house, out of your child's bedroom, where it is used as a family resource and entertainment source.
- Encourage your child to play *educational, non-violent* video games. They are more beneficial for problem solving and improving hand-eye coordination.
- Play video games with your child so you are aware of the game's content and can adequately discuss the implications of playing certain types of games.
- Limit one "tech activity" a night during a school day, preferably to one hour, whether it is watching a television show, going on the computer (non-academic-related), or playing a video game.

Due to the multitude of factors that contribute to the onset of violent attitudes and behaviors, there isn't one approach to effectively preventing violence. Teaching children early on how to deal with their emotions without resorting to violence and to accept other children from different racial and ethnic backgrounds can greatly minimize violence. By limiting your child's exposure to violence and modeling appropriate behaviors, he or she will be able to learn how to resolve conflict in a more peaceful way.

It's hard to completely eliminate violence. However, teaching your child to be respectful, tolerant, and accepting of people from all backgrounds, in all capacities, can make a big difference.

Gambling

The Invisible Yet Insidiously Growing Addiction

"Even kids as young as nine years are learning about gambling. They may not be gambling with money, but they're learning concepts of gambling. They see it."[1]

—Dr. Jon Kelly (CEO of the
Responsible Gambling Council of Canada)

*M*illions of people worldwide participate in gambling in all of its forms, whether it is at casinos, racetracks, purchasing lottery tickets, or online gambling. It is widely promoted throughout the Internet, on television, and on billboard advertisements, and has become a widespread activity among adolescents. For some young people, however, gambling has become an addiction, just like alcoholism or drug use, that has led to some serious problems.

THE INSIDIOUS NATURE OF GAMBLING

My friend's nephew *Tommy* started playing different online games when he was a little boy. By the time he was ten years old, his parents had divorced and Tommy had spent most of his free time playing games on the computer. In the beginning, what seemed like innocent play on the computer turned into an addiction.

Problems escalated as Tommy entered middle school. His mother struggled to get him off the computer to do much of anything else. Tommy spent most of his time after school and during the weekends glued to the computer playing interactive online games with his friends. His interest in things had shifted and activities he used to enjoy doing such as basketball, art, and fishing had suddenly faded.

A couple of years later, Tommy demonstrated outbursts of anger and neglected personal, school, and family responsibilities. He often complained of being sick and refused to attend school. He was completely defiant toward his mother. On one occasion, Tommy got caught ransacking the home, stealing money from his mother.

Most days, Tommy stayed up into the wee hours of the night playing on the computer and would not wake up until the middle of the afternoon. Tommy's mother grew increasingly frustrated with her son's behavior and didn't know what to do about it. One day, Tommy's aunt saw a message appear on her nephew's Facebook wall that said he was playing slot machines, poker, and Texas Hold'em. She told Tommy's mother about what she saw and expressed her concern that Tommy had a gambling problem and needed help.

At that time, Tommy's mother lost her job and was in denial about her son's gambling problem. After talking with Tommy's father, both parents decided that it would be best if their son lived with the father, hoping that Tommy would get back on the right track. However, time and time again, the father noticed the same behavior patterns that the mother witnessed and threatened to remove the computer if Tommy didn't go to school and do his homework. But that strategy only worked temporarily until Tommy's grades slipped so badly that he dropped out of school at seventeen years old and continued to gamble online—sleeping during the day and gaming throughout the night.

Gambling problems in adolescents have historically not garnered as much attention as other addictive problems facing youth. Gambling by adolescents, however, can greatly influence their development and make them vulnerable to other risk-taking behaviors. Adolescents, as compared with adults, have been found to have high rates of problem and pathological gambling. Males are more likely to have gambling problems than females. The average age at which a child first gambles is twelve years old, which is younger than the average age for first time use of alcohol, tobacco, or other drugs.[2] The accessibility of online gambling makes it that much easier for kids to start gambling at an early age. This underscores the importance for parents to prevent and be on the lookout for risk factors associated with problem or pathological gambling.

GAMBLING AND YOUTH SPORTS

Brandon Bivins was a coach and president of the Fort Lauderdale Hurricanes, with one of the best winning records for youth football teams in South

Florida. Bivins was also an owner of a barbershop where men walked down a long hallway into a room with three windows where they regularly placed bets on NFL and college football games, MLB, and even little league games. This place was a front for an elaborate, high-stakes gambling operation where nine youth football coaches and associates were involved in promoting and organizing illegal wagering on these little league football games, which came to be known as "Operation Dirty Play."[3]

This story was featured on ESPN when "Outside the Lines" showed video surveillance of large crowds of men in their twenties and thirties openly exchanging money in the stands, on the sidelines, near the front entrance, and sometimes even feet away from police officers. They were betting anywhere from hundreds up to tens of thousands of dollars on youth football games in a football league comprised of children ages five to fifteen.[4]

One nine-year-old began playing in this league and soon garnered notice from off-the-field betters for his superb talent. He admitted that he was paid for playing football, sometimes in the thousands if he played a good game. He recalled one kickoff that he returned in which one man said to him that if he ran it back for a touchdown, then he would be given one hundred dollars. The boy ran it back for ninety-nine yards and by the end zone, he ran past the coolers where the man gave the money to him.[5]

What the little boy didn't realize at the time was that the money he received was part of the payoff from men who won bets from his performance. Former players, parents, and coaches openly told their stories of how many other players were paid hundreds of dollars for individual plays made during the games.

Head coach in the league and Broward County sheriff's deputy, Ron Thurston, witnessed firsthand the negative effects from paying youth for their performance on the field. He said that many of the kids in the juvenile unit, where he worked, had played youth football in that league and were there for crimes such as drugs and robbery.

It didn't take long for the young player to get pulled into that crowd. He dropped out of high school and was convicted of a felony for cocaine possession. Like so many other kids who possessed outstanding abilities and could have taken their talents to higher levels, their futures were cut short due to the influences of gambling and other things that follow with it.

RISK FACTORS ASSOCIATED WITH YOUTH GAMBLING

Gambling is the fastest growing teen addiction; it prevails as the most severe type of addiction among today's youth.[6] Louisiana State University reports that individuals in juvenile detention are at about a four times greater risk to have a gambling problem as their peers. Roughly two-thirds of the youngsters in juvenile detention have openly admitted to stealing, specifically to finance gambling.[7]

So why has gambling become so popular among youth? Today's generation of children is surrounded with gambling in more venues than ever before. Television is cashing in big time on attracting youth to the gambling arena. Internet gambling has become one of the most popular and lucrative businesses. Many young people think that this is a cool thing to do and an easy way to make money. But how does this compulsive behavior all begin?

For many gamblers, it's not only about making money, but also about the *excitement* and *adrenaline rush* of playing. The ill effects from losing, however, become a downward spiral for so many young people who get involved.

Some teens gamble out of curiosity, boredom, or loneliness, while others use it as a distraction and a way to escape problems at home. It could start as innocently as playing a video game online. Video games have a special appeal with the flashing lights, dynamic sounds, and enthralling excitement. Research shows that the more often youth play video games, the more likely they are to believe that their playing skills are related to gambling success.[8]

Although studies have shown an association between different types and frequency of video game play and gambling-related problems, additional factors such as family/peer/social influences, personality, and values may also explain why some teenagers experience gambling-related problems.

Kids are taught that "practice makes perfect." Many kids, however, don't realize that there isn't a specific system or skill set that they will develop to "master the art of gambling." No amount of practice will make a child become a successful gambler, but rather can lead to more serious problems such as dropping out of school, stealing, and addictions.

A growing number of kids' heroes and icons today have shifted from athletes and rock stars to gaming legends on the poker table. Many young wagers possess grandiose ideas of becoming the next poker star and use gambling as their personal path to acquire wealth and power. They fall in love with the excitement and rush of gambling and hear success stories of winning grand prizes worth millions of dollars.

Many individuals decide to take it to the next level by studying how to become professional gamers. They read books, take classes, get personally mentored, and play online in rooms, preparing to one day play with the big timers for a chance to win big pots. They play poker, Texas Hold'em, Omaha, Black Jack, Card Stud, and other games.

As kids become more involved in gambling, they derive their self-esteem from their earnings and losses and the activity becomes a compulsion. When gambling leads to more continued losses, the compulsive gambler may start to borrow money and find a thrill in chasing back the money that was lost. Hence, the player feels that the only way they can "earn back the losses" is to commit to gambling in order to restore the debt.

National statistics indicate that 96 percent of adult male recovering compulsive gamblers began gambling before the age of fourteen.[9] These people remain attached to gambling for quite some time, even though their family and friends around them have become adversely affected. Despite the problems that continue to arise, these people continue to gamble.

Many adult gamblers reported serious gambling as early as nine and ten years old. Some individuals were fortunate to have quit, realizing that they had exhausted too much time and money and were causing a strain on relationships with family and friends, while others noticed other aspects of their lives that suffered during the process and struggled to find a way out of gambling.

THE EFFECTS OF YOUTH GAMBLING

While researching the topic of gambling, I came across a story about *Pete*, who loved hockey; he started betting on the games when he was fifteen years old. The amount first began at $5, then increased to $100, and finally exploded to even higher amounts. He was consistently winning thousands of dollars a month on sports gambling. He even got recruited to get paid to make picks for other people.

For a while, things were going good for Pete. However, he got to a point when he found himself not being able to live an hour without having to place a bet on something. He was completely immersed into the thrill of every game being different and feeling like a "king" when he won. But when he lost a game of online blackjack, he would get angry and blow away an entire bankroll and max out all of his credit cards and resources.

Unfortunately, years later, Pete was still gambling and reached a point of hopelessness where all he thought about was the games and how much he won and lost. His mind was consumed with point spreads and full statistics of all the teams and players.

Pete expressed, "It doesn't matter how much I make at work because I will just blow it all on gambling. I am constantly going through *anxiety* and *depression*. It's gotten so bad that I have isolated myself from a lot of my friends and I would just gamble. Everyday seems like a struggle to me filled with anxiety and insomnia and continuous thoughts of suicide."[10]

Casual gambling for money at an early age has the strong possibility of leading to more serious problems down the road, including smoking, alcohol, vandalism, robbery, widespread violent behavior, substance abuse, selling drugs, bankruptcy, divorce, depression, and suicide. The National Council on Problem Gambling also reports that among young people who gamble, 50 percent are likely to binge drink and 75 percent are likely to smoke marijuana.[11]

Legalized gambling has been claimed by politicians as a way to raise taxes effectively and painlessly. Additionally, supporters propose that it will get rid of illegal gambling and drive new revenue to help plug budget gaps. Several states in the United States are taking steps to authorize online gaming. A California lawmaker from Orange County sees legalizing online poker in California as an opportunity to decrease the state's financial debt and hire more teachers and social service workers.

Proponents of legalized gambling, however, do not take into account the hidden *social impact* that legalized gambling has on today's youth. They assume that all people will gamble anyway, so why not make it legal and in turn, the state could collect profits. The statistics show that in states with different numbers of games, participation rates increase steadily and sharply as the number of legal types of gambling increases. States that lack legalized gambling possess less than half as much social betting, as compared to states with three legal types of games: 35 percent to 72 percent, respectively.

If you are concerned that your child may be addicted to gambling, look for these early warning signs:[12]

- Becomes more affixed with sports scores and point spreads
- Increased knowledge of betting-related events
- Drastic mood shifts for no apparent reason
- Loss of interest in other activities
- Poor coping skills
- Shift in the group of friends to gambling acquaintances
- Appearance of sudden wealth that cannot be explained
- Frequent requests for money
- Stealing and lying
- Missing money and/or possessions in the house
- Increased irritability, impulsivity, defiance, and/or hostile behavior
- Sleep problems
- Missing school or work
- Seeing gambling merchandise around the house (e.g., books, CDs, DVDs, scratch offs, lottery tickets, etc.)
- Begins to sell personal belongings
- Depression, unexplained anger, and/or suicidal thoughts/attempts

How can you step in and address the issue of gambling with your child before it becomes a serious problem? Here are specific ways to intervene with your child:

- Monitor your child's activities on the Internet and impose specific limits for its use. Be aware of unusual amount of time spent on a phone, computer, or any other electronic devices.
- Deny access to cash, debit cards, and credit cards so your child isn't able to use them for gambling, in any capacity.
- Communicate with your child about the negative effects of gambling, before the habit becomes too serious of a problem.
- If your child seems to be displaying many of the warning signs of compulsive gambling and your interventions are not working, insist that they seek additional help. There are different addiction treatment programs available, along with educational and informational resources, for teens and young adults about compulsive gambling. For information on the best gambling addiction rehabilitation programs in your area, check out www.rehabs.com.

Gambling is a serious problem that is glamorized on television and in the movies and is inaccurately addressed throughout many areas of the media. They construct a prophecy to the public that "gaming"—although they don't call it what they truly mean, "gambling"—helps build a child's social, mathematical, and problem-solving skills, self-discipline, concentration, and skills in reading mannerisms of people.

Not all adults see a concern with kids playing a game of poker either at home or with friends. But there is cause for concern because the adolescent brain is not yet fully developed and some kids are more prone to risk-taking behaviors than others.

Many young people can get caught up in the excitement of gambling and bet over their means. The social impact of gambling begins as one person's addiction, but then becomes a much more serious matter, negatively affecting the lives of individuals close to them. The more a person gambles, the more they want to venture for higher stakes with greater risks. This could cross over to other areas of a person's life, thus resulting in co-occurring serious, life-altering addictions. There are no clocks in gambling, just a ticking away of a young person's future.

———◦◦◦———

Protect your child from gambling and talk about its negative effects.

———◦◦◦———

Sex

How It Can Change Your Child's and Your Life Forever

"Given a choice between hearing my daughter say 'I'm pregnant' or 'I used a condom,' most mothers would get up in the middle of the night and buy them herself."[1]

—Joycelyn Elders (American pediatrician
and public health administrator)

I've been lecturing on adolescent sexuality for quite a few years. I recall the first time I had to teach a lesson on the reproductive system. I was standing on the platform in the front of my classroom and you could hear a pin drop. It was the "boys' day" and I was about to discuss the male reproductive system and its involvement in sexual reproduction. I said to myself, "How on Earth am I going to teach this lesson without the whole class feeling uncomfortable and embarrassed?" I clicked to the next slide and said, "And this is the male reproductive organ called the penis."

Confused, excited, embarrassed, and frightened are all adjectives used to describe the reactions of my twelve- and thirteen-year-old students. Some students' eyes were fixed to the full-size image on the board and couldn't believe what they were seeing. Other students started to giggle, while blushing and feeling embarrassed. Another group of students turned their heads away, while others started to whisper to nearby classmates. I was determined to figure out a way to get through the discomfort and speak to the students so they could focus and grasp this all-important information that would guide them in making important choices as they went through adolescence and into adulthood.

TEENAGE PREGNANCY

Despite the significant decline in the number of babies born to teenagers over the years, approximately 300,000 births by teens aged fifteen to nineteen years take place each year in the United States, according to the CDC.[2] The reality television series *Teen Mom* exemplifies the struggles that teenage mothers go through as they raise their children. One of the four featured teen moms, Maci Bookout, was described as the classic teenage overachiever who had everything going for her. She was well liked by her peers, athletic, and was successful in her academics. She had aspirations of going away to college with her friends until that all changed when she became pregnant.[3]

Maci was forced to grow up quickly, having to juggle parenthood, school, and work. She also became frustrated with the lack of help she received from her son's father, Ryan, which led to their splitting apart. Maci stated that a major reason for her going on this show was to make teenage girls more aware of the daily challenges involved in being a teen parent.

There has been a dramatic decline in teen pregnancy and abortion rates in the United States. Some experts claim that teens are having less sex, and that contraceptive use has risen for those who are actively engaged in it. According to the National Survey of Family Growth, there has been an increase in the amount of students who have never had sexual intercourse (14 percent for female and 22 percent for male teenagers) over the past twenty-five years. However, the United States still ranks as having one of the highest teen pregnancy rates in developed countries. Experts attribute this to American teens' lack of proficiency at using contraception when compared to teens in other developed countries.[4]

SEXUALLY TRANSMITTED DISEASES

For so many years, preventing teen pregnancy has been a large-scale focus. There has been an emphasis on the different choices that are available for preventing it. However, the topic of *disease prevention* has been somewhat squandered, and it has taken a back seat to teen pregnancy. Few regular scientific-based discussions take place in school that adequately address how sexually transmitted diseases (STDs), such as chlamydia, syphilis, gonorrhea, herpes, human papilloma virus (HPV), and HIV, can change a young person's life forever.

I have addressed the topic of STDs in my class and how they have become what public health officials call a "hidden epidemic" that is exploding throughout the lives of teenagers. Consider that this year in the United States alone, there will be an estimated 19 million new cases of STDs contracted. Almost half of these cases occur among youth between the ages of fifteen and twenty-four, with about 4 million affecting solely teenagers.[5]

Oral sex has become a growing trend among teens. While it won't get a girl pregnant, it can cause serious problems for both boys and girls. There are stories of middle and high school students having oral sex in the back of a bus, at movie theaters, or at home when parents have left. To teens, this isn't viewed as "real" sex because they are avoiding penetration, which means that they haven't lost their virginity and are playing it safe from catching a disease—or so they believe. This perception, however, is far from the truth.

Studies show that oral herpes has dramatically increased from 25 percent of all cases of herpes infections to 75 percent. Many of these infections can spread from any sexual contact, including mouth to penis/vagina and semen to skin, without intercourse. Researchers have established a link between oral sex, HPV—the same virus that causes cervical cancer—and throat cancer.[6]

In my teaching career, I recall one of my former female students coming into my classroom to speak with me about a few things that concerned her. At the time, she was in eighth grade and I hadn't seen her in months. I immediately noticed a drastic change in her physical appearance. Her once brown hair was now colored tar black. She wore black clothes and had a row of piercings going up along the sides of her ears, accompanied by a piercing on her nose.

I wasn't quite sure what to say to her when she came into my classroom besides, "How are you doing?" She said she wanted to ask me something scientific. By the look on her face, I knew this conversation was going to be serious. As she talked, I could see how agitated she was and that something was bothering her. She blurted out a series of questions: "What is HPV? How do you get it? Can I get cancer from it?"

For a moment I was taken off guard and wanted to probe into why she had asked me those questions. But I had a strong sense of why she was curious and wanted all of these answers. After addressing her concerns as objectively as possible, the girl asked me another question, which really concerned me: "Why do I feel so depressed?"

She described how she did something "inappropriate" with a high school boy at his house. She described it to me as "not having the real thing." As she was telling me the story, I could see how saddened she was by what she had done. She felt disgusted with herself and mentioned how she would get angry at her mother for no apparent reason. To make matters worse, word spread at school and many boys were sexually harassing her, calling her bad names, which caused her self-esteem to plummet and hurt her relationship with other girls.

I could see how much this situation had affected her. I often wonder how many more students wander the halls of middle schools and high schools feeling depressed or upset about engaging in similar sexual events. Teenagers seem to be especially misinformed about the STD risks associated with oral sex. Some teens are having it at parties, in groups, and don't see anything wrong with this type of behavior.

One of these parties—the so-called rainbow party—has gained attention in the media and alerted parents to possible sex acts going on among teenagers. Rainbow parties are alleged group oral sex events in which females wear various shades of lipstick and take turns fellating males—one after another—leaving behind a trail of rainbow colors. The idea of a rainbow party was first publicized on *The Oprah Winfrey Show* in 2003 and was featured as a topic of discussion on *The Doctors* with dozens of teens, parents, and professionals.

Many sex researchers and adolescent-health professionals say that this is more media hype than reality and that this is not a big part of teenage sexual behavior. However, some guidance counselors feel that these parties are a real concern and that they do take place. But they are not sure to what extent it is actually happening.[7] Providing this type of scenario, whether real or fantasy, demonstrates the importance of teaching children about the dangers of different forms of sex.

We are living in a hypersexualized society where a large emphasis is placed on sex and body image. Television, movies, music, magazines, and advertisements portray a fun, carefree nature to having sex—without any repercussions involved. *Friends*, one of the most popular sitcoms of all-time, featured topics about sex, love, and relationships where six main characters were shown sleeping around with each other or with other people. The only ramifications seen for their actions were a broken heart or an occasional pregnancy. Very rarely was there a reference made to acquiring an STD, which statistically should have happened to at least one character in the show.

In the music media, there are more sexually provocative music videos with salacious images of artists exposing their bodies in suggestive ways than ever before; these images can infiltrate a child's mind. Millions of tweens and teens from all socioeconomic backgrounds are regularly listening to these megastars and reciting their lyrics—oftentimes explicit—in public, as if they were reciting their ABCs. Many of today's current artists are singing songs that contain sexually explicit lyrics and vulgar themes. Both female and male performers glorify the idea of casual, meaningless sex, and yet very few acknowledge in their personal lives the very dangers of those topics about which they sing. Instead, young boys and girls are taught to idolize these performers and to ignore the real dangers that can arise when such activities are acted upon.

SEXUAL ACTIVITY AND EMOTIONAL HEALTH

Sexual activity among teens is connected to substantial problems with emotional health. Studies suggest that there is a relationship between teen sexual activity and depression.[8] However, which one is the cause and which one is the effect, is unclear. Substantial data do not demonstrate, for certain, that early sexual activity leads to depression or that depression leads to early sexual activity, for that matter. However, the significantly lower levels of happiness and higher levels of depression among sexually active teens lead to an increase in emotional stress and reduction in happiness and overall well-being.[9]

So why do teenagers choose to be sexually active in the first place? They respond to their family and school life in a variety of ways. Various social forces play a role in a child engaging in sexually active behaviors, such as a family's socioeconomic background, which may contribute to emotional stress and instability. Premature sexual activity can be triggered by a low-income background, little or no parental supervision at home, difficulty in school with grades, and poor relationships with peers. Other factors such as race, gender, and age have been compared, and they were not shown to have a significant effect on this link between teen sexual activity and depression/suicide.

How do adolescents really feel when they take that step to have sex for the first time? Studies have shown that while guys experience a boost in self-esteem after losing their virginity, women experience feelings of depression.[10] Some girls have expressed that depression started to kick in and they didn't want to go to school, eat, or do much of anything. Others expressed that they never felt anything this bad in their entire life.

Many young girls experience the emotional pain for months afterward, and the internal battle with themselves and their boyfriends, now that they have crossed the line. Many have expressed guilt because they didn't want to go through with the act but did anyway. They hated themselves, the person they lost their virginity to, the people at school, the movies, and television shows that glamorize sex as being wonderful and intimate. They wished that they had more information given to them from sex education about how it really was and the emotions that come with having sex.

For many teens, having sex fulfills the need for an emotional connection with someone, anyone. It is a perceived solution for acquiring happiness in their lives for where they feel it is lacking. A study from the University of

Southern California indicates that teenagers who engage in *sexting* are more likely to engage in real-life sex. Data from a survey given to Los Angeles high school students suggest that sexting is not a substitute for sexual intercourse but perhaps a precursor leading to it.[11]

SEXTING

Sexting is the act of sending sexually explicit photographs or messages, primarily between mobile phones, and is illegal in the United States with varying degrees of punishment. Depending on the state laws, minors who are caught sexting are subject to juvenile delinquency proceedings, misdemeanor charges, or even felony charges under the state's child pornography laws, regardless of age.

It is always better to be proactive and talk with your child about the ramifications of a person's actions before the damage has been done. Teenagers, however, can make impulsive, poor decisions, especially during social interactions. Boys may feel pressured by friends to prove their masculinity by sharing provocative photos and/or messages that their partners have sent them.

You can start a discussion with your child by highlighting the importance of maintaining a positive digital footprint. Stress the importance to your child about treating everyone with respect and standing up to peer pressure when asked to share sexually explicit photos, messages, or videos. Discuss how falling prey to peer pressure could hurt them and someone else in the near future and later in life when applying for college or trying to get a job in the workforce.

Needless to say, not all children can see beyond tomorrow and grasp the concept of digital permanence and as a result, they end up making poor decisions. Encourage your child to ask themselves the following questions before sending a message or picture of another person to anyone:

- How will this make the other person who is the subject of the message or picture feel?
- Will this text leave a positive or negative digital footprint for me?
- Could I get in trouble for sharing this with others?

PORNOGRAPHY

What do you do if you find out that your child has been watching pornography online? First and foremost, you want to remain calm about the situation.

As embarrassing as it may be for the both of you, it is important to confront your child about what has happened and find out if it was accidental or intentional. Ask them why they made such a decision and clearly express that something of this nature is unacceptable and cannot happen again.

There are a number of reasons why kids look at pornography in the first place. Some kids are curious after hearing that such websites exist. For others, it is to impress their friends and show that they are cool, or for boys, that they are masculine. Other times, it is for stimulation when they are by themselves.

No matter what the reason is for their actions, you don't want to shame your child by saying to them that they are a bad kid for doing these kinds of things. You also have to be careful in how you discipline your child. Overreacting by taking the phone or computer away, without regard to intention, could close off future communication between you and your child and spur them into wanting to view more of it.

Use the situation, instead, as an opportunity to talk about how sexuality can be exploited online, and reinforce values about men, women, and relationships. Furthermore, discuss Internet safety and restate or initiate rules about Internet use. At that point, it would be appropriate to follow up with natural consequences such as removing the phone or computer for a certain period and having them work to earn back your trust.

There is only so much you can do as a parent to protect your child from exposure to pornography and other sexualized media online. Parental supervision and pornography blocking software can help protect your child to a certain degree, but does not solve the problem. A parent's job is to monitor and shape their child's behavior to the best of their ability. That means knowing your child's passwords for any electronic devices, their e-mails, and social networking and sitting down with your child to have a conversation that is age appropriate, helping instill morals, care, honesty, and respect for other people. How you respond to your child's actions can have more of a lasting effect than the exposure itself.

SOCIAL MEDIA

Some teenagers get involved in "virtual relationships" and chat with complete strangers in online forums. This emotional fantasy can become an obsession, wreaking havoc on a child's psyche. These behaviors usually persist because someone expresses interest and kindness and fills a lonely and frustrating void in a child's life.

According to data from the Pew Research Center, 81 percent of teens are on social media.[12] In addition to monitoring your child's activities on social media sites such as Facebook, Instagram, and Snapchat, there are dating apps, many of which are open to anyone above the age of thirteen, that many teens are using such as Tinder, MeetMe, Skout, Badoo, OkCupid, Blendr, MiuMeet, Hot or Not, Omegle, Grindr, and so on.

Some of these dating apps require full name, age, and zip code, upon registration. They may also lack privacy settings and ask permission to use location services on your teen's mobile device, which can reveal the exact whereabouts of your child. It is also easy to falsify information on these apps, and on many social networks, to pose as either an adult or a teen.

Many of these dating apps contain sexually explicit, obscene content and can be a forum for potential stalkers and pedophiles targeting children. There have been multiple cases of alleged rape involving adults who have posed as teenagers on these apps.[13]

People, in general, are wired to build relationships and emotionally connect with others. When children are curious or starved for attention, they may travel down these dangerous, all-consuming paths that can lead to more problems later on. In a study conducted by the Kaiser Family Foundation, 23 percent of sexually active teens and young adults, ages fifteen to twenty-four in the United States, reported having unprotected sex as a result of drinking or using drugs at the time. Twenty-four percent of teens, ages fifteen to seventeen, stated that their alcohol and drug use led them to be more sexual than they had intended.[14]

SEX EDUCATION

Because today's culture doesn't censor "all things sexual" the way it once did and kids have easier availability to hear and watch sexually related content, tweens and teens must receive accurate information from parents and educators about what sex is, in all of its forms, as early as the elementary school years.

All states are involved in sex education for public school children in the United States.[15] There are many different facets to educating children about sex and sexuality and so many different beliefs and opinions of how parents and educators feel about the subject exist. Getting accurate information about sex, sexual health, and relationships plays a crucial role in helping young people make healthy decisions that can impact their lives.

So when is a good time to start talking about sex with your child? You, as the parent, should be ready to discuss this topic with your child at any time and preferably sooner than later. Don't wait until your child has a question.

Everyday events can serve as teachable moments to open up a conversation with your child. Begin when they are little by talking about body parts while they are taking a bath. Use music, television, and movies as opportunities to discuss sexuality. A pregnancy or birth in the family is a great opportunity to discuss how babies are conceived and born.

If your child asks questions, try not to look embarrassed or too serious. Be concise and age appropriate with your responses and let your child's reactions to your responses be your guide. As early as eight years old, your child is able to comprehend that sex is something that happens between two people who love each other. That would be a good time for starting a discussion about how sexually transmitted diseases (STDs) can be spread, how to protect against them, and how to prevent pregnancy.

It is also important to reinforce and discuss the topic of sex with your child at home, following a lesson in sex education class at school. Your child's definition of "sex" may be completely different than yours. Whatever the definition, your child is listening and wants to hear your input—even if you think they don't.

I realize that having this kind of talk with your child may be easier said than done. But at the end of the day, you are the expert and remain the primary influence in your child's life. Even though the topic of sex may not be the most comfortable to talk about, it is crucial to discuss it with your child *early on* in their life and is more effective than just telling your child to simply say "no" to sex.

ABNORMAL SEXUAL BEHAVIOR

While it is important to understand sexual behavior, it is also essential that you understand the signs and symptoms of abnormal sexual activity. Teens that go beyond the realm of curiosity and display sexually maladaptive behaviors, such as making inappropriate sexual contact with other children or adults, making crude movements associated with sexual acts, exposing oneself in public, touching the genitals of animals, or asking other children or adults to engage in sexual activities with them, endanger their physical and emotional well-being, as well as those around them.[16]

Children and adolescents who exhibit these behaviors are typically victims of some form of sexual abuse. Brain imaging studies have shown that these individuals have variations in their brain structures compared to those who do not engage in this kind of behavior. Some researchers attribute these discrepancies to mistreatment or as a result of a birth defect. Parents who do not establish appropriate boundaries, abuse alcohol and/or drugs, or are absent from a child's life put a child at risk for displaying these sexually inappropriate behaviors.[17]

DISCOURAGING PREMATURE SEXUAL ACTIVITY

Here are some ways to address the topic of sex with your child to help reduce or prevent your child from engaging in premature sexual activity:

- Discuss the theme of relationships and intimacy. Have regular conversations to discuss appropriate ways to treat others in a relationship. Your input helps to guide and inform your child about these topics, which they might have questions about.
- Discourage early, frequent, and steady dating. Voice your opinion clearly and maintain a standard that you have deemed age appropriate to begin dating. Group activities among young people are one thing, but dating early can lead to serious problems. Research conducted from the University of Georgia showed how students who date in middle school are four times more likely to drop out of school; report twice as much alcohol, tobacco, and marijuana use than their single classmates; and have significantly worse study skills.[18]
- Discuss pregnancy prevention by addressing various contraceptives available. As awkward as the situation may seem at the moment, the repercussions for not firmly addressing these issues, early on, can become quite severe, not just for your child, but also for you and other family members.
- If your child is about to go away to college, reemphasize your values. If they are entering into a steady relationship, communicate the importance of being proactive and setting limits in the relationship, from the start, in order to prevent out-of-wedlock births or STDs.
- If your child talks to you about a sexual experience that they had, react calmly to the situation. Many teens have trouble dealing with their own feelings, let alone approaching their parents on this topic. Teens who report having open communication with their parents about sex are more likely to delay sexual activity.
- Discuss sex openly from an early age, focusing first on the biological aspects of reproduction and sex. As children get older and start exploring their sexuality themselves, be open and honest with them about the topic, rather than judgmental or secretive. Listen to what they have to say and provide them with truthful, relevant, and accurate information. It is perfectly fine if you don't have answers to all of your

child's questions. Compliment your child on asking questions and tell them that you are not sure and together you will find the answers.

- Work in tandem with the health education curriculum and ask a health teacher for any literature that they can provide you to better discuss this topic with your child and complement what they are learning in school.
- Set limits about dating and clearly explain the reasons for setting them such as preventing teen pregnancy and contracting venereal diseases.

Kids should understand that *caring* and *intimacy* promote *commitment*. Sexual desire and activity should be a natural byproduct of a strong, already developed intimacy. A healthy and loving relationship involves *support, trust,* and *open communication between two partners* and your influence, as the parent, can go a long way in your child's understanding and application of these concepts. Listening to your child from an early age and encouraging open discussions about any and all life topics provides a reliable, honest source that your child can turn to for answers about anything throughout their life.

Talk with your child about the topic of sex. Discuss the risks of early pregnancy and contracting STDs.

Drug Abuse

The Seductive Gateway Addiction

"Children are often the silent victims of drug abuse."[1]

—Rick Larsen (Congressman)

*A*real problem persists with millions of adolescents experimenting with a variety of drugs and becoming addicted to all different kinds. There are many factors that are involved in why kids start using drugs. Some kids say they rebelled against authority, were bored, or just curious about its effects, while others say it enhanced their performance and made them "feel good." Many, however, tried it because supposedly "everyone's doing it," and they were influenced by a "friend" who had no idea of the true nature of addiction and the long-term consequences.

Hospital staff removed sixteen-year-old *Eva*'s breathing tube and stopped all medication and nourishment at 1:15 p.m. on December 16, 2012. Only morphine dripped into her body as her family stood by her bedside in what appeared to be her final moments. Eva was an A and B student, full of happiness and laughter, until the day she decided to experiment with synthetic marijuana. She saw her friends doing it and chose to follow suit.

The drug Eva used was sold as "potpourri" at convenience stores and advertised as a "legal" alternative to weed but often labeled as "unfit for human consumption" to avoid laws preventing its manufacturing. Synthetic marijuana, also referred by different brand names, such as "K2" or "Spice," is a blend of herbs sprayed with chemical compounds that is said to be even more potent than marijuana. Drug enforcement officials and users say that it's difficult to guess what will happen after you smoke or ingest it because the chemists who manufacture it are always changing the main ingredients.

That day, after Eva tried the drug, she complained of a migraine and took a nap at her house. When she awoke, a drastic turn of events took place.

Her family described Eva's behavior at that moment as erratic, stumbling, and hallucinatory. After realizing that Eva had experimented with some drug, they immediately dialed 911. The police showed up, along with the paramedics, and had to restrain a very violent Eva as they transported her into the ambulance.

When she was brought into the hospital, she bit guardrails and attempted to bite hospital staff. As doctors noticed that she was becoming a danger to herself and others, they placed Eva into an induced coma where she spent the next four days in the intensive care unit. After being in a sedated state and doing multiple tests on her brain, an MRI revealed that Eva had several strokes, which had caused intense vasculitis—a swelling of the blood vessels.

Parts of her brain were permanently damaged as a result of the blood vessels being severely inflamed. The vessels going into her brain were constricting and causing a reduction in oxygen flow, thus resulting in oxygen deprivation. The doctors had no choice but to perform emergency surgery on Eva. They had to drill a hole into her skull and insert a tube to drain the excess fluid and reduce the pressure and inflammation. For the next hour, Eva's family anxiously waited, not knowing if they would ever see her alive again or in the condition she was prior to the tragedy.

Following the surgery, the neurologists met with Eva's family and showed them her brain scans and pointed out how over 70 percent of her brain appeared permanently damaged. The prognosis appeared grim and without a breathing tube, Eva's throat would close up, as that part of her brain was functionless. Additionally, she would never be able to eat on her own again or regain function of her arms and legs. In essence, her family came to the hard conclusion that Eva would not be able to function on her own any longer and was in a complete vegetative state.

Just four days before her seventeenth birthday, Eva's family decided to take her off life support. But three days later, she was still alive. Eva was miraculously able to breathe on her own. Even though she couldn't move, was blind, and could barely understand what was happening around her, she was able to laugh with her family as they made jokes. According to Eva's sister, they were happy to still have her alive, fighting for her life.

More than a month after the life-changing night, Eva was transferred to a rehab hospital where she underwent physical, occupational, and speech therapy. Since then, Eva had a long road to recovery. She expressed that she had her vision, but her brain couldn't make sense of what she was seeing. According to Eva, she wasn't able to get a job or do much of anything but hopefully would be an inspiration for others dealing with something similar.[2]

SYNTHETIC DRUGS

Most parents would never fathom that they would have to make a decision of this nature and all because of a decision to experiment with a dangerous drug. According to a national survey conducted by the University of Michigan, one in every nine high school seniors admitted to having tried "fake weed."

Synthetic marijuana has been sweeping the country among today's teens, ranking as the second most commonly used illicit drug by them, only behind marijuana. Synthetic marijuana was linked to 11,407 drug-related emergency department visits in 2010, and jumped to 28,531 in 2011, most of them being children ages twelve to seventeen.[3] According to the CDC, the number of deaths from synthetic marijuana had tripled from January to May 2014 to the same period in 2015. During that time frame, the number of reports of adverse effects documented by the National Poison Data System had increased by 330 percent, and the number of calls to the poison control centers had increased by 229 percent.[4]

The federal government has referred to this as a "growing public health threat that needs to be stamped out." In July 2012, U.S. president Barack Obama signed legislation banning five common chemicals used to make synthetic marijuana and an emerging family of drugs known as "bath salts," containing an amphetamine-like stimulant. During that month, the Drug Enforcement Administration (DEA) was able to seize nearly 5 million packets of synthetic marijuana in its first national sweep of the drug.

You would assume that with legislation around the country proposing to ban the sale of synthetic marijuana and all of the anti-drug messages provided over the years from parents, teachers, commercials, guest speakers at schools, recovering family members, biography stories, and movies about what drugs can do to someone, young people would be fully aware of the dangers and consequences involved and drug use would drastically plummet. Sadly enough, we are seeing this is not the case. For that matter, this emerging problem of synthetic marijuana can strike any child anywhere in the world.

Another tragic incident occurred for a seventeen-year-old boy who suffered severe consequences from using a synthetic drug called 2C-I, also known as "Smiles," given to him by his eighteen-year-old friend. The boy was at a McDonald's with his friends when he fell ill from the effects. He had hyperventilated and hit his head against the ground. Several hours later after his friends took him home, the boy stopped breathing. His friend was charged with third-degree murder and second-degree manslaughter.[5]

Over the past few years, synthetic drugs have become increasingly popular with teens and young adults. Sometimes it is hard to tell if someone uses these kinds of drugs. Also, they don't usually show up in drug tests, which is another reason for the growing boom among adolescents. As much as it oftentimes goes undetected in the bloodstream, doctors recognize the ill effects. These synthetic drugs have been documented in causing seizures, kidney failure, and fatally high blood pressure.

MARIJUANA

According to a Monitoring the Future survey of U.S. secondary school students, marijuana use among teens rose for the fifth straight year, despite a drastic decline that had taken place in the previous decade. Marijuana, however, is still ranked as the most popular drug of choice; approximately one in two twelfth graders have admitted to trying it at least once and 29 percent reported current use.[6] The effects of this drug are frequently overlooked. Considered a "gateway drug" by many experts, its active intoxicating chemical ingredient is THC—tetrahydrocannabinol—which alters the functions of various nerve cells in the brain to produce a high feeling.[7]

In a groundbreaking, unprecedented decision back in 2012, Washington and Colorado became the first two states—and the first two jurisdictions in the world—to legalize the production, distribution, sales, and recreational use of marijuana, which has led to a growing number of states that have followed suit.

Despite the dangers that accompany drug use, different states are still considering legalizing its recreational use. For starters, marijuana sales have generated an increase in revenue, especially with the higher tax added on all pot transactions. According to the Colorado Department of Revenue, in the first month of legal recreational marijuana sales in Colorado, retailers amassed $1.24 million in tax revenue and in the next three years collected more than $88 million, while Washington had collected over $83 million.[8]

The Drug Policy Alliance reports that violent crime has declined in Washington and other crime rates have remained stable since the passage of Initiative 502. Law enforcement has reported that they have been able to focus on "more serious crimes," rather than arresting over 750,000 people a year for possessing small amounts of marijuana.[9]

What does this mean for marijuana use among youth in these states that have legalized recreational use compared to other states? According to the latest study conducted by the Rocky Mountain High Intensity Drug Trafficking Area, Colorado is 55 percent over the national average among teens and young adults using marijuana.[10] While some people may argue that legalization drives up youth marijuana use, others disagree and feel that higher use creates legalization.

Dr. Michelle Cretella, president of the American College of Pediatricians, has examined the results of the study and noticed a spike in the number of auto fatalities and accidents related to marijuana use, as well as students coming to school high on marijuana.[11] This begs the question, "Is gaining revenue from tax dollars more valued than the welfare of children when it comes to the root of the decision behind the legalization for the recreational use of marijuana?" This is serious food for thought for policy makers in other states who may be considering jumping on the legalization bandwagon.

PRESCRIPTION DRUGS

Prescription drugs, especially painkillers, are next in line behind marijuana as most frequently used by young individuals. They are inexpensive compared to illicit drugs, widely available, and easily accessible. When abused, these drugs can alter brain activity and give an individual a false sense of a high, thus resulting in irreversible damage over the long term. Abusers may experience a heightened state of arousal, euphoria, and energy, which can lead to serious long-term problems, both mentally and physically.[12]

Many middle and high school students have the ability to easily access these drugs from their own homes and then enter school and distribute them during lunchtime, in the bathrooms, in locker rooms, after school on or off school grounds, at friends' homes, on the streets, at parties, or through Internet sales. There are young people who commonly abuse tranquilizers, stimulants, pain relievers, and even glue for many reasons, including curiosity, trying to appear cool among peers, and/or they are experiencing family troubles.

In the past few years, non-medical use and abuse of prescription drugs have become one of the fastest-growing addictions among today's youth. Hospitals are receiving more cases in the emergency room of young people overdosing on combinations of prescription medication. The Partnership for a Drug-Free America (PDFA) has coined a term describing this generation of substance abuse among teens and young adults: "Generation Rx."

A reported one in four teenagers in the United States has misused or abused legal prescription painkillers.[13] Prescription painkillers, such as OxyContin, Vicodin, Percocet, and codeine, have become popular prescription drugs of choice providing numb, euphoric effects. Stimulants such as Ritalin, Adderall, and Dexedrine are being used more frequently to increase energy levels and achieve a euphoric state, especially by older teens and college students. A reported one in ten teens has abused cough medicine to achieve a hallucinogenic effect.[14] In addition, inhalants such as various aerosol cans, butane lighters, glue, paint thinner, nail polish remover, and other solvents are also being abused for their mind-altering, intoxicating effects.

Teens have admitted to getting their ideas about using different psychoactive substances from the Internet, sharing their experiences with other peers, and simply experimenting and seeing what happens. They often feel invincible and do not think through the consequences that could happen and disassociate themselves from becoming addicted.[15]

The abuse of legally prescribed drugs by today's youth is seen as a way to get around the restrictions and laws. The availability and access to obtain these products are much easier, considering the fact that many families have leftover pills in their medicine cabinets from a surgery or illness. The casual theft from home and transactions on and off school property make it very easy for these drugs to get around. Many Internet pharmacies are distributing these drugs without much of a medical consultation. Some kids have even gone as far as faking to be sick in order to acquire some medication.

In having spoken with recovering prescription drug users, here are statements that they have shared regarding its use:

- "It's just easier to pop a pill at school without people noticing."
- "It's more socially acceptable."
- "They are easy to get from home."
- "I used it for a prescription and then it became addicting."
- "These are medicines. It's much safer than doing bad drugs."
- "They don't smell on my breath or body so they are easy to hide."

There are a variety of methods that kids employ when ingesting prescription drugs:

- Swallowing the pills
- Crushing the pills and snorting them
- Crushing the pills and taking them with a drink
- Smoking the powder

Potential consequences from sustained periods of abuse include:[16]

- Respiratory failure
- Permanent brain damage
- Depression
- Heart attacks
- Seizures
- Frequent mood shifts
- Hostility

- Paranoia
- Anxiety
- Nausea
- Diarrhea
- Muscle and bone pain
- Restlessness
- Liver damage
- Kidney damage
- Other organ injuries

Here are some suggestions to help prevent your child from *abusing prescription drugs*:

1. Discuss the use of prescription medicine and educate your child on the dangers that these types of drugs can have both mentally and physically, if taken without a medical reason. Prescription medicine is powerful and can benefit a sick person, but it can have a drastically negative effect on a healthy person.
2. Emphasize with your child that prescription drug abuse can be just as addictive and lethal as illicit drug abuse. For example, painkillers are made from opioids, the same substance found in heroin.
3. Remain active in your child's life and monitor the group of friends that they associate with on a regular basis. Discard leftover medications and urge the parents of your child's friends to either hide or dispose of their medications.
4. Keep all prescription medicine hidden. Rather than storing it in a typical medicine cabinet, put it in a less conspicuous area. If you suspect that your child has taken some, do an inventory count and monitor pill quantities and medicine levels.
5. Educate your child on the misconception that prescription medicine use is safer than illegal, street drugs because doctors approve prescription drugs.
6. Monitor your child's activities and time spent on the Internet, and impose limits on the websites they are allowed to visit.

Monitor your child's behavior. Look for any observable warning signs of abuse:

- Drop in grades
- Chronic absence from school
- Being frequently sick
- Change in group of friends

- Change in mood, eating patterns, and overall attitude
- Appearance of strange paraphernalia such as pipes, rolling papers, small medicine droppers, bongs, and/or butane lighters
- Being uncooperative and frequently breaking rules set forth
- Disappearance of medication, money, and/or credit cards

CLUB DRUGS

Another group of dangerous and popularly used drugs among teenagers and college students is "club drugs." These are often found at bars, nightclubs, parties, and concerts. They include MDMA (Ecstasy), GHB, Rohypnol, ketamine, methamphetamine, and LSD. Research has shown that use of these drugs is linked to an increase in reports of sexual assaults committed by "slipping someone's drink." The dangers of these drugs are augmented when taken in combination with alcoholic beverages.[17]

HEROIN

Heroin use among teens has been on the rise faster than any other hard street drug, including cocaine and meth. It is particularly gaining popularity among teenagers in suburban areas. According to the Substance Abuse and Mental Health Services Administration, heroin use has significantly increased by 80 percent among twelve- to seventeen-year-olds, across most demographic groups, since 2002.[18] Experts feel that heroin's sudden surge in popularity by teens in suburban areas as first time users can be largely attributed to high costs of prescription pain pills. Hence, adolescents are turning to a cheaper and more accessible fix in what is typically an impure form of heroin, leading to large overdoses and emergency room visits.[19]

THE EFFECTS OF DRUGS ON CHILDREN

The effects that drugs have on children at school are extensive. They can alter moods and energy levels, reduce the ability to focus at school, increase sickness and days absent from school, affect organization and ability to follow through on assignments, diminish motivation, and may create changes in brain development that put youth at risk for becoming addicted to other drugs.[20]

Young people often feel that their bodies are indestructible. What many adolescents don't take into consideration is that early damage can have a later, more severe and lasting impact mentally, emotionally, socially, and physically. It can also put them at risk for other addictions or result in overdosing that can lead to death.

Regrettably, there is a lot of information being thrown at kids from many different directions about the use of drugs. Children may not find the topic of drug awareness and prevention as something that is particularly relevant to their lives and consequently, may fail to absorb the impact of the conversation the first time that it is presented to them. That is why it is very important and necessary for children to hear about drug awareness and prevention multiple times from parents and educators before it becomes a problem. Sometimes, the best way for children to understand how drugs can impact their lives is not by teaching them what's right and wrong, but instead focusing on what is best for them and the people they love and how thoughtful, informed decisions can directly impact their lives and others around them.

A TALE OF THREE MEN

In my mid-twenties, I had an opportunity to live in New York City for a summer. During that time, I witnessed people high on drugs and most of them happened to be homeless. One evening I watched three men, all unshaven, wearing layers of ripped clothes, carry their cardboard boxes in the rain as they stumbled down 32nd Street toward Madison Ave. They were shaking their change buckets along the way, while asking people for donations. I couldn't bear to see the three men struggle any longer, so I offered to bring them into a local diner and bought each of them a hot meal.

That night was an eye-opening experience and truly special for me, as I sat down and had dinner with these three individuals who were all from different backgrounds and had a story to tell about how their drug addiction led them to the streets of NYC. We spent over two hours together at the diner talking about life and all of its trials and tribulations. I asked them some candid questions about their circumstances and how they ended up homeless.

Two of the three men were ex-heroin addicts. Both were previously married and had children who they were no longer seeing. One of the two men had contracted HIV. And the third man had been running with the wrong crowd in the Bronx and was kicked out of his house when he was eighteen years old for stealing and vandalizing properties. When I asked them how long they had been on the streets, their responses were shocking to me. One of them said, "It could be three years. It could be five. I have no idea how long I've been out here for." Another guy said, "Maybe five or ten years on the streets. I don't know. I lost track of time a while ago."

Before leaving the diner that night, I hugged all three men and asked them one final question: "What dreams did you have when you were a kid?" One man said he wanted to be mayor of his hometown, another a radio host, and yet another said he wanted to be a doctor. They also mentioned that never in a million years could they have envisioned this kind of life. One man said, "Not this. No way. Not me. Not where I am now. That's for damn sure. Now it's too late." This just shows that at one point these individuals were also children with dreams and never thought they would become homeless and battle addictions.

PEER INFLUENCE

Many kids start using drugs due to a *strong peer influence*. Children develop friendships based on similar interests, beliefs, behaviors, and attitudes. A child begins to form perceptions early in life about accepted behaviors, expectations, and actions in order to obtain social acceptance and status. Children who associate with peers using these substances are more likely to try them, due to the increased exposure and availability. Peer pressure can be subtle in the form of passing around a drug from person to person or overtly asking or persuading someone to try it. Over time, this can reshape a young person's values and become a perceived accepted behavior.

Peer pressure took its toll on gifted writer and high school basketball star Jim Carroll, who ran with a tough crowd on the streets of New York City in the mid-1960s. Carroll fell deep into a world of drugs and crime. He and his friends went from being high school basketball stars to teenage junkies.[21]

Carroll kept a detailed diary of his experiences growing up on the streets of New York City and his growing dependency on drugs. His memoirs vividly highlighted his downward spiral, his drug use, and his willingness to do almost anything to pay for his addiction. As time passed, Jim got suspended from school and kicked out of his mother's house. To get his next fix, Jim desperately engaged in acts of homosexual prostitution, stealing, mugging, and even murder.[22]

Carroll's detailed recollections were compiled and published into a book, *The Basketball Diaries*, which was later made into a film starring Leonardo DiCaprio—portraying Jim Carroll. His memoir included graphic depictions of the harsh reality of a life mixed with drugs and the painful and destructive effects that they had on a young person, his family, and friends.

EDUCATING YOUR KIDS ABOUT DRUGS

The most effective weapon against young people going down this road of drug use is *education*. Research shows that positive parenting practices have a protective effect against substance abuse.[23] Having early, regular conversations with your child about the harsh realities of substance abuse goes a long way toward future decisions your child will make when confronted with opportunities to experiment with drugs.

A powerful way to convey anti-drug messages to your child and help them realize the serious ramifications involved in drug use is through sharing with them the words of young people who have experienced the consequences firsthand:[24]

> *"It started with the weed, then the pills (Ecstasy) and acid, making cocktails of all sorts of drugs, even overdosing to make the rushes last longer. I took copious amounts of these chemicals every day for as long as two years until I had a bad trip one night and went into toxic psychosis. I prayed and cried for this feeling to go away. I had voices in my head, had the shakes and couldn't leave home for six months. I became very withdrawn and thought everyone was watching me. I couldn't walk in public places. Man! I couldn't even drive."* —Ben

> *"My goal in life wasn't living . . . it was getting high. I was falling in a downward spiral towards a point of no return. Over the years, I turned to cocaine, marijuana, and alcohol under a false belief it would allow me to escape my problems. It just made things worse. I had everything, a good job, money, a loving family, yet I felt so empty inside. As if I had nothing. Over twenty years of using, I kept saying to myself, I'm going to stop permanently after using this last time. It never happened. There were even moments I had thought of giving up on life."* —John

Studies have shown the different mental and physical effects that drugs have on children:

- Disturbed energy levels, which contribute to a lack of motivation to do much of anything
- Disrupted concentration in class, homework completion, and study time
- Impaired memory for learning information
- Altered respiration and heart rates
- Changed physical composition of the cells and its genetic material, which can alter one's life span

- Drastic mood swings—"highs" followed by extreme "lows" (e.g., euphoric states followed by a strong wave of depression or suicidal notions)
- Insomnia
- Impotence
- Organ damage
- High blood pressure, strokes, blindness, convulsions, and cardiac failure

Here are some major reasons why kids start experimenting with drugs in the first place:

- Afraid to say "no" to peer pressure
- Curiosity
- Boredom
- Feel bad about themselves
- Desire to feel accepted
- Unestablished standards and ethics ingrained in a child
- Escape from painful situations at home, in school, and in the community
- Rebellion against authority
- Lack of self-discipline and control in one's life
- Having anything desired because of overindulgence

How can you be most effective at carving the message into your child's mind that drugs should be avoided without them rebelling against you? It is imperative to first understand the pressure-packed choices that children have to make, day in and day out, that affect how they are treated and perceived among their peers. This is their world at the time and it is often difficult for them to see beyond the scope of tomorrow.

The best time to discuss the harmful implications of drug use with your child is as early as possible. Your children develop their beliefs, attitudes and values at a young age, which will have an impact on decisions they will make throughout the rest of their lives. As influential as a child's peer group can be, you have the *most important role* in impacting your child's life. By teaching children decision-making strategies and problem-solving skills, they will be well equipped to cope in society as a young person and an adult with life's challenges and pressures.

The Foundation for a Drug-Free World is an organization that provides empowering information for both parents and children about the dangers of substance abuse and real stories, told by people, who suffered from drugs.

Take the time to sit down with your children and discuss how drugs can drastically affect their lives forever. These continuous discussions will help your children learn about the life-changing effects of drugs and will significantly lessen the chance that they will experiment with them.

If you suspect, however, that your child is using drugs, here are suggested statements to express to him or her:

- "I am worried that something different is going on in your life. Let's talk about what's bothering you. I am here to listen."
- "Even if a person thinks everything is under control, it is not. Drugs slowly take hold of a person and never let go. They will ruin your entire life and those you love, and I would never want to see that happen to you."
- "I don't want to see you ruin your life because of one poor decision to do drugs. It's just not worth it."
- "Drugs destroy the people doing them and negatively affect their families. That is a lot of lives for one person to ruin for making the choice to use drugs."

TREATMENT

If you find that your child struggles with drug use, treatment options are widely available, both inpatient and outpatient services, and the rehabilitation process usually involves different forms of therapy. If the adolescent is substance dependent, detoxification and withdrawal management may be required. For those who are not substance dependent, the most commonly used therapies include the following:[25]

- Counseling—a casual, informal setting with a mental health professional to help discuss the habit and other problematic issues that may be going on in a young person's life.
- Cognitive behavioral therapy—helps an individual identify the underlying causes for their actions and behaviors and learn coping skills to prevent relapse.
- Motivational interviewing—a non-judgmental, non-confrontational approach to help a teen open up by asking open-ended questions and help the individual see and understand the risks and consequences of their actions so they become interested and committed to change and recovery.

- Contingency management—a type of clinical behavior analysis therapy that offers teens rewards for adhering to their drug treatment plan. This can help an individual seek a reward or prize that is something other than the substance that the young person's brain comes to expect whenever they feel they've "earned it."
- Adolescent Community Reinforcement Approach—a behavioral treatment that helps youth and families replace factors that have previously reinforced drug use with the goal of helping support an adolescent's recovery.

The Substance Abuse and Mental Health Services Administration (SAMHSA) has an online resource that locates drug and alcohol abuse treatment programs in your area.[26] If you find, however, that your child is reluctant to accept professional help, discuss how drugs will destroy their life and emphasize that getting the right kind of help will give them back control of their mind and personality, resurrect their self-worth, and restore a positive outlook for the future.

———◦◉◦———

Discuss with your children how drugs can negatively impact them and their loved ones. Start by having open discussions and watching documentary videos with them about the dangers and consequences involved in different kinds of drug use.

———◦◉◦———

· *16* ·

Alcohol

Educate Early to Prevent a Depressing Future

"When we are no longer able to change a situation, we are challenged to change ourselves."[1]

—Viktor Frankl (neurologist, psychiatrist, Holocaust survivor)

Monique was homecoming queen, cheerleading captain, class president, and honor student in high school. She was well liked by her peers and had the total package for a bright future ahead. But when Monique went off to college at Colorado State University, things turned tragic; she attended the college's largest social event and consumed somewhere between thirty and forty beers in an eleven-hour time frame. Monique's friends left her alone to "sleep it off" in a fraternity house where she was found dead the following day.[2]

Just twelve days later, close by at the University of Colorado, an eighteen-year-old male was found dead at another fraternity house. He, too, had died of alcohol intoxication after consuming an excessive amount of alcohol in a hazing ritual.[3] These stories are two in thousands of real-life tragedies of adolescents dying each year after binge-drinking episodes.

Approximately 10 million people in the United States who are under the legal drinking age of twenty-one consume alcohol. It is the most popular drug used by high school seniors and college students. Nearly 80 percent of twelfth grade students reported having experimented with alcohol at least once, as compared to 71 percent of tenth grade students and 52 percent of eighth grade students. In fact, 62 percent of twelfth graders, 49 percent of tenth graders, and 25 percent of eighth graders reported having been drunk at least once.[4]

Alcohol is a factor in approximately 600,000 accidents and 100,000 cases of sexual assault or rape each year in America. Furthermore, alcohol abuse is linked to as many as two-thirds of all sexual assaults and date rapes of teens and college students.[5]

Alcohol takes no prisoners and can lead to serious problems. This substance has been the cause of many premature deaths among youth. In fact, it has been a contributing factor in youth suicides, homicides, and fatal accidents.

During a graduation trip with her senior classmates, an eighteen-year-old girl engaged in excessive drinking. Police reports mentioned that she had been drinking on the trip every day, all day. According to statements from her classmates that were on the trip, she began her morning with cocktails and drank excessively to a point where she didn't show up for breakfast on two occasions.[6] The last time that her classmates saw her was when she had left a bar and night club around 1:30 a.m. with a group of boys.[7] Authorities searched extensively for the missing girl around the island and surrounding waters but were unable to find her.

Another tragic incident involving alcohol use claimed the life of an eighteen-year-old freshman who was receiving a bid to pledge Sigma Chi Fraternity at Purdue University in Indiana when police officers arrived to break up the late-night party where he and other minors were imbibing. The young man became scared and tried to evade authorities. He attempted to swing from the fifth floor balcony to the floor below. In the process, he lost his grip on the banister and fell down five stories, landing on the first floor where a guest at the party and the responding officer found him laid out unconscious and bleeding. He was immediately taken to the hospital in critical condition but later died from his injuries. That weekend alone accounted for more than two hundred arrests on Indiana college campuses.[8]

Experimenting with alcohol can start as early as elementary school. The Governors' Spouses' initiative, *Leadership to Keep Children Alcohol Free*, was designed to make childhood drinking prevention a national health priority. This is a unique alliance of governors' spouses, federal agencies, along with public and private organizations that specifically target prevention of alcohol consumption in the nine- to fifteen-year-old age range.[9] Alcohol use by this cohort of children is an overlooked yet very serious problem in the United States.

But who has the greatest influence on a child's behavior, whether they decide to experiment with alcohol or not? Research shows that three out of four teens say that their parents are the primary influence on their decisions about using alcohol. According to a study conducted from RI International and the University of North Carolina at Chapel Hill, an astounding number of parents believe that exposing a child to alcohol early in life in the home will discourage later use during adolescence and help prevent alcohol abuse.

The study revealed that 40 percent of mothers, out of the 1,050 who were surveyed, felt that attempting to prevent children from tasting alcohol would make it more inviting, a "forbidden fruit" that they would desire when they got older. In addition, statistics show that one in every three third graders had already tried alcohol in some form.[10]

Many parents feel that teaching "responsible drinking" early on is having children try it under parental supervision. They believe that this is the way kids will behave with their peers when in a different setting. The majority of research, however, shows that adolescents are unlikely to model responsible drinking behaviors of their parents when out partying with their friends. Fifth-grade students whose parents introduced them to alcohol were actually at double the risk to report using alcohol in seventh grade.

According to the Substance Abuse and Mental Health Services Administration (SAMHSA), nearly half of kids between the ages of twelve and fourteen who drink get their alcohol from their family. An estimated 709,000 kids in the United States between these ages drank alcohol in the past month and 93.4 percent of them got it for free the last time they drank. Moreover, about 111,000 kids in that age range received it from a parent or guardian.[11]

A HALLOWEEN STORY

While growing up, I also witnessed my peers engaging in underage drinking as early as the seventh grade. It was Halloween morning when I was at home dressing up for the best-costume contest at my school. That morning, my mother was painting my face to look like a professional clown. Along with my multicolored wig, I had on a disturbing clash of a blue and yellow shirt with purple suspenders. Below the belt buckle, I was wearing baggy white and green–striped pants, exposing my red and white–striped calf socks and flopping around in my father's size eleven and a half wingtip blue-checkered shoes that were three sizes too big for me, serving as ideal clown shoes.

The clown makeup stayed on perfectly and I was receiving quite a few compliments on my outfit. It was now lunchtime and teachers walked around with a paper to cast their votes for the annual Halloween Best-Dressed Contest. I felt that I had a decent chance to win because there weren't many other kids dressed up in the first place and those who were didn't have colorful makeup or clothes as clashing as I did.

One of the teachers walked over to the microphone in front of the cafeteria and announced, "And the winner of the Best Dressed Halloween Costume is . . . the clown!" I had won the best costume contest! I was so excited to win and walked to the podium to receive a gift certificate for a free ice cream cone at a local ice cream shop.

When I returned to the lunch table with my prize in hand, everyone there wanted to see it. About a minute or so later, one kid at the table asked us if we wanted to do something "more fun" than go out trick-or-treating that night. He told everyone that his parents were not going to be home and that he wanted to have a bunch of people over his house to do vodka shots.

I thought his request was ridiculous and flat out declined his invitation. Many kids, however, at the lunch table were intrigued and attended his party that night. I remember this kid's "popularity ranking" skyrocketing among his peers that year. That crowd of kids thought he was cool, which encouraged him to have more of these kinds of parties throughout middle and high school.

EARLY ONSET OF ALCOHOL USE

The most recent data from the National Survey on Drug Use and Health on the onset of alcohol use at a young age are compelling and demonstrate the need for a prevention campaign:[12, 13]

- Unlike adults who drink, young people tend to consume large quantities of alcohol at one time, or "binge" drink.
- Approximately 40 percent of adults who started drinking before age fifteen expressed having signs of alcohol dependence.
- Twice as many eighth graders drink, as compared to using illegal drugs. About 76 percent more eighth graders drink than smoke.
- Approximately 36 percent of ninth graders report binge drinking.
- Among ninth graders, girls consume alcohol and binge drink at rates almost equal to boys.

Research reveals that early alcohol use can have serious adverse consequences on mental, physical, and social development that may persist into adulthood. The most recent studies indicate that alcohol may actually impair cognitive processes in young people, causing them to remember 10 percent less of what they learn than their non-drinking peers. Early alcohol use is also linked with poor school performance, depression, suicide, criminal and violent behavior, and risk taking that can lead to serious injuries and death. Moreover, it can lead to premature sexual activity, with exposure to sexually transmitted diseases and/or resulting in unplanned teen pregnancies.[14]

NEGATIVE EFFECTS OF ALCOHOL

Here are some statements that may serve as powerful messages to share with your child about the negative effects of alcohol on a young person's life:[15]

- *"When I was thirteen, friends would make fun of me if I didn't have a drink. I just gave in because it was easier to join the crowd."*
- *"I was only sixteen but my liver was badly damaged and I was close to killing myself from everything I was drinking."*
- *"Kicked out of my home at age sixteen, I was homeless and started begging for money to buy drinks. After years of abuse, doctors told me there was irreparable harm to my health."*
- *"By the time I was in my mid-twenties I was locked into drinking."*
- *"If I had to go without a drink, I would go through shakes and sweats. I couldn't go for more than a few hours without a drink."*
- *"This past year I have gone to work drunk, blacked out in clubs and bars, and can't remember getting home. Ashamedly, I slept with someone and could not even remember the person coming home with me until we bumped into each other the next day."*
- *"My addiction built steadily and, before I realized it, I had become a morning as well as an afternoon drinker. I decided to stop drinking. I lay awake most of that night, and by noon the next day every bone in my body ached. In a blind panic, I nervously poured a glass full of gin, my hands shaking so violently that I spilled half the bottle. As I gulped it down, I could feel the agony gradually lessening. Then I finally knew the terrible truth: I was hooked. I couldn't quit."*
- *"I spent the next eight years in and out of detox and hospitals, trying to figure out what the hell happened to me, how was it possible I couldn't quit. It was the worst and longest nightmare."*

The specific consequences that can result from alcohol abuse include the following:[16]

- Doing irreversible physical damage to the body
- Destroying relationships between partners and friends
- Impairing academic performance
- Reducing concentration and focus on tasks
- Decreasing study time
- Increasing truancy/missing classes at school
- Ruining physique
- Engaging in risky, disease-contracting sexual behaviors

- Disturbing sleep patterns
- Destroying brain cells
- Having long-term health problems
- Feeling depressed and/or suicidal
- Disappointing loved ones
- Creating family stress
- Putting a limit on one's future

Alcohol abuse contributes to

- 28 percent of college dropouts,
- 66 percent of student suicides,
- 40 percent of academic problems, and
- 60 percent of STDs (including HIV).

The millions of alcoholics who are in recovery are examples of people who have taken the initiative to make up for lost time and turn their lives around. After speaking with recovering alcoholics personally, they have indicated that alcohol has not helped their lives in any means, but certainly has shaped it. It taught them harsh lessons about experiencing "rock bottom" and the struggles to reclaim their lives, which they carry with them each day, one day at a time. They stated that if they could do it over again, they wouldn't have started drinking in the first place. They would have chosen to pass on having a drink, rather than waste precious years being dependent on alcohol.

I attended an Alcoholics Anonymous meeting many years back to support a friend who was in the 12-step recovery program at the time. I sat in a circle for about an hour with him, listening to some of the most mind-blowing stories that I have ever heard in my life. The people there were males and females of all ages, from teenagers to elderly. There were accounts of near-death experiences, blackouts, violence, and torn apart relationships. During the meeting, I thought to myself how lucky these individuals were to be alive and recount their stories.

One young man, in his early twenties, shared his tragic alcohol-related experience with the group. It was difficult to hear him relive his story, as he was very emotional describing what happened to him one fateful night when he was driving back home drunk from a friend's house. He had inadvertently swerved and crashed his car into a tree and while fading in and out of consciousness, he saw images of a boy pinned between the car he was driving and a tree. He remembered rescue workers using the Jaws of Life tools to cut away the car. But unfortunately it had been too late. The boy had not made it and died right then and there in front of his eyes.

The painstaking agony written all over this young man's face as he recalled that night told the grim story of how he had to bear this memory with him for the rest of his life. I recall him mentioning how he "continues to cause pain to his family and himself every day." While sobbing, he continued to say, "I am afraid that when I leave this meeting that I will return back to the bottle and repeat this tragedy all over again."

According to a government report, nearly 88,000 people die each year from alcohol-related accidents.[17] If your child is ever involved in a situation where their friends are drinking, tell him or her to never take a ride with any friends who are under the influence. Rather, have your child give you a call to come pick them up. This plan of action can save many people's lives, including your own child. You can assure your child that they won't get in trouble if they call, but will rather be commended for making a responsible, life-saving decision by not getting into a car with friends who have been drinking.

There are many factors that may influence a child's decision to drink:[18]

- Teenagers may associate alcohol use with becoming an adult.
- Drinking may appear to be a societal norm and a regular, acceptable behavior in the adolescent's peer or cultural group.
- Portrayal, advertisement, and marketing of alcohol in the media.
- Parental use of and attitude toward alcohol.

Many factors may increase the chances of a child engaging in heavy drinking:[19]

- Feeling disconnected from family, school, or community.
- Family history of alcohol problems.
- Having emotional or psychological problems.

Warning signs that a child is using alcohol include the following:[20]

- Behavioral changes—having school-related problems (e.g., low grades, poor attendance, getting in trouble), poor hygiene, disheveled appearance, rebellious behavior, switching peer groups and not allowing you to know anything about these individuals, decrease in motivation and involvement in things that once interested them
- Emotional changes—displaying radical shifts in mood, becoming hostile, irritable, and defensive, and becoming apathetic toward things
- Mental changes—having memory lapses and poor concentration
- Physical changes—lethargy, slurred speech, lack of coordination, and bloodshot eyes

If you're concerned that your child may be exposed to underage drinking, here are some suggestions that you can implement to help discourage him or her from alcohol use:

- Engage in regular conversations with your child. Demonstrate respect for your child's point of view by actively listening, without interruption. The more you show respect for your child's viewpoint, the more likely your child will listen and respect what you have to say. If there is something that is unpleasant to hear, refrain from outbursts of anger and take a few deep breaths to calm down and continue to listen to your child.
- From an early age, regularly talk with your child about the use of alcohol and the consequences associated with underage drinking. According to the U.S. Department of Health and Human Services, the average age when boys first try alcohol is eleven years old, for girls it is thirteen years old.[21] The earlier the addiction, without any early intervention, the more difficult it is to treat.
- Talk with your child about the meaning of "true friendship" and how to stand up to troubling situations when peer pressure strikes.
- Educate children on how alcohol portrayed in the media can affect actual drinking behavior.
- Share stories and videos of real-life cases of people who have ruined their lives from alcohol abuse.
- Encourage children to partake in positive extracurricular activities. The more active they are, the less time they have to engage in alcohol use.
- Be actively involved early on in your child's life. Provide a set of rules for them to follow, monitor their peer group closely, and look for any warning signs of alcohol abuse such as a change in attitude, drop in grades, smell of alcohol on their breath, change in friends, and withdrawal from family. Parents who drink influence their children's decisions. Studies show that teens are less likely to engage in drinking if they know their parents are against it.[22]
- Become actively involved in early prevention programs to reduce underage alcohol use and driving while under the influence such as Mothers Against Drunk Driving.

HOW TO TALK TO YOUR CHILD ABOUT ALCOHOL

Alcohol has become the unfortunate topic of discussion for millions of people's lives. Unfortunately, it can become a tragic fate that completely consumes or even ends the lives of adolescents. Teens have a tendency to take risks, explore, and ignore the important life-saving messages given from authority figures about alcohol's harmful effects.

Having an alcohol problem is like having a mental obsession. The thought of "having a drink" is always there and can only be relieved when alcohol is consumed. The progression from one or two drinks to five or six and later on to ten or twelve occurs in an insidious manner over time, until it either destroys the individual or makes them realize that they have a serious problem that requires immediate help.

If you suspect that your child is engaging in underage drinking or find evidence of alcohol use, speak with your child privately and express your concerns openly and honestly by saying something to the effect of "I am concerned about what I found in your room and wanted to talk with you about it."

Be assertive and let them know that you have specific concerns—whether it is drastic changes you've seen in some aspect of their life or finding a beer bottle in their room. Allow your child to convey what is going on. Your child may deny that they are using alcohol or that they have a problem; however, listen without judgment or expressing any frustration. Avoid getting into an argument or discussion about other issues. Remain focused on the matter at hand and point out how your child's behaviors are affecting certain areas of their life and how you are there to support them and together come up with a solution for the problem.

When your child finishes speaking, reiterate what you heard and allow them to clarify any misunderstandings. Provide your child with information about alcohol use, alcoholism, and associated risks, while emphasizing the importance of avoiding alcohol use due to health reasons. While working to encourage your child to consider the health risks and willingly change their behavior, establish expectations and hold your child accountable for their actions (e.g., for coming home by a certain time, informing you of where they are and who they are with). Avoid using bribery, threatening, or lecturing to make your child change their behavior. Also, don't make excuses for your child's actions as that will not correct the issue and only make the problem grow worse over time.

Talk with your child's school about starting an alcohol awareness program, if they don't already have one. Studies have shown the benefits of school-based alcohol education and life skills programs in a child's knowledge and awareness around alcohol.[23] If you notice that your child is struggling with alcohol abuse, the Substance Abuse and Mental Health Services Administration (SAMHSA) has an online resource that locates drug and alcohol abuse treatment programs in your area.[24]

It is not uncommon for many tweens and teens to feel that things are out of control in their lives, they are not understood and/or accepted by others, or they are simply not good enough. No matter the circumstances, it is vital to encourage your child to speak about their feelings openly and honestly, without suppression. This opens up doors between you and your child and helps to get to the root of different problems they may be dealing with at that moment.

Keep your child safe by delaying alcohol exposure for as long as possible. Monitor your child's peer groups and discuss the ramifications that alcohol can have on a person's life.

• 17 •

Smoking

Why Kids Start and What You Need to Do to Prevent It

> *"I don't operate on smokers. I tell cigarette smokers that I can operate on you, I get paid the same. And you might even do well. But it's the wrong thing to do. So I refuse to operate on you until you stop smoking."*[1]
>
> —Dr. Mehmet Oz (cardiothoracic surgeon,
> author, and television personality)

*W*hen I was in third grade, I remember my teacher Mrs. Paternostro talking to our class about the effects of smoking on the body. That day she did a class survey aloud asking, "How many of you have at least one parent who smokes cigarettes?" As she tallied the numbers on her clipboard, she asked us to stand up. About six to eight of us got out of our chairs as she said, "I'm sorry to confess that one in every four of you will end up smoking when you get older."

I remember sitting back down in my chair thinking how awkward this topic was and wondering how she knew who would end up smoking later in life. Then, just a few seconds later, Mrs. Paternostro said, "Stand up if both of your parents smoke." I rose out of my chair and noticed all of my classmates staring at me from their seats, while I anxiously awaited the teacher's response. She told me, "It's hard for me to tell you this, Douglas, but you are most likely going to smoke when you get older."

I stood there embarrassed and in disbelief and insisted that I wasn't going to smoke. The teacher replied, "Let me explain. The reason behind why you will most likely smoke is because parental smoking is the biggest reason why kids start smoking in the first place and continue to do so as they get older."

According to research conducted by the Seattle Social Development Project, which examined the development of positive and problem behaviors among adolescents and young adults, twelve-year-old children whose parents smoke are twice as likely to smoke on a daily basis between thirteen and twenty-one years old than are children whose parents don't smoke. According to Karl Hill, director of the University of Washington's Seattle Social Development Project, parental smoking is the biggest contributor to children initiating smoking.[2]

From an early age, I was around cigarettes. They were on the counters all around the house. And I agree that it truly is a matter of a parent's *actions* over their *words* that make a big difference when it comes to a child's decision to start smoking or not in the first place. However, research has also shown that there are key factors that help prevent a child from smoking such as consistent supervision, established rules for a child, a strong emotional attachment within the family, and not involving a child with a parent's smoking habit.[3]

Certainly, the "do as I do" motto has a stronger impact than the "do as I say" one. However, I credit my parents, in particular my father, for doing something more with his words than simply reiterating the fact that smoking is bad and making threats about what he would do if he caught me smoking.

My father was very much addicted to nicotine and couldn't resist smoking a pack and a half of cigarettes a day. He openly expressed how he couldn't go more than a half an hour without having a cigarette. He said that he tried his first cigarette with some friends when he was around fourteen or fifteen years old and didn't think anything of the consequences. But before he knew it, he was addicted. From that point, my father had planned all his day-to-day activities around smoking.

He said, "Douglas, I never wanted to start smoking in the first place. I am not an example of what you should follow. I am addicted to cigarettes and wish I never started." He kept emphasizing the dangers of smoking to me and mentioned how his grandfather got emphysema and other health problems as a result of this habit.

While growing up, my father always enjoyed playing sports, but he realized how much his endurance levels had been affected because of smoking. Consequently, he was unable to compete at a high level, which prevented him from becoming a great athlete. Instead of shoving words down my throat without reason, my father's viewpoint on smoking and his honest explanation about how kids get introduced to this bad habit and its harmful effects had a profound influence on me. It translated into not only never trying a cigarette in my life, but also being able to successfully handle all different kinds of peer pressure and resist temptations, such as alcohol and drugs, as I got older. After many years of smoking, I am happy to say that both of my parents eventually kicked the habit and never looked back.

For some older generations, smoking was promoted for their health as the consequences had not been fully revealed. In fact, back in the 1930s and 1940s doctors were proclaiming that cigarettes weren't harmful or that certain brands were less irritating than others. A majority of physicians smoked and smoking had become a norm for both men and women at that time.[4]

That is until the report of the Advisory Committee to the Surgeon General of the United States in 1964 showed a link between lung cancer and chronic bronchitis and cigarette smoking. Despite the surge in public awareness about the dangers linked to smoking, ad campaigns persisted on television until the Public Health Cigarette Smoking Act was passed in 1970. They also continued throughout magazines until 2005 when tobacco advertisements were removed from the school library editions of *Time*, *People*, *Sports Illustrated*, and *Newsweek*.[5] In 2009, the Family Smoking Prevention and Tobacco Control Act became active and placed further restrictions on tobacco marketing and sales to youth.[6]

Although the number of younger Americans who smoke has declined since the late 1990s, the rate of smoking among eleventh and twelfth graders is still higher than adult smokers and the use of some tobacco products, such as electronic cigarettes and hookahs, has risen. Approximately 90 percent of adult smokers tried their first cigarette at or before age eighteen. About 50 percent of high school students have tried cigarette smoking at least once in their lives. Nearly 25 percent of high school students and 8 percent of middle school students currently use some type of tobacco product.[7] The younger a person is when they first use tobacco, the more likely they will be using it as an adult.[8]

A CHILDHOOD TALE

Throughout my middle school years, smoking and chewing tobacco became more prevalent. I remember playing basketball at my friend's house down the street one Sunday afternoon. There were about ten of us, all thirteen to fourteen years old, having a slam dunk competition on my friend's eight-foot hoop. That afternoon was the first time my peers and I were asked to try something new and forbidden.

One of the kids pulled a tin of dipping tobacco out of his backpack. I remember we watched him "pack the tin" with one hand, similar to how you would pack cigarettes. The boy told everyone that he got it from his older brother and asked us to go across the street to try some. He was also telling us how his brother and friends all enjoyed doing it.

To my knowledge, at least half of those kids didn't have parents that smoked, but I also knew that peer pressure was a strong influence on any of us to try something new that we would rather not. The threat of exclusion from the group was high if we didn't follow the crowd. But it was at that moment that my father immediately popped into my head, and I thought back to our conversations on the consequences of smoking.

Right then and there, I decided my fate and walked back home alone; it was the right and most rewarding thing to do. As I sauntered down the road and between the two lakes, I remember watching those boys go behind the local church and disappear into the woods. I made the decision at that moment, albeit an unpopular one, not to follow the crowd but rather go back home of my own accord, and I thought how fortunate I was to escape the situation. I can honestly say to this day that the decision I made at that time largely shaped the course of not only my life, but also the lives of many of those boys in their later involvement with cigarettes, alcohol, and drug use.

DANGERS OF TOBACCO USE

Tobacco use is the leading cause of preventable death in the United States. Tobacco products have been responsible for debilitating millions of lives, causing various cardiovascular diseases and cancers, and claiming the lives of more than 6 million people each year.[9] The tobacco industry has been largely successful in protecting their assets and continuing to distribute cigarettes to people throughout the world. After years of research that proved the addictive and harmful nature of cigarettes, it is mind-boggling to imagine that this industry still continues to grow the way it does.

The devastating effects of smoking took hold of a fourteen-year-old boy named Shawn who moved into a new town with his family and had a difficult time making friends. His way of building new relationships was through cigarettes that he stole from his father and gave to kids at school. Shawn started smoking at an early age and unfortunately, sixteen years later, he was diagnosed with throat cancer. After going through radiation treatments, Shawn still didn't want to give up the cigarettes. It wasn't until the doctors removed his larynx, and he was forced to breathe through a hole in his neck, that Shawn finally quit.[10]

For decades, the American Heart Association has strived to reduce the number of deaths and smoking-related diseases by working with Congress to pass bills to have smoke-free communities. Although Congress hasn't attempted to pass a federal bill banning smoking in all enclosed public places yet, many states have enacted bans on smoking in workplaces, schools, restaurants, night clubs, and bars across the nation to promote clean indoor air.

People who choose to smoke are required by many places to go to a designated area.

There are many young people, however, who can't escape secondhand smoke. Annually, an estimated 126 million Americans are regularly exposed to secondhand smoke. Over 53,000 of them die from diseases caused by secondhand smoke exposure. Secondhand smoke has more than 4,000 substances, including several compounds that are carcinogenic and increase the risk of children experiencing debilitating health effects. Especially considering their small size and increased rate of breathing, developing children have the greatest risk for health problems.[11]

Most exposure to secondhand smoke takes place in the homes and workplace. The story of a little boy named Aden shows the impact that secondhand smoke has on a young person's life. At three years old, Aden was diagnosed with asthma. Although his mother, Jessica, was not a smoker, Aden was exposed to secondhand smoke when his grandmother smoked around him while watching him during the day. The smoke triggered Aden's asthma attacks, which almost cost him his life. These attacks increased in severity to the point of the boy being sent to the emergency room, spending multiple nights in the intensive care unit, and having to be put on different medications.

With all of the knowledge about the dangers of secondhand smoke, pioneering communities such as San Rafael, California, have gone as far as to restrict smoking in the households. There are even towns that are going as far as banning smoking in the entire community and having only a few designated smoking areas. In an effort to prevent and decrease purchases of tobacco products, there have been discussions at the state, county, and municipal levels, about increasing the excise tax on them.

PEER PRESSURE AND SMOKING

So why do kids start smoking in the first place? For the same reason many kids try alcohol and drugs—peer pressure. Pressure from "the tribe" seems to be the greatest factor in why a child begins to smoke in the first place. Around 4,400 children become regular smokers each year. As stated earlier in this chapter, 90 percent of adult smokers started at or before the age of eighteen.[12]

Peer pressure is not the only factor involved in why a child decides to smoke. Other factors include the following:

- Parents are smokers
- Rebelling against authority and showing independence
- Doing something that is seen as forbidden in society

- Curious about the taste
- Wanting to be more "adult-like"
- Seeing everyone else around them smoking and thinking that they should
- Wanting to appear cool among friends
- Media's portrayal of smoking as sexy, cool, fun, attractive, and adventurous
- The "high" they get from the nicotine

The Family Smoking Prevention and Tobacco Control Act is aimed at preventing young individuals from starting to smoke. It "restricts tobacco product advertising and marketing to youth by directing FDA to issue regulations on tobacco products." There are also tighter restrictions on the purchase of cigarettes and smokeless tobacco products. Furthermore, this act "requires bigger, more prominent warning labels for cigarettes and smokeless tobacco products."[13]

It can be very difficult for young people to express their opinions freely to their peers out of fear of rejection or humiliation, especially when they are trying to explain their reasons to a smoker, who may already be addicted and get upset if other people don't conform. If children aren't taught to say "no" and to make good decisions, it will be much easier for them to succumb to peer pressure and be lured into the crowd.

Here are some replies that your children can use when confronted with a difficult peer situation involving tobacco:

- "No, I'm good. I need to stay in shape for basketball season and this will ruin everything."
- "The smoke will get all over my clothes and there is no way that I am going home smelling like smoke all over my body."
- "This stuff is nasty and makes me really sick."
- "This stuff is disgusting. It will make my breath smell gross and yellow my teeth. I'm all set."
- "I have asthma, and I can't smoke or I could have an attack."
- "I can't stand the smell of cigarettes."
- "It's so unhealthy."
- "Cigarettes make me jittery."

EDUCATION LEVEL AND SMOKING

The view of a smoker can be stigmatized as a dirty, smelly, low-class habit. In fact, studies have shown an inverse relationship between education level and smoking, in which the least educated are more likely to smoke than adults with college degrees. But the reasons for this disparity have not been established until recently. A long-term study conducted at Yale University collected data over a fourteen-year period and showed that educational discrepancies in adult smoking are linked to characteristics, experiences, and choices made in childhood.[14]

Long before a college education is or isn't obtained, research has shown differences in smoking by completed education as early as twelve years of age. The study examined features such as social networks, future expectations, and school experiences prior to a child regularly smoking to predict smoking in adulthood. Data regarding school policies, peers, and health expectations were collected at ages thirteen to fifteen and shown to predict smoking at ages twenty-six to twenty-nine. Also, smoking status at sixteen years old was shown to predict both completed college education and smoking in adulthood. It is important to take advantage of this knowledge to determine these characteristics before the adolescent years in order to help a child stay committed to school and prevent them from initiating smoking.

LIFESTYLE CONSEQUENCES OF SMOKING

In addition to the severe health effects associated with smoking, your child should be made aware of the major lifestyle consequences of smoking:

1. **Smoking controls how you plan your day.** Needing to find a place to smoke all of the time becomes a priority for a smoker, as opposed to enjoying time doing a healthy activity alone, with friends, and/or with family.
2. **The amount of money wasted on cigarettes.** A person who smokes a pack a day for ten years spends approximately $20,000 to $40,000 that could be invested more intelligently.
3. **Non-smokers don't want to be around smokers.** Relationships with others may become affected. There is tension when a smoker is around a non-smoker for a certain time frame. If someone decides to light up a cigarette, a room becomes polluted for many non-smokers, making it unfair for them to have to breathe in harmful chemicals.
4. **Smoking increases the risk for mental health problems and aggressive behavior.** Individuals who smoke are at a greater risk for getting into a physical fight, carrying weapons, engaging in sexual behaviors, and having mental health problems such as depression and attempting suicide.[15]

5. **Smoking increases the risk for many diseases.** These include lung cancer, cardiovascular disease, stroke, and atherosclerosis. In addition, smoking affects skin color, causes wrinkles prematurely, and accelerates aging.
6. **Smoking decreases lung function and the body becomes starved for oxygen.** A smoker cannot physically keep up with a counterpart non-smoker, ultimately leading to a more sedentary lifestyle and not obtaining the proper amount of daily exercise.
7. **Smokers are more likely to start accidental fires than are non-smokers.** Fires triggered by smoking have the highest fatality rate among residential fires.[16]
8. **Smoking is linked to erectile dysfunction in men.** This can have a negative effect on a person's sex life and relationship with their partner.[17]
9. **Smoking can result in acquiring emphysema.** This is an irreversible lung disease that can also damage a person's heart. There is no cure for this disease once you acquire it.[18]

IF YOUR CHILD IS ALREADY SMOKING

If your child is smoking or using tobacco-based products, it's not too late to take action:

1. **Encouraging your child to express their concerns.**—Avoid threats of punishment and lecturing your child about the dangers of smoking. Instead, show interest in what your child has to say in a non-judgmental, non-threatening manner by engaging them in conversations about why they are smoking and what they feel are the negative aspects and consequences of smoking. Appeal to their image; explain how smoking will cause their breath and clothes to smell bad and result in a smoker's cough, low energy, shortness of breath, premature wrinkles, and yellow teeth and fingernails.[19]
2. **Discussing the weekly, monthly, and yearly cost of smoking and how that can affect a person long term.**—From there, ask them what changes can be made in their life to help them quit and help them set goals to accomplish these changes.
3. **Being a role model for your child.**—If you smoked and have already quit, talk with your child about your experience so they can better relate to you. If you are still smoking, strongly consider quitting your own habit. Modeling the positive behaviors that you desire to see

your child display is much more effective than simply expressing your opinions without actions to back it up.

4. **Being supportive of your child through the process of quitting smoking.**—Nicotine is a highly addictive drug that acts on the brain's reward center to create feelings of pleasure or satisfaction—like heroin and cocaine—and can cause a person to become dependent after only a short time of using the substance. The good news is that individuals who quit smoking before age thirty will reverse much of the damage incurred by tobacco use.[20]

To help prevent your child from smoking, here are some tips that you can use:

- Lead by example and don't smoke. If you do, make a conscious effort to quit as soon as possible for you and your family's welfare. Your child sees the value in your words, along with your actions. If you do smoke and have a hard time quitting, express to your child that you would have never started in the first place if you had known about the addictive nature of cigarettes.
- Monitor your child's peer groups and where they regularly play.
- Check for any unusual smells on clothes, such as cigarette smoke or a cover up fragrance. If you sense that your child has smoked, immediately sit them down and address the issue head on. Smoking is a killer and if you sense that your child has experimented with tobacco, you should intervene as soon as possible.
- Talk about the dangers of smoking with your child at an early age. Discuss the risks associated with cigarette smoking and using other tobacco-related products. Risks include ulcers, chronic bronchitis, heart disease, emphysema, stroke, atherosclerosis, and lung and many other types of cancer.
- Discuss the addictive quality of nicotine and how people who quit have a very difficult time dealing with the physical and psychological withdrawal symptoms, including irritability, anxiety, sleep disturbances, nervousness, headaches, fatigue, nausea, and cravings for tobacco.
- If you smoke, try to quit. If you choose not to, avoid exposing your child to secondhand smoke. Refrain from smoking in the house, car, or anywhere that your child is present. Secondhand smoke exposure can increase your child's chances of having ear infections, allergies, asthma, wheezing, pneumonia, and frequent upper respiratory tract infections.
- Visually display the negative effects that smoking has on a person's body. Present your child with pictures or a model of a smoker's lungs,

and compare them to a pair of healthy lungs. Children can understand the negative effects of smoking that much better if they can visualize them.

Stay patient with your child through the recovery process as there very well may be mood swings that come from nicotine withdrawal and other challenges along the way. If your child is tempted to start smoking again, discuss the natural consequences that would happen if they went back to smoking, such as declining health, wasted money that could be used on other things, smelling like cigarettes, and being dependent on something that will control much of their day-to-day living.

Educating your child on making good choices and taking responsibility for their actions can make a big difference in your child's life. A bad decision will get your child bad results. Despite all the health warnings today, teenagers continue to become addicted to tobacco; they think they are immortal and the consequences won't apply to them. But life as a smoker is an expensive, risky, and unhealthy life of addiction that can and should be prevented.

You can find more information and additional resources for quitting smoking at www.cdc.gov/tobacco or call 1-800-QUIT-NOW (784-8669).[21]

———<©>———

**From an early age, teach your child about the consequences
of smoking and how to stand up to peer pressure to prevent a
life of nicotine addiction.**

———<©>———

· 18 ·

Depression and Suicide

The Warning Signs That Could Save Your Child's Life

"If you are chronically down, it is a lifelong fight to keep from sinking."[1]

—Elizabeth Wurtzel (American writer and journalist)

Life for many young people is a painful tug-of-war filled with mixed emotions from developmental changes while growing up to stressful situations that children experience among family, friends, peers, teachers, coaches, and other individuals in their lives. As children go through various changes throughout childhood, they deal with gender issues and sexuality, and start to assert their independence. As a result, conflict between a parent and a child ensues, which can cause an overwhelming sense of sadness, confusion, frustration, and/or anger for a child.

Some kids respond to stressful events by doing something fun, playful, or relaxing. They may try to figure out solutions to their problems or get support from their friends. However, other children fall into a depressed, self-loathing, self-mutilating, and unbalanced mental state that can seriously impact every aspect of their lives.

When people think of depression, they generally picture someone who is sad and withdrawn. People who feel sad when something bad happens, but can manage to cope and quickly bounce back without treatment, are not considered depressed. Depression is a serious mental health condition that can happen to anyone at any age. It often recurs and can persist into adulthood.[2]

Major depressive disorder is the most severe form of depression and can affect children as young as preschool. Before puberty, males and females are equally likely to develop depression. Depression lasts for at least two weeks and negatively affects a young person's ability to perform daily activities, to complete tasks, and to interact at school and at home. According to the

National Survey on Drug Use and Health, more than 11 percent of youth aged twelve to seventeen—2.8 million adolescents—had a major depressive episode (MDE) during the past year. The percentage of youth aged twelve to seventeen who experienced an MDE and an MDE with severe impairment in the past year is higher than the percentages a decade ago—ranging from 7.9 to 9.1 percent.[3]

Two main triggers of depression are *family* and *friends*, which are also, ironically, the two primary sources of support for young people. Kids go through maturational and situational crises at home, at school, and with peers; they are triggered by tension, pressure of expectations, conflicts, and tragedies in life. Therefore, it is important not to overreact to your child's struggle to gain independence, respect, self-worth, friendship, or love. At the same time, it is critical that you recognize the factors that put your child at risk for depression:[4]

- **Genetic predisposition**—An inherited tendency or vulnerability for a person to be affected by something. If there is a history of depression and/or other psychiatric disorders in your family, then your child may be predisposed to this condition.
- **Effects of medications**—Young people may experience depression from the effects of certain medications or when discontinuing its use. Depression can co-occur with conditions such as ADD/ADHD, anxiety disorders, other disruptive behavior disorders, eating disorders, and substance use.[5]
- **Negative social events and psychological distress**—Significant changes that take place in your child's life, such as financial status, divorce, sudden illness, injury, loss of a parent or family member, and/ or increased arguments with a parent and/or family member, can be triggers for feelings of depression. Negative/traumatic events, such as bullying, rejection from a peer group, and/or a breakup with a boy/ girlfriend, can be factors that lead to depression as well.

IRRITABILITY OR DEPRESSION

Adolescents usually rely on adult figures, such as parents and teachers, to notice their feelings, recognize their suffering, and get them the help they need. However, it isn't easy to spot the differences between typical teenage irritability and depression. Furthermore, it is difficult for children and adolescents to seek help and express their feelings when they feel that no one understands their situation or cares to listen to them.

How would you know if your child is simply in a bad mood or suffering from depression? People who are depressed show it in different ways. If you are wondering if your child is depressed or not, consider the major warning signs and symptoms that are linked to *depression*:[6]

- Persistent sadness, anxiety, or apathy
- Feelings of guilt, helplessness, worthlessness, and/or hopelessness
- Loss of interest in once pleasurable leisure activities
- Loss of memory and concentration on tasks and decision making
- Increased tiredness and loss of energy
- Changes in appetite and weight
- Poor self-image or self-esteem
- Feelings of restlessness and irritability
- Physical problems such as headaches, pain, and digestive complaints
- Sleep disturbances
- Suicidal thoughts or attempts

If your child exhibits any of the signs or symptoms of depression as dramatic differences for two or more weeks, then there are underlying issues that are prominent and must be appropriately addressed to prevent any physical self-injury from taking place. In summary, consider the following three factors if you are unsure if your child is suffering from depression or not: [7]

- The duration the symptoms have been exhibited.
- The severity of the symptoms.
- A sudden, radical change in behavior. If your child suddenly becomes more violent, obsessive, anxious, withdrawn, and isolated, then there are underlying issues that they are dealing with that need to be immediately addressed.

CUTTING AND SELF-HARM

A child's life could turn into a downward spiral that can lead to other serious problems. Some of the hardest and scariest times of my teaching career came when I found out that one of my twelve-year-old female students had been "cutting." Cutting is a form of self-injury that involves making cuts on the skin of the arms, legs, hips, abdomen, or some other part of the body with a sharp object.

There are many reasons why someone would decide to cut themselves in the first place. Depression is a major risk factor for cutting. Adolescents who are depressed, have an eating disorder, have lower self-esteem, have difficulty coping with stressful situations, partake in more risky health behaviors, and feel a sense of relief from anger, shame, or frustration have been reported to participate in non-suicidal self-injury.[8]

My student told me that she had been cutting herself, on a daily basis, for a little over three months. She couldn't explain why exactly she had started doing this, but mentioned how some of her "friends" were laughing at her, making fun of her, and talking behind her back. She indicated that she felt different from everyone else, unpopular, and unattractive.

I asked her if she ever talked to anyone about what was bothering her. The girl told me that her mother wasn't taking her seriously and she only saw her father on the weekends—and they didn't share in open conversations about personal topics. She also expressed that she couldn't confide her true feelings in anyone because she would be laughed at, not listened to, or not taken seriously.

What really got me concerned was when the girl told me how much she hated herself for living this way and felt that she was a failure and a burden to others. I remember the point at which she rolled up her sleeves and showed me the cuts along one of her forearms. It then hit me that she was struggling with her self-identity and needed help.

She also told me she had more cuts in hidden areas along her hips and across her abdomen. She admitted that once she started cutting, she couldn't stop because it was the only way she was able to relieve her pain. The cuts got deeper, longer, and more painful each time. She admitted how every night she cried herself to sleep because she wanted to feel normal again.

I was heartbroken in hearing how this girl was feeling so much inescapable pain and how each waking moment turned into a devotion to pursue control that would bring her a temporary release. Despite her knowing the physical harm involved, she expressed that "seeing the blood was like seeing the pain disappear and escape her body." This spurious reasoning actually caused her more tears and anger, making the problem worse.

Most young people who self-cut are females—64 percent females compared to 36 percent males.[9] From the discussions I had with adolescent girls who cut themselves throughout my teaching career, I found that the basis for this behavior lay in a desperate attempt for them to gain power over something in their lives they felt was out of their control. They said that cutting was their comfort and the pain helped bring them a sense of relief at that moment.

There is a difference, however, between self-injury and suicidal acts. Individuals who cut themselves or engage in other self-injury behaviors typically do not have an intention to commit suicide, but want to rid themselves of pain and feel a relief from anxiety and agitation or stimulate themselves out of mental states such as depression, hopelessness, and apathy toward life. On the other hand, individuals who have the intent to commit suicide have a goal to end their lives so they don't have to feel pain any longer. However, individuals who cut themselves can also have suicidal ideation, which can lead them to suicidal attempts.

If you suspect that your child is engaged in this kind of behavior, take matters seriously. The key to supporting a child who self-injures is to listen to the person's concerns without making judgments. Communicate that you understand what the person is going through. You don't have to agree with their actions, just acknowledge it. It is important that young people going through these kinds of experiences feel they are heard and understood.

It is important to know that your child is longing to gain control and restore balance in their life. The act of cutting is an example of a maladaptive coping mechanism used to relieve mental anguish. If you see this behavior exhibited by your child, it is important to seek professional help right away. If the self-injury behavior is associated with a mental health disorder, such as depression or a personality disorder, the treatment should focus on the disorder, as well as the behavior.

Effective psychological treatments are available that can help an individual learn skills and strategies to improve their self-image, manage stress, regulate emotions, become better problem solvers, develop skills to improve relationships and social skills, and effectively identify and handle situations that trigger self-injuring behaviors.

Some types of psychological therapies have been shown to be effective in treating individuals who suffer from depression and self-injuring behaviors:

- **Cognitive behavioral therapy**—helps individuals recognize unhealthy, negative beliefs or thoughts and channel them into positive ones. It helps those suffering from depressive behaviors by scheduling regular activities that bring a sense of joy and satisfaction to their lives.[10]
- **Family support and therapy**—helps the family change any existing behavior and/or communication patterns to best support the relationship between all family members and reduce or prevent conflict within the family.[11]
- **Trauma-focused cognitive behavioral therapy**—helps children, adolescents, and their caregivers overcome traumatic events. It incorporates elements of cognitive behavioral and family support and therapy for traumatized children. The treatment is designed to reduce negative emotional and behavioral responses or any distorted perceptions or beliefs following a traumatic event such as loss of a family member, domestic

violence, sexual abuse, and other traumatic-related events. This therapy also helps provide parents with strategies to effectively handle their own stress and develop skills to best support their children.[12]

- **Mindfulness-based cognitive therapy**—helps individuals who suffer from recurrent bouts of depression by breaking negative thought patterns through meditation, breathing exercises, and stretching. This therapy helps reduce anxiety and depression and enhances an individual's overall well-being by being in the present moment, rather than focusing on past and/or future events.[13]
- **Interpersonal psychotherapy**—helps individuals resolve conflicts with other people and develop better relationships.[14]
- **Dialectical behavior therapy**—a type of cognitive behavioral therapy that teaches individuals different strategies to best handle stress and manage emotions effectively.

AN UNEXPECTED TRAGEDY

It was the beginning of my teaching career and I vividly recall one Friday afternoon when I was getting ready to leave school for the weekend. As I bent down to pick up my bags, three of my former students entered into my classroom. I was surprised to see these girls still here after school, considering that the late bus for the extracurricular activities had already left more than thirty minutes ago.

One of the girls seemed particularly excited about seeing me and telling me how well she was doing in her classes. She asked me, "Do you have any special plans for this weekend?" I couldn't think of anything in particular that I was doing and replied, "Nothing special, how about you?" She replied, "It's going to be a busy weekend. Well, thanks for everything last year, Mr. Haddad. I just wanted to let you know that you're the best teacher ever."

She also went on to tell me that she *didn't owe anything* to any of her teachers. I was pleased to see that she had made friends and appeared happy and enthusiastic. In the past, I remember this girl being withdrawn and keeping to herself, more so than other students. As she left my classroom that afternoon, she said goodbye to me, and I didn't think anything of it besides that it was nice to see her again.

The following Monday, I received a phone call from a member of the school crisis team indicating that an unexpected tragedy had taken place over the weekend involving one of my former students taking her life prematurely. The student who suffered the tragedy was in fact the girl whom I last spoke with that Friday afternoon before leaving school. In shock to say the least, hearing this news was by far the worst feeling and experience that I have had in my teaching career—and I will never forget it.

For quite a while, I wondered if I could have done something to save her life. I thought if only I had picked up on the clues earlier or saw the "whole picture" better, I could have gotten her help and possibly saved her life. At that time, I had only been teaching for a couple of years and didn't have any experience with situations of this nature.

Thinking back, I found it peculiar how she mentioned that she *didn't owe anything to anyone, largely expressed her gratitude toward me, was uncharacteristically expressive* and *different looking in her overall appearance* than what I was used to seeing her wear, and *said goodbye as if she would never come to visit me again.* I had a hunch that something was out of the ordinary that afternoon, but I couldn't pinpoint what it was and dismissed that feeling. Things appeared fine on the outside, but I had no idea how she was truly feeling inside. The thought of suicide didn't even cross my mind; I didn't think something like that was possible for a kid so young, let alone one of my students.

WARNING SIGNS

The warning signs of suicidal behavior are often overlooked or may be difficult to detect for parents, family members, or educators. The prominent outlook of modern medicine is that suicide is a "mental health concern, associated with psychological factors such as the difficulty of coping with depression, inescapable suffering of fear, or other mental disorders and pressures."[15]

Suicide has tripled since 1960 among fifteen to twenty-four year olds. It ranks as the third leading cause of death among ten to twenty-four year olds and the second leading cause of death among college-age youth. Lesbian, gay, bisexual, and transgender youth who are living in the closet, being outcast by someone or a particular group, or being ridiculed are at an increased risk of suicide.[16]

Although depression is more often diagnosed in females than males, young men tend to commit suicide more than women.[17] White men complete over 72 percent of all suicides and 79 percent of them are accomplished with the use of firearms.[18]

Two powerful effects that cause extreme feelings of pain and can promote emotions of violence are shame and guilt. *Shame* motivates anger and violence toward others, while *guilt* evokes these feelings within the individual.[19]

Psychoanalyst Helen B. Lewis explained, "The experience of shame is directly about the self, which is the focus of evaluation. In guilt, the self is not the central object of negative evaluation, but rather the thing done by the individual is the focus."[20] Similarly, in their book *Facing Shame*, Merle Fossum and Marilyn Mason stated, "While guilt is a painful feeling of regret and responsibility for one's actions, shame is a painful feeling about oneself as a person."[21]

People who feel *shame* perceive it as stemming from other people and target the anger toward those individuals, while people who experience *guilt* perceive the problem as being within themselves and some of these people believe that the only way to eliminate the guilt is to eliminate its source—which is thyself.

Discussing feelings of shame and guilt with your child and emphasizing open and honest lines of communication are ways of helping your child if they are suffering from depression. Keeping firearms out of the household and prescription drugs in a safe, inconspicuous location can help thwart impulsive suicide attempts.

Here are the *suicidal warning signs* to look for in depressed children:[22]

- Saying, texting, or making online posts like "I wish I were never born," "I'd be better off dead," "There's no hope," "I can't go on," "I feel so depressed," "There's no way out," "Everyone would be better off without me," "If I see you again . . ."
- Seeking out lethal means such as guns, knives, a rope, or other objects that could be used to commit suicide
- Actual talking or joking about committing suicide
- Saying goodbye to family and friends as if it were for the last time
- Poor communication with parents
- Increased risk-taking behaviors such as experimenting with alcohol, prescription drugs, and/or illicit drugs
- Drastic changes in personality, eating, sleeping, studying, grades, clothes, overall appearance, style of music listened to, peer groups, likes/dislikes, quitting activities that were enjoyable, and so on
- Social isolation
- Written notes, online posts, text messages, e-mails, stories, or poems about death or suicide
- Morbid thoughts glorifying death
- Violent or rebellious outbursts
- Giving away prized possessions
- Apathy
- Increased sensitivity
- Recent suicide of a friend or family member
- Saying that they have nothing to live for

- Attempted suicides before
- Impulsive actions/prone to accidents
- Rejection by a boyfriend or girlfriend
- Sudden sense of calmness and happiness—this could mean that they have made a decision to actually carry out their suicidal mission

STARTING A CONVERSATION

If I see these warning signs with my students, I immediately start a conversation with them by saying something to this effect: "I have noticed something different about you lately. I was just wondering how things are going and how you, personally, are doing." This typically sparks a conversation and opens the door for more specific questions to follow, as well as support to be offered.

If you are unsure if your child is suicidal, don't be afraid to start a conversation and ask how they are feeling. You cannot make children become suicidal by asking questions about their emotional well-being. The following questions can be used in your conversation to see if your child exhibits any suicidal warning signs:

- When did you start feeling this way?
- Is something going on that feels out of your control?
- Do you feel like no one understands what you are going through?
- Have you thought of asking for help?
- How can I best support you right now?

Starting a conversation can be very difficult, especially if you are concerned that your child might be emotionally unstable. However, expressing your concern is a powerful first step in preventing suicide.

Be sure to show empathy for what your child is going through and tell them that feelings of suicide are completely normal and that help is available to discuss healthy solutions for dealing with the problem. Determine your child's reaction and see if they appear apathetic to your words or say something like "What's the point of living anymore?"

If so, those are high risk warning signs that it's time to ask the following tough "how, when, and where" questions to evaluate the level of planning your child may have to carry out the act.

- "Have you decided *how* you would like to kill yourself?"
- "Have you decided *when* you plan on doing it?"

- "Have you decided *where* it will take place and if you have everything necessary to carry it out?"

Be aware that there may be other risk factors, such as alcohol or substance use or previous suicide attempts to be on the lookout for that may make the individual more susceptible to carrying out future suicide attempts. When a young person feels that someone truly cares, understands, or can relate to their situation, then a significant breakthrough has been made and can be the difference between their life and death.

If your child is demonstrating some, or many, of the warning signs that they may be suicidal, you can assist them with encouraging statements during your conversations:

- "I may not be able to exactly relate to how you are feeling right now, but I had something similar happen to me when I was your age. So, I have some idea how you might be feeling."
- "I am so glad that we are talking right now and just know that you are not alone. I am on your side and here for you every step of the way."
- "You are at a stage in your life right now where there are many mental and physical changes going on and some things may feel like the end of the world. It is completely normal to feel this way and everyone experiences these kinds of emotions. You may not believe it right now, but trust me when I say that this feeling you have is not going to last forever. Things are going to turn around for you and change for the better."

On the other hand, here are some things you *don't* want to say or do during a conversation with your child:

- Demean your child's depression and try to talk them out of being depressed.
- Lecture and provide advice without listening.
- Get into an argument or go against your child by saying things like "You have so much to live for," "What you're doing is wrong," "Suicide will hurt your family."
- Promise that you won't tell anyone else.

SOCIAL FACTORS

An individual's interpersonal relationship with their surroundings and others can be a major cause of depression. After age fourteen, girls are at twice the risk for developing major depression or dysthymia (persistent depressive disorder) as opposed to young boys. It is important to examine the *social factors* that your child experiences and how they impact *depression* and *suicide*: [23]

- Problems within the family, including the loss of a loved one, pregnancy, divorce, abuse, and/or unemployment.
- Childhood experiences of abuse.
- Social isolation due to intolerance of one's race, ethnicity, sexuality, and/or socioeconomic status. These long periods of loneliness can lead to a long lasting feeling of depression.
- Children who grow up in an impoverished environment are more vulnerable to abuse.
- Media's display of the "ideal image" can result in an obsession to be perfect in many young individuals, especially girls.
- Spreading of rumors online and through texting gives a person less control of what is said behind their back, causing increased feelings of anxiety.
- Academic pressures to achieve at high levels.
- Not feeling understood by family, friends, teachers, and other close individuals.
- Feeling unable to express their true feelings to someone.
- Too many responsibilities, expectations, and social pressures from a child's primary and secondary groups.

STRATEGIES

Many young people go through difficult situations at some point in their lives that can trigger depression. Here are some strategies that you can use with your child if they exhibit the warning signs of someone who appears *depressed* or *suicidal*:

- Provide emotional support and listen to your children. An atmosphere that is kind, caring, and free of negativity allows children to freely express and share their pain with someone who cares. Encourage open conversation realizing that your assistance may be the difference between life and death.
- Be patient, calm, accepting, non-judgmental, and sympathetic to the situation. If your child is unwilling to communicate with you at that moment, reassure them that your door is always open to talk later. If

your child is uncomfortable speaking with you about an issue, encourage them to speak with someone else who is trustworthy.

- Invite your child to participate in an activity, such as sports, watching a movie, playing a game, or attending a social gathering, to keep their mind diverted away from negative emotions and focused on something positive. If your child declines, refrain from pushing too much. Many demands may increase feelings of failure and hopelessness.
- Offer to help your child set *short-term goals*. Dividing large tasks into smaller pieces helps relieve anxiety and pressure to accomplish an entire task.
- Help boost resiliency skills. Children who cope well with stress and challenges are able to ward off the negative effects of pressures and avoid risky behaviors, compared to those who don't.
- Be aware of the warning signs and symptoms of depression and/or suicide, and take them seriously. Almost everyone who commits or attempts suicide has given a clue or warning along the way. If you have attempted other strategies to help your child but don't see positive changes taking place, immediately see a specialist with your child.

Going through different developmental stages is a stressful time for children and is filled with major social, mental, and physical changes. Most people who commit suicide don't want to die. They are just blinded by feelings of hopelessness, despair, self-loathing, and isolation and can't find any other way to relieve the pain other than through death.[24]

The greater awareness that you have of your child's everyday life, the better able you will be at addressing warning signs of depression and suicide and constructing interventions to facilitate their emotional development. If you or someone you know is in suicidal crisis, call 911 or a suicide hotline such as the National Suicide Prevention Lifeline at 1-800-273-TALK (8255). Other prevention hotlines include 1-800-SUICIDE (784-2433) or 1-800-799-4TTY (4889) for text telephone for individuals with speech and hearing impairments. You can also visit www.suicide.org for a more comprehensive list of suicide prevention hotlines by state in the United States.[25]

Be aware of the warning symptoms and signs for depression and suicide. Be patient, accepting, non-judgmental, and sympathetic when listening to your child's feelings.

Eating Disorders

Why (Not) Eating Yourself Skinny Can Be Life Threatening

"Beauty is eternity gazing at itself in a mirror. But you are the eternity and you are the mirror."

—Kahlil Gibran (writer, poet, artist, philosopher)

*N*ow and then, you will hear a celebrity, usually a woman, come forth about her struggle with eating disorders. Singer and songwriter Lady Gaga admitted to suffering from anorexia and bulimia since she was fifteen years old. She had been called "meaty" and was told that she had "piled on the pounds" when pictures of her performing showed her appearing heavier than her usual look.[1]

After losing out on a part in a school musical to a much thinner singer, pop rock singer Kelly Clarkson began her battle with bulimia as a freshman in high school. Former *Jersey Shore* star Snooki said that she became anorexic in high school out of fear of being replaced on the cheerleading team by thinner, younger freshmen.[2] These celebrities are just a smattering of those who have been afflicted with these kinds of problems in the highly superficial world of entertainment.

Public figures that promote unhealthy body forms can influence impressionable young girls and boys who try to emulate an often unhealthy, hard-to-attain look. This "slenderness mania" marks the onset of eating disorders and other problems for millions of young people, particularly girls, around the world.

THE STORY OF *ADRIANA*

When my wife was working as a volunteer counselor for young people with eating disorders, she told me a story about a girl, *Adriana*, who suffered from anorexia nervosa for many years. Starting in seventh grade, Adriana, who from first sight didn't look any different from her peers, started comparing herself with her friends and noticed she was a little bigger and chubbier than the other girls.

While growing up, Adriana was called "fat" by her older sister. Her aunt didn't help the situation either and made comments like "Adriana, you look like you put on some weight." This made Adriana more self-conscious about her body and in turn, she started to exercise at home and noticed that her stomach became flatter. Even Adriana's sister started asking her how she managed to stay so thin.

Direct or indirect encouragement to slenderize may be derived from family members. Consequently, the individuals receiving these messages may become obsessed and more self-conscious about their bodies, which can lead to developing an eating disorder.[3]

Many individuals are obsessed with achieving this "perfect body" and go to extremes to get it. Going to the gym is no longer looked at as a choice, but rather a necessity for so many young people. Chris Shilling, author of *The Body and Social Theory*, describes that in postmodern society, the body becomes like a machine, perceived as a body without organs, which can be reconstructed and maintained by exercises, diets, and health programs.[4]

The opinions of a child's friends, largely influenced by the ideals of society, can also cause an individual to be conscious about one's body and in Adriana's case that is very well addressed. When the time came to graduate from middle school and enter high school, Adriana had a difficult time transitioning. She had trouble fitting in and making friends. Kids kept asking her if she gained weight and told her that she appeared heavier than before. She was regularly called names like "fatty," "chunky," and "chubby."

When Adriana came home from high school, she poured out her emotions and cried incessantly for weeks. The girl could barely hold back her tears in school when she started thinking about the pleasant memories from elementary and middle school. Adriana, in a quandary, lost the ability to connect with people and felt socially awkward. Before she knew it, she was afraid of interactions with her peers and began to lose the ability to intermingle with people. Adriana isolated herself from others and emotionally shut down.

One thing led to the next and Adriana started eating less and noticed that her clothes became looser. She started pulling out some older clothes from her closet that she wore in her middle school years and after trying them on, Adriana was excited when she realized that she could fit into them again. From that point, her lone mission was to continue losing more weight.

The whole slimming process was very pleasurable to this girl and made her feel in control of something in her life; it helped her restore a lost happiness—or so she thought. Within a few months, at five foot eight inches, Adriana went from being 132 pounds down to 92 pounds. Her temporary contentment turned into a world of confusion, as she always wanted to be the best in everything she did. Adriana yearned for being the smartest, most beautiful, and most talented girl in all ways. Her desire for perfection was a big risk factor for the development of an eating disorder.

Developing an eating disorder is not simply the result of a desire to be thin or fear of getting fat, but is rooted in deeper emotional and psychological problems. Individuals with eating disorders, which include anorexia nervosa, bulimia nervosa, and eating disorders not otherwise specified, view their self-worth largely based on their body shape and weight and their ability to control them. The National Institute of Mental Health reports approximately 30 million people in the United States have an eating disorder of some kind.[5]

Although eating disorders are typically more prevalent in females (at 4 percent) than males (at less than 2 percent), there are a growing number of boys and young men coming forward that express having an eating disorder. Eating disorders typically emerge between eighteen and twenty years old, but almost half of individuals with eating disorders have reported their first episode between the ages of sixteen and twenty, a third of them reported starting between ages eleven and fifteen, and 10 percent reported the onset of an eating disorder at age ten and younger.[6]

Adriana wasn't happy with the relationship she had with her parents. The relationship largely impacted her "overachieving mentality." Her parents demanded a lot from her academically, putting a great deal of pressure on her to achieve in school.

The girl expressed that she wanted her father to listen to her more, while she felt that her mother was too controlling and intervened in every single situation of her life. Adriana's parents had been divorced for a while and no matter which household she went to, Adriana felt that she was lacking a main cohesive source of support and stability.

Family dynamics greatly affect a child's perception of what is deemed appropriate and acceptable. The family that values externals, such as appearance and/or achievements and how others will perceive them, has a strong influence on giving power to the importance of *self-image*. Overprotective parents may have an influence on a child's identity formation and leave them wondering, "Who am I?" Most girls with eating disorders also come from problematic families that experience problems such as violence, divorce, alcoholism, loss of a close person, criticism of appearance, and a distant relationship between one or both parents.[7]

As her obsession tightened its grip, Adriana's compulsion with dieting and perfection led to multiple attempts to commit suicide. Several studies have found a link between negative body image, depression, and suicide. Suicidal thoughts and attempts are much more common when young people perceive themselves as too fat, regardless of how much they weigh.[8] Adriana demonstrated that cycle as she became very depressed and trapped in a no-win situation where she starved herself and then binged. Instead of dealing with the consequences of putting on weight and "becoming fatter," she resorted to attempting suicide.

On one occasion, Adriana took fifteen pills before going to sleep and started violently vomiting. She had to be rushed to the hospital where the doctors pumped her stomach to save her life. Another time, she tried to inject air into her veins with a syringe. Thankfully, the amount of air that was administered wasn't enough to stop her heart from beating. If that wasn't enough, Adriana tried to take her life a third time through alcohol intoxication. Yet again, she was rushed back to the hospital to save her life. Individuals who have a distorted self-image of their bodies and think obsessively about their appearance are forty-five times more likely to commit suicide than people in the general population.[9]

ANOREXIA NERVOSA

Anorexia nervosa is an eating disorder characterized by "deliberate weight loss, induced and sustained by the patient." It is a specific mental illness whereby an individual has a "dread of fatness and flabbiness of body contour." A person sets a low weight standard, severely restricts caloric intake, and becomes malnourished to a certain severity.[10]

Anorexia has one of the highest death rates of any mental health condition and many individuals who become afflicted do not fit the typical anorexic profile. This problem is not simply isolated to the Western Hemisphere, but has become widespread cutting across age, gender, race, and ethnicity.[11]

In 2007, French actress and model Isabelle Caro appeared in a controversial advertising campaign titled "No Anorexia." It displayed shocking and unforgettable images of her fifty-nine pound emaciated frame, showcasing her vertebrae and facial bones that were protruding from her body. Caro's intention was to be an example and show young girls what anorexia looked like and warn them about the dangers of this affliction. In 2010, Caro died at the age of twenty-eight after battling anorexia for fifteen years.

Anorexia strikes people of all age groups, but predominately affects adolescents and young women. There are even children as young as ten years old and under who refuse to eat and are unable to provide an explanation for their actions.

A girl named *Sophie* was diagnosed with anorexia nervosa when she was only six years old. She first gave up sweets and then restricted her food portions. To further exacerbate the situation, Sophie exercised compulsively on the monkey bars, burning off additional calories when she could.[12]

The little girl admitted that she was not eating her school snacks and lunch. She had experienced dizziness, itchy skin, and constipation, all symptoms of malnutrition. One night when Sophie's mother was tucking her into bed, Sophie confessed, "Mommy, I have a problem. I am hungry all the time and I can't eat. A voice in my head is telling me not to eat."

Because all of her anthropometric measurements appeared to be in the healthy percentiles on the charts, Sophie's parents were unaware that their daughter was developing anorexia. When Sophie was finally diagnosed in first grade, she hadn't gained a pound for ten months and had dropped from the sixtieth to the nineteenth percentile on the weight charts.

It is difficult to say for certain what exactly triggered Sophie to restrict her diet. However, her mother expressed how Sophie followed rules to the hilt, better than anyone else. She recalled Sophie's teacher telling the students to eat healthy. This may have aggravated the problem and triggered the condition to present itself early on. Sophie's mother described her daughter as "a perfectionist" and as always being an "anxious kid."

No matter how minuscule the comment, individuals with anorexia are very sensitive to *criticism* and *failure*. It reinforces their own negative perception that they are "no good," or "not good enough." Experts state that the earlier the disorder is spotted and treated, the greater the chances for full recovery.[13]

The key to Sophie's progress lies in weight restoration. Sophie's mother had learned, in family-based therapy, how to re-feed her child by structuring the environment where eating was a requirement for Sophie, before she was allowed to play or enjoy other activities. Sophie, along with an estimated 20 million women and 10 million men in the United States, struggles with eating disorders such as anorexia nervosa, bulimia nervosa, and binge-eating disorder.[14] The validity of that number may be skewed due to the fact that boys tend to conceal their illness better than girls.

CHILD BEAUTY PAGEANTS

Individuals even as young as preschool aged children are aware of their body physiques and how they compare with other children their age. Sexualization of young girls is occurring even among toddlers. We have seen this over the years in popular reality television programs featuring child beauty pageants with contestants as young as two years old, with full makeup and elaborate hairdos; dressed in tight, revealing two-piece costumes; dancing around with attitude; and vying to win a competition.

Young girls in these contests become aware of the importance of physical appearance on the outcome of the pageant. A three-year-old contestant who was on the once-popular reality show *Toddlers and Tiaras* commented, "All those girls are ugly," prior to an upcoming pageant in Las Vegas, where she went on to win the Grand Supreme title, among dozens of other trophies and sashes that she had won.[15]

REALITY TELEVISION SHOWS

The Girl Scouts Research Institute conducted a study looking at the effect reality television had on young girls. Of the 1,141 interviews conducted with girls aged eleven to seventeen, 38 percent of regular reality show viewers feel a girl's value is based on her appearance, compared to 28 percent who do not watch these types of reality shows.[16]

Mass media, with its popular, slim, sexual, and beautiful woman's body appearance, can also be a major reason why girls "catch the illness." Many times, young girls who are not happy with how they look strive to achieve this "ideal image" through dieting and overexercising. They are made to believe that in order to be accepted and fit in, they must be thin. Drastic measures are taken by many children to achieve this valued status in our society. They feel that if they lose weight, then they will "look good, be popular, loved, and accepted," which ultimately can become a dangerous obsession.

Children witness this "display of beauty" while they are standing in the checkout line at the grocery store with their parents. The covers of many popular magazines portray a picture of a model or female celebrity appearing thin and happy. These magazine covers also include messages such as *"Lose 10 pounds this week," "Melt flab away," "Miracle pill that melts fat,"* and *"Mary lost 100 pounds in just five months."*

Diet and exercise commercials appear on television more than ever. The subliminal and outright weight loss messages given influence young people into believing that once they shed the pounds, then they will be happy. Children watch shows that exhibit most actors and singers as lean. What they don't realize is that many celebrities have endured hours of daily exercise and have battled with eating disorders to achieve this state. They also radically reduce their food intake, which deprives them of proper nutrition, just to maintain a slim physique that is "socially accepted and glorified."

Unrealistic and unhealthy images that "girls must be thin" are regularly portrayed throughout the media and often lead girls into not only developing eating disorders, but getting plastic surgery as well. Our society places a high premium on physical attractiveness and rewards those who are slender, good-looking, and youthful. The big craze about the slender body started in the mid-to-late 1960s, when British model Leslie Hornby, nicknamed "Twiggy" for her stick-like figure, burst onto the scene. At five foot six inches and ninety-one pounds, she became one of the first international supermodels that took the fashion world by storm. From then on, the diet industry exploded and models gradually became taller, younger, and thinner.

Females are especially concerned about their body weight and shape, while males are more concerned about their size and strength, building muscles, and sculpting a chiseled appearance. Research suggests that nearly eight out of ten girls and young women feel dissatisfied with their body appearance and desire to lose weight.[17] A negative body image can lead to a severe loss of self-esteem, resulting in depression, as well as eating disorders.

If you are concerned that your child may be developing anorexia, here are the warning signs:[18]

- Sudden decrease in weight
- Dry and yellowish skin
- Refusal to eat meals and/or specific foods
- A dramatic decrease in clothes size
- Frequent comments of feeling fat or overweight despite losing weight
- Anxiety about gaining weight or being fat
- Denial of hunger
- Development of food rituals such as eating foods in certain orders, excessive chewing, rearranging food on a plate, and so on
- Giving regular excuses to avoid mealtimes or situations pertaining to food
- Excessive exercise despite fatigue, illness, injury, or inclement weather
- Withdrawal from usual friends and activities
- Lack of a menstrual cycle
- Shift in attitude/behavior indicating that weight loss, dieting, and control of food have become the main priority in the child's life

Along with the social and emotional effects that anorexia has on an individual, here are the associated potential health consequences:[19]

- Decrease in bone density—thus increasing the risk for osteoporosis
- Muscle wasting and weakness

- Severe dehydration—which can result in kidney failure
- Fainting, lethargy, and overall weakness
- Dry hair and skin, and commonly hair loss
- Growth of a downy layer of hair called lanugo all over the body, including the face, in an effort to keep the body warm
- Abnormally slow heart rate and low blood pressure, which means that the heart muscle is changing (risk for heart failure rises as heart rate and blood pressure levels drop)

BULIMIA NERVOSA

Anorexia nervosa, oftentimes, leads to another eating disorder called bulimia. *Bulimia nervosa* is a disorder characterized by "recurrent and frequent episodes of binge eating and a feeling that one lacks control over eating."[20] These actions lead to a pattern of overeating followed by vomiting or use of purgatives.

While researching this topic, I came across many videos and blogs of young girls sharing their personal stories about their daily struggles as bulimics. I was touched by the story of Shaye Boddington, a young lady from New Zealand, who had suffered from bulimia since the age of eight.[21]

I spoke with Shaye and she agreed to share her personal story about her struggles with bulimia.[22] Shaye expressed that dieting or restriction for her was the first phase of the binge/purge cycle characteristic of bulimia. She started dieting and restricted herself from foods because she felt that in order to be popular and successful, she needed to be thin. She used to say to herself that she would only eat fruits and vegetables, starting the next day. That caused her to eventually binge and purge. From there, a cycle of bulimia began that she couldn't stop for years.

This subconscious food restriction makes the body think that there is a deprivation, which causes an individual to go in search of it. When a person "cannot eat" certain foods, then it becomes a psychological problem. The body doesn't truly know the difference between starvation and diet. Therefore, this behavior triggers a deep internal drive or urge to overeat.

Shaye's strong negative belief kept her bulimic for a long time and caused her to begin dieting at a young age, which led to daily episodes of binging and purging. It wasn't until Shaye changed her beliefs to healthier, alternative ones that things started to improve for her. She started by working on a positive core belief that "despite her body size, she would be loved and accepted." This took some time and required a lot of persistence and repetition.

As with anorexia, more females than males, approximately 80 percent, suffer from bulimia. The binge-eating episodes mask deep-rooted unresolved psychological issues that have presented themselves as serious pressures in an individual's life.[23] These forces affect self-image and self-esteem. Both anorexia and bulimia have similar ramifications, causing feelings of depression and tying into emotional, verbal, physical, and sexual abuse. The ability to spot a bulimic is not that easy, as compared to many, but not all, suffering anorexics. Individuals who struggle with bulimia may appear to have a normal body weight or even be slightly overweight, and unless you catch them in the act of bingeing or purging, you may never guess that they have a problem.

Bulimics have a different medical concern than anorexics in that a constant purging of food causes tooth decay and results in many digestive tract problems. The esophagus can be severely damaged due to the constant regurgitation of stomach acids. As a result, the body can have an irregular heartbeat and an electrolyte imbalance, become severely dehydrated, and experience bowel movement problems. Bulimics can die from ulcers, ruptures in the intestinal lining, kidney failure, strokes, and heart attacks.

If you are concerned that your child may be developing bulimia, here are the warning signs to look for, according to the National Eating Disorders Association:[24]

- Evidence of binge-eating, including disappearance of large amounts of food in short time frames or the existence of wrappers and containers—indicating the consumption of large amounts of food
- Excessive exercise despite fatigue, illness, injury, or inclement weather
- Unusual swelling of the cheeks or jaw area
- Calluses on the back of the hands and knuckles from self-induced vomiting
- Discoloration or staining of the teeth
- Creation of schedules or rituals to make time for binge-and-purge sessions
- Withdrawal from regular friends and activities
- Frequent trips to the bathroom following meals
- In general, behaviors and attitudes indicating that weight loss, dieting, and control of food are becoming a main priority and concern

Along with the social and emotional effects that bulimia has on an individual, here are the associated potential health consequences, according to the National Eating Disorders Association:[25]

- Electrolyte imbalances that can lead to irregular heartbeats and possibly heart failure and death (electrolyte imbalances are caused by dehydration and loss of potassium and sodium from the body as a result of purging behaviors)

- Inflammation and possible rupture of the esophagus from frequent vomiting
- Tooth decay and staining from stomach acids released during frequent vomiting
- Chronic, irregular bowel movements and constipation as a result of laxative abuse
- Gastric rupture is an uncommon, but possible side effect of binge eating

BINGE EATING

A third eating disorder classified as "eating beyond the point of satiety at least twice a week" is known as *binge eating*. This eating disorder is characterized by episodes of binge eating, without the purging events that follow. This has become the biggest eating disorder in the United States, outnumbering those individuals suffering from anorexia and bulimia combined.[26]

This behavior of out-of-control eating is a contributor to a rise in obesity. With the growing stresses and responsibilities that adolescents take on as they get older, their life may feel unmanageable, and food is used to control feelings of anxiety and depression. Individuals who indulge in such a manner express shame and guilt over their eating behavior.[27]

Along with the social and emotional effects that binge eating disorder has on an individual, the associated potential health consequences, according to the National Eating Disorders Association, include high blood pressure, high cholesterol levels, heart disease, type 2 diabetes, gallbladder disease, fatigue, joint pain, and sleep apnea.[28]

Psychiatric researchers at Harvard University Medical School indicate that among the U.S. population,[29]

- 1 percent of women and 0.3 percent of men suffer from anorexia,
- 1.5 percent of women and 0.5 percent of men suffer from bulimia, and
- 3.5 percent of women and 2 percent of men suffer from binge eating disorder.

Eating disorders are likely to result from many different social factors, including social pressures, family influences, genetic predisposition, neurophysiological vulnerability, moral values, and personality variables such as perfectionism, the need for control, and poor self-esteem. According to Dr. Ruth Striegel, professor of psychology at Wesleyan University, a common factor shared among those who suffer from eating disorders, which happens to be the same psychological implication, is a *miscued self-perception.*[30]

Many young people who suffer from eating disorders realize that they do have a problem, but cannot find a solution. Below is a ten-question body image test that you can give your child to see where their self-perception lies in regard to their personal appearance. If they answer "YES" to three or more questions, then they may have a negative body image.[31]

1. Does consuming a small amount of food make you feel fat?
2. Do you worry or obsess about your body not being small, thin, or good enough?
3. Are you concerned your body is not muscular or strong enough?
4. Do you avoid wearing certain clothes because you think they make you feel big?
5. Have you ever disliked your body?
6. Do you look in the mirror and see yourself as fat and/or ugly?
7. Do you feel badly about yourself because you don't like your body?
8. Do you want to change something about your body?
9. Do you compare yourself to others and feel that you fail in comparison?
10. Have you avoided playing sports or working out because you didn't want to be seen in gym clothes?

WHAT YOU CAN DO

Here are some tips to help prevent the onset of eating disorders in your child:

- Evaluate your own attitudes, beliefs, and behaviors about food, weight, body image, physical appearance, health, and exercise. If you are always concerned about your weight and desire to be thin, chances are your children will develop similar beliefs and values about weight loss.
- Educate your children about healthy eating habits such as eating when you are hungry, rather than inadvertently telling them not to eat something that could make them fat and deprive them of a meal.
- Encourage moderate exercise and balanced eating, including a variety of foods, three healthy meals a day, a few snacks, and plenty of water.
- Avoid using food as a reward for desirable behavior.
- Love, respect, listen to, acknowledge, encourage, appreciate, accept, and value your child out loud. Teach your child to accept people for

who they are and emphasize that all people are unique and come in all different shapes and sizes.

- Help develop your child's self-esteem, self-worth, and self-identity early on in life. Feeling confident and having a sense of balance and control in life are key factors for a healthy mind, body, and spirit.
- Develop a value system based on internal values that focus on cooperation, individuality, caring for others, self-awareness, ambition, motivation, curiosity, confidence, and a good sense of humor.
- Your kids long for control over their lives. Even if you are going through personal challenges, it is important to be a lynchpin for your child, a source of strength and stability. Also, provide opportunities for your children to feel in control of something by allowing them to make choices once in a while—what to have for dinner and different family activities. Allow your children to make decisions in their lives, as long as it doesn't negatively affect their well-being.
- Allow your child to freely discuss their concerns on a daily basis. Body image disorders arise from a variety of bottled up physical, emotional, social, and family problems. Make time for your child to express their emotions with you. The more open the lines of communication, the less suppressed the emotions, thus helping to prevent a manifestation of an eating disorder.
- Directly address the cultural obsession of slenderness (females) and strength (males) as physical, psychological, and moral issues. Help your child think critically about the intentions of the mass media in their portrayal of an "ideal image."
- Foster your child's self-respect and respect for others in a wide array of environments by promoting diversity in race, ethnicity, gender, sexuality, body size, athleticism, intelligence, and popularity. Emphasize the importance of people's character over physical appearance.
- Involve your child in various group activities that allow them to obtain physical activity in something safe and enjoyable. Help your child accept and feel good about their body.
- If you suspect that your child may have an eating disorder, it is important to take action as soon as possible. Seek advice from a professional such as an eating disorder specialist, a doctor, a psychologist, or a nutritional counselor to see what further steps need to be taken to accurately address the problem.

If you have concerns that your child may have an eating disorder, have an open, non-judgmental, respectful conversation and allow them to discuss other concerns that are not related to food, weight, exercise, or body image.

Eating disorders oftentimes co-occur with depression, anxiety, and substance use disorders.[32] Speaking about what is bothering them provides a sense of relief that someone else acknowledges their problem and cares about them.

If you find out that your child is battling an eating disorder, early treatment increases the chances of a full recovery.[33] Young people with an eating disorder may not think they have a problem or may refuse treatment for a number of reasons. Overcoming eating disorders is a long-term process that requires support, patience, and sensitivity to a young person's emotions and fears. Mental health professionals can address psychological and behavioral aspects of the disorder by utilizing therapies for other mental health disorders such as cognitive behavioral therapy, family therapy, and interpersonal psychotherapy. Nutritional counselors can provide meal planning and education on healthy eating choices to help restore a healthy weight.

Anorexia and bulimia are very complex disorders that are rooted in serious unresolved emotional conflicts or expressions that often start in adolescence. A series of traumatic events from early in life largely contribute to these behaviors, whether they are major occurrences like severe physical or mental abuse or less severe traumas where expectations for being thin strongly emanate from family, friends, past relationships, and/or society. Eating disorders can get out of hand and are hard to overcome. For any hope of a full recovery, early intervention and treatment by a professional are required.

For additional resources, available treatments, and stories of recovery from individuals with eating disorders, visit the National Eating Disorders Association website (www.nationaleatingdisorders.org). They have a confidential helpline at 1-800-931-2237, offering support and guidance with compassion and understanding.[34]

———=◉=———

Be a role model and promote healthy eating and moderate exercise. Help your child understand the media's distortion of an ideal body and encourage the celebration of all shapes and sizes.

———=◉=———

Poor Eating Habits and Physical Inactivity

What Needs to Be Done to Bring Your Child to Health

> *"Follow your dreams, work hard, practice and persevere. Make sure you eat a variety of foods, get plenty of exercise and maintain a healthy lifestyle."*[1]
>
> —Sasha Cohen (United States figure skating champion)

*T*welve-year-old *Carlos* was one of the first boys that I personally mentored through the Big Brothers Big Sisters program when I was in college. He lived with his mother in a one-bedroom apartment in a crime-ridden section in Hartford, Connecticut. Most afternoons, Carlos was home alone for about three hours. He usually ate a snack consisting of potato chips and a can of soda. Carlos watched television and played video games until his mother came home from work. For dinner, his mother usually brought something home from a fast-food restaurant.

Carlos's mother was being treated for hypertension and Carlos's pediatrician had expressed concerns about the boy's rapid weight gain. The mother knew this lifestyle wasn't the healthiest way to go for neither Carlos nor her, but given her work schedule, it was very hard for her to find time to cook. Also, she indicated that buying anything more expensive at the store was not an option, considering her limited, fixed income.

You may struggle in situations similar to this one and find it hard to make healthy changes at home, due to financial and/or time constraints. As difficult as it may be, developing proper eating and exercise habits is essential to your child's overall well-being. In order to positively influence your child's lifestyle habits, you must reduce the environmental risk factors or circumstances that are contributing to the family's health problems, which may include the following:

- Family not eating meals together
- The availability of junk food
- Dysfunctional family situation (divorce, single parent, alcoholism, drug abuse, chronic depression, other health-related issues)
- Busy schedule
- Frequent traveling
- Lack of knowledge about healthy eating and the importance of daily physical activity
- Economic hardship
- Poor eating habits modeled at home

Adequate daily nutrition depends on consuming a variety of foods in sufficient amounts. Your child's nutritional status greatly impacts many facets of his or her life, including behavior, the ability to focus, learning experiences at school, and physical activity levels.

When I arrived to meet Carlos for the first time at his middle school, the principal greeted me and we reviewed the boy's background history. Carlos had been diagnosed with ADHD, had difficulty getting to school on time, and had a low motivation for academics. When I was first introduced to Carlos, I was expecting this hyperactive child who would be jumping off the walls. On the contrary, he appeared shy, withdrawn, and lethargic. I could see that something was affecting him, and I wanted to make a positive difference in his life.

Carlos and I decided on doing something that we both liked—and that was playing basketball. We went down to the school's gymnasium and Carlos asked me if I knew any trick shots. I picked up a basketball and took a few dribbles, flipped the basketball behind my back and caught it off the backboard. In mid air, I caught the ball, put it between my legs, and spun 360 degrees for a lay-up. Carlos was enthralled with all these fancy moves and from that moment, he and I had made a connection.

Over the course of that school year, Carlos and I did many sports-related activities together. I noticed, at times, that Carlos got easily tired, so I expressed my concern to his mother about Carlos being dizzy and fatigued after we played. I discovered that Carlos ate high-sugar cereals in the morning and bought hot lunch at school every day. Unfortunately, lunches offered at his school were high in fat, calories, and salt, which contributed to his weight gain.

After discussing some healthy alternatives with Carlos's mother, she was able to get her son into a regular habit of eating a low-fat yogurt and a banana when he got home from school. On a few occasions, I surprised Carlos with a salad, a yogurt, or a chicken sandwich and discussed healthy eating habits with him. I also got him a basketball, tennis racquet, and football, and introduced him to different games and sports throughout the school year.

My experience with Carlos went beyond just playing different activities with him to exposing him to new ideas, lifestyle habits, and opportunities that he could carry with him for the rest of his life. After nine months of interacting with this boy, I had seen him make significant improvements in his motivation, academics, and overall health. As he took a more active role in making his lifestyle healthier, he had more energy to do things and sculpted a leaner physique.

Eating and exercise habits are learned behaviors that stick with a child well into adulthood. After over four decades of government health campaigns promoting healthy living, we still continue to have a long-standing problem with *healthy eating* and getting kids into *better shape*.

MAKING HEALTHY FOOD CHOICES

Today we are living in a society plagued with unhealthy food choices. When it comes to a child's health, parents are the most influential figures for shaping their child's lifestyle habits throughout their formative years. However, the corporate food advertisements foisted upon children can be quite frustrating in what often seems like futile attempts at getting kids to eat healthy.

The food industry presents colorful cartoon characters on cereal boxes to get a child's attention. The response is usually something like "Look, Mom, it's Tony the Tiger!" or "I want the cereal with Toucan Sam!" Moreover, research has found a correlation between advertisements for non-nutritious foods and increased rates of childhood obesity.[2]

Most parents are part of a highly stressed out working population juggling many responsibilities throughout the day. Many parents lack energy to do anything when they get home from a long day at work and just want to kick back and relax. When living a busy, on-the-go, stressed-out lifestyle, it may be more convenient to pick up cheaper, fast-food meals or throw a frozen dinner in the oven than to make a home-cooked, highly nutritious meal.

In today's economy, many families are barely making ends meet and sadly sacrificing meals for paying the bills. Although understandable, this repeated pattern has many negative implications for a child's overall health and wellness.

Concerns for unhealthy food consumption lie in the choices kids are given on what to eat when they are with their family and when they are on their own. This is largely shaped by the eating patterns that kids acquire while growing up. Research has found that children who eat the same food as their parents, rather than being given kids' meals, are far more likely to have healthy diets.[3] There shouldn't be one meal made for you and another made for a child. As they say, what's good for the goose is good for the gander.

Your children require a nutritionally balanced diet with proper caloric intake for optimal growth and development. They need to eat their fruits and vegetables, as experts have said for years. However, a lot of children tend to dislike the taste of vegetables, and many to the point of refusing to eat them at all. Vegetables have strong tastes, can be bitter and mushy, are fibrous, and low in calories.

GET YOUR CHILD TO EAT THOSE VEGGIES

Children are born with ten thousand taste buds and as they get older, the number of taste buds decreases. This accounts largely for the reason why many kids don't enjoy eating vegetables because they tend to be on the bitter side. As kids grow up, their aversions to bitter flavors tend to ease and they typically enjoy eating more vegetables. In the meantime, what can you do to get your child to eat those veggies without constant resistance?

First off, your child needs to *acquire* a taste for vegetables. It may take multiple efforts to get them to eat a piece of broccoli or cauliflower, but the bottom line is that they should consume vegetables and plenty of them. It does take time for your child to learn to like these foods. The more frequently you introduce vegetables to your child, the earlier their brain will learn to like the taste.

You can use a little trickery on your child by disguising the bitterness of vegetables by adding extra virgin coconut or olive oil, various nut butters, and/ or different seasonings to enhance the flavor. Several cookbooks and websites offer tips on how to make typically "gross" foods more palatable to children. There are ways to "hide" veggies in sauces, baked goods, and other dishes, but it's also good to present children with healthy food in its natural form in order to train their taste buds to enjoy healthy foods.

Offering fruit for dessert from a young age can also help encourage children to make healthier choices. Children require more fat intake compared to adults anyway, so increasing fat consumption, especially healthy fats, is not a concern. Topping green salads with fresh fruits and veggies of different colors is not just nutritious, but colorful, too. Children like contrasting colors. Playing the rainbow color game with them is a great way to get them to eat an abundant amount of fruits and veggies in a surreptitious way.

Another method to stealthily pack in your child's daily requirements of vegetables is by mixing them with fruits to make a smoothie. Creatively play around with a variety of mixes, including oranges, grapefruits, apples, pears, kiwi, raspberries, strawberries, bananas, blueberries, carrots, cucumbers, and butternut squash. For additional protein and calcium, you can add organic low-fat yogurt, chia and hemp seeds, and/or nut butter to the drink. As a result, children receive an excellent source of vitamins and minerals this way and may actually look forward to the next healthy drink.

CHOOSE ORGANICALLY GROWN

It is best for the human body to consume organically grown products such as pesticide-free fruits and vegetables, hormone-free meat products, organic eggs, and wild, not farm-raised fish. According to the National Cancer Institute, scientists reported that at least 80 percent of cancer cases are caused by environmental factors such as agents in the water and air, as well as lifestyle factors such as smoking, drinking, and diet.[4]

It is vital to minimize pesticide exposure to babies and young children in order to increase the odds for healthy development. Exposure to pesticides and toxic chemicals at a young age can cause detrimental, developmental effects throughout childhood and into adulthood. A child's nervous, reproductive, and endocrine systems can be permanently affected by exposure to toxic substances in utero or throughout early childhood that, at the same level, would not cause considerable harm to adults.[5]

Organic food, in general, is more expensive than conventional, but that should not be a deterrent for purchasing these foods even if you're on a budget. By comparison shopping and keeping an eye out for coupons and sales, you can significantly cut costs and purchase these health-promoting foods as part of you and your child's regular diets and reduce the risk of various diseases.

Here are some tips for affordably purchasing organic fruits and vegetables:

- **Look for sales, specials, and coupons**—Check your local newspaper, online, and at the grocery stores for special discounts. Oftentimes, you can get better deals by visiting chain grocery stores. They can buy in volume, which can lower the prices for the consumer. Also, sign up for a membership card to receive additional discounts.
- **Buy in bulk**—Compare the price and the number of servings from fresh, canned, and frozen forms of the same fruit or vegetable. Canned

and frozen fruits or vegetables may be bought in large quantities, last longer, and be less expensive than fresh produce. For canned fruits, choose 100 percent fruit juice and for canned vegetables, choose "low sodium" or "no salt added" on the label. Be sure that the cans are BPA free.

- **Buy fresh fruits and vegetables regularly in small amounts**—If you notice that you are throwing away fresh fruits and vegetables each week, buy smaller amounts more often. If you can't make it to the store a couple of times a week, then consider canned or frozen forms.
- **Shop after you eat**—You will save money shopping after you've eaten. You will be less tempted to splurge for sugary, high salt, and fatty foods.
- **Plant your own vegetables**—Take advantage of the warm seasons by involving your child in planting a variety of vegetables and herbs in your backyard. If you only have a small space on a deck, buy a few pots and plant a few vegetables and herbs.
- **Support local organically grown produce**—Visit a local farmer's market to pick from a variety of fruits and vegetables. Locally grown organic produce is more nutritious and costs less than what is sold at conventional grocery stores.

GENETICALLY MODIFIED FOOD

It is estimated that between 70 and 75 percent of all processed foods in U.S. grocery stores may contain ingredients from genetically engineered plants.[6] We are unaware of the actual percentage because the food manufacturers and the biotech companies are not yet required to notify the U.S. Food and Drug Administration (FDA) that they are bringing new genetically engineered products to the market. However, there is new hope for genetically engineered food labeling. Labeling proposals for genetically modified (GM) food products have been introduced into various state legislatures and are likely to expand nationally.

GM foods are genetically modified to grow faster, bear more fruit, or develop their own insecticide. Long-term safety testing of genetically engineered food has not been conducted. Different scientists, some within the FDA, mention the potential dangers in altering the genetic makeup of a food crop and how unexpected food allergies can be triggered, toxins can be created in the food, and antibiotic-resistant diseases can develop.[7]

Scientists have also investigated the relationship between artificial food coloring additives and hyperactivity in children. Although there is no conclusive evidence that has shown food dye to directly cause attention deficit hyperactivity disorder (ADHD) in children, some studies have suggested a link between the two.[8] Food coloring is often added to processed foods, drinks, and condiments. Regardless of whether a child suffers from this condition or not, kids should consume very few processed foods, if any at all.

Processed sugars produce a rapid increase in blood glucose levels because they enter the bloodstream quickly. This activates the hormone insulin into action to counteract this surge in blood sugar, which can lead to adult-onset diabetes. Many children as young as three years old are already developing hypertension, hyperlipidemia, high blood glucose, and high cholesterol levels, which increase a person's risk of heart disease, stroke, and diabetes.[9]

Diabetes is part of a metabolic syndrome where an individual is not able to produce a sufficient supply of insulin or various cells do not respond to the insulin that is produced and thus cannot appropriately regulate blood sugar levels in the body. Studies have shown a 21 percent increase in the number of individuals aged ten to nineteen who have been diagnosed with type-2 diabetes over the past decade or so.[10] When you examine the non-nutritious foods that many kids eat nowadays, along with their increased sedentary lifestyle, it is not surprising to see a sharp increase in this condition.

SETTING FOOD GUIDELINES

What is alarming is that this statistic is quite high, considering the fact that children rarely have control over their food choices at home and at school. They eat what is available or served to them on a daily basis. That is why it is important for a child to be provided with healthy food choices and encouraged to be physically active each day.

Foods that are calorie dense and potential sources of excessive caloric intake—which could lead to obesity—include whole milk, sugar-sweetened beverages, different pastries, other high-fat foods, and fast foods. On the other hand, eating fruits, an abundant amount of vegetables, and whole grains satiates the appetite, due to the fiber content in these foods, and offsets high-caloric intake.

It is important to set guidelines to when and where food should be eaten. Kids tend to make better food choices when there are guidelines set for them. Children who eat meals with their families tend to consume more fruits and vegetables and less sugary drinks and fried foods.

Children require a variety of foods that provide balanced energy requirements on a daily basis to support optimal growth and development. Refer to the American Heart Association's Dietary Recommendations for Children for specifics on grains, fruits, vegetables, and dairy by age and gender.[11]

Carbohydrates are the primary source of energy available for the body. They are classified into two main groups: simple and complex. Carbohydrates with a low-glycemic index, those that are digested and absorbed into the bloodstream slowly, are the most desirable kind. In addition to fruits and vegetables, here are some other examples of low-glycemic carbohydrates that are good for your child's developing body:

- Sprouted 100 percent whole grain bread
- Oatmeal (steel-cut or rolled)
- Whole-grain cereals with organic milk (for children under two years old, choose whole milk; for older children, 1 percent or 2 percent milk)
- Salads containing protein such as chicken, turkey, or fish

Breakfast is the most important meal of the day and fuels a child with energy and brain power. Just like other meals, a child should eat a variety of foods that contain enough protein, carbohydrates, fats, vitamins, and minerals.

Here are some breakfast options that you can choose for your child each morning:

- Whole-grain cereal with milk; fresh fruit on the side
- 2–3 egg whites with whole-grain/multi-grain bread with coconut oil or a butter substitute (without the partially hydrogenated oil, additives, and preservatives)
- Whole-grain toast with nut/seed butter
- Yogurt with fruit and/or nuts
- Smoothies (fresh blend or frozen fruits with low-fat yogurt)

While breakfast energizes and fuels a child throughout the morning, lunch helps a child focus and function throughout the rest of the school day. Here are some flavorful foods to pack in your child's lunch bag:

- Turkey or chicken breast sandwich on whole wheat tortillas or whole grain/wheat bread (with lettuce and tomato on the side)
- Salad with grilled chicken, fish, or turkey added
- Low-fat yogurt
- Carrots, broccoli, and/or celery sticks with hummus
- Apple slices with dips made from yogurt
- One or two fresh fruits
- Drinks made from water with a hint of flavoring or 100-percent fruit juice, as opposed to sodas or artificial sugar-laden juices

When your child is home after school or during the weekend, here are some healthy snacks for them that are packed with fiber, protein, healthy fats, whole grains, and vitamins:

- Fruit and vegetable smoothies
- Peanut butter and jelly on toasted whole wheat, or multigrain bread/waffles
- Grilled cheese sandwich on a piece of whole grain/multigrain bread
- Sliced fruit with peanut butter or yogurt dip
- Fruit and cheese kebobs
- Homemade guacamole or salsa and tortilla chips made with organic corn
- Healthy trail mix such as raisins, dried pineapple rings, dried cranberries, unsalted almonds, walnuts, cashews, and sunflower seeds. Check the ingredients to make sure the items don't contain sulfur, added salt, sugar, preservatives, and/or partially hydrogenated oil.

THE BENEFITS OF PROPER NUTRITION

A child's body requires proper nutrition. The adequate intake of energy and nutrients is necessary for children to achieve their maximal growth and developmental potential. When eating a healthy diet, children:

- have more energy for a good performance in school,
- have a more regulated and stable mood,
- have blood sugar levels that remain balanced so they can concentrate,
- are able to be more active and get the proper amount of exercise they need,
- begin to make the association between "feeling good" with "eating healthy," and
- have a better chance at developing a lifelong habit of healthy eating, which reduces the risk of various diseases.

WHAT YOU CAN DO

Here are some strategies to help you get your child into a *healthy eating* habit:

- **Stock your home with healthy foods** – When your children are hungry, they will eat what is available at home. Take your children shopping with you and allow them to explore different foods. Point out the nutrition facts on food labels and teach them about the contents in various foods and how they work to promote growth and development. Encourage them to compare the macromolecules, nutrients, and vitamins for different foods by reading the labels.

- **Teach about food moderation** – Your children should be fed consistent meals and snacks at regular intervals. Eating at least one meal a day together as a family is important and is a great time to introduce new, healthy foods into your child's diet. Breakfast is the most important meal of the day and should be the highest caloric meal. There should be a balance of protein, healthy fats, carbohydrates, vitamins, and minerals. Jumpstart your child's metabolism for the day with brain foods such as oatmeal, eggs, high protein/low-sugar whole grain cereals, and fruits.
- **Make mealtime special and get your child involved** – Have your child help set the table each night. You could make it a weekly ritual to involve your child in picking a meal from a menu of healthy food choices. You could also allow your child to help create a menu filled with healthy food choices.
- **Don't use food as a reward or punishment** – When foods are used as rewards for achieving good grades, doing well in an activity, and/or showing affection, a child may learn to use food in coping with stress or other emotions in different life situations. Instead, offer short words of praise, hugs, and kisses. Scolding your child for not eating certain foods can foster a negative relationship between you, your child, and food.
- **Involve your child in making a snack or cooking a meal** – Kids love eating foods they make. Know your child's abilities and consider safety first. You can include your child in helping to add, pour, stir, mix, or pick out the ingredients. Also, your child can help to cut up or peel foods and also clean up the area.
- **Allow room for a special treat** – Although it is important to regularly make healthy choices for your child's growth and development, having a special treat once a week or even once a day such as a cookie or an occasional ice cream is an enjoyable experience and will help your child gain a healthy sense about a balanced diet.
- **Limit "tech time"** – When children are sitting down in front of the computer or watching television, they have a tendency to snack on non-nutritious foods. Instead, encourage physical activity because the more time that children are active, the less time they will be mindlessly snacking and ruining their appetite for a healthy nutritious meal.

- **Eat at least one meal together as a family every day** – Make televisions, radios, phones, and other devices off limits during family mealtimes.

CHILDHOOD OBESITY

Today's society has drastically changed from the days when kids used to run around and play outside in the neighborhood until it was time to eat dinner. Nowadays, many children are spending less time doing physical activities and more time on their phone, in front of the television, on the computer screen, and/or playing video games, which have become acceptable leisure activities for today's youth. The problem isn't necessarily in the activities, but rather in the excessive time frame spent on them.

A major problem influencing today's children is that anything they desire is a click away. There is a massive amount of technology available where today's generation of kids can watch television, play video games, text and talk with their friends, and listen to their favorite songs, all at the same time, without ever having to leave the room.

In the last decade or so, technology has exploded, particularly as it relates to the sophistication and graphics of modern-day video games and the popularity of online social networks. This generation of parents has an additional challenge on their hands that past generations didn't have, which is *preventing children from becoming overweight or obese.*

Childhood obesity has grown to pandemic levels across a large population of the world. Globally, over 43 million children under the age of five are overweight, as are 200 million school-age children. Of those, 40–50 million are classified as obese.[12] This translates into approximately one out of every three kids being classified as overweight or obese. North America, Europe, and parts of the Western Pacific have the highest prevalence of overweight children in the world at approximately 20 to 30 percent.[13] So, what actions are being implemented to reverse this curse of low activity and rising percentages of overweight and obese children?

Communities around the United States are putting forth an initiative to reverse the trend. Grants are being written across the nation to acquire federal funding for health and wellness programs for today's youth, in the form of health education or actual health and fitness programs at schools. Former First Lady Michelle Obama developed the Let's Move! initiative to solve the problem of childhood obesity for today's generation of kids. Its goal is to ensure that children have a healthy future by offering parents and caregivers the tools, support, and information they need to make healthy choices and live a healthy lifestyle. The equation is simple: *healthy nutrition* + *physical activity* on a daily basis = *better overall behavior* and *academic performance* of a child throughout the day.

Children who are overweight or obese can suffer severe emotional and psychological abuse from their peers. A video on YouTube titled "Fat Kid Fights Back" garnered the attention of media outlets around the world showing fifteen-year-old Casey being teased, slapped, and punched in the face by another boy. The incident ended with Casey body slamming the boy onto the concrete ground and both kids getting suspended from school.

After the incident, Casey was interviewed on television and asked how the bullying for him first began. Ever since he could remember, Casey said that he had been picked on. His peers taunted him about his weight, which took a huge toll on his self-esteem to the point of Casey considering killing himself. On a television interview, Casey said, "Kids would call me 'fatty' and tell me to lose some weight. I started to put myself down. All the crap just kept piling on. All I wanted was for the bullying just to stop."[14]

Being stigmatized as a "fat kid" can result in the emotional torment of being bullied, depression, violent outrage, and thoughts of suicide. Many kids who struggle with weight issues need help to develop effective strategies to improve their self-esteem during their transitory years of childhood and prevent potential health risks associated with a higher body mass index. They also would benefit from strategies to improve their daily level of physical activity. This would help restore their energy levels and motivation both in and out of the school environment.

Childhood obesity is a multi-factorial issue combining environmental factors such as family, school, peers, community leaders, media, one's own mental perception, and motivation, in combination with genetic factors. Psychological issues can also result from long-standing obesity—poor self-esteem, depression, eating disorders, and negative family dynamics.[15] A support system that consistently encourages an overweight or obese child to eat nutritious foods and exercise regularly accounts for a bulk of the solution. It turns out that exercise is good for learning, as well as having a positive effect on anxiety, depression, ADHD, addiction, hormonal imbalances, and aging.[16]

Approximately 60 percent of overweight children and adolescents have at least one additional risk factor for cardiovascular disease.[17] Overweight children are also more likely to have broken bones and joint problems. This poses a double negative because musculoskeletal pain often leads to reduced mobility, agility, and consequently, decreased levels of physical activity. Evidence suggests that some children are at an elevated risk for becoming overweight adults. Children who have overweight biological parents are twice as likely to become overweight in adulthood, as compared to children with parents of a healthy weight.[18]

Awareness concerning this issue is necessary because for the first time, there is an unfortunate possibility that this generation of children may not live as long as their parents in terms of life span. Considering the fact that the gene pool of today's kids has not changed from the previous generation of kids or their parents, only environmental effects on energy balance can account for the increased incidence of overweight and obese children. How often children play video games, talk on the phone, watch television, and spend time on the computer translates into time not spent getting a healthy dose of physical activity in their daily schedule. It is important not to let these multimedia pieces of equipment take the job of the babysitter. It is easy for them to occupy a child's attention until it is time to eat and then time to go to sleep.

ENCOURAGE PHYSICAL ACTIVITY

Putting limits on the use of electronics is paramount to reducing the effects of excessive media use on a child's mental, physical, academic, and social well-being. There is not much we can do about having fast-food restaurants, video games, cell phones, televisions, and computers in our society. There is, however, something that you can do about restricting your child's time using electronics and influencing their choices about eating healthy and being physically active.

Here are some strategies to help get your child *more physically active*:

- **Get your child involved in an age-appropriate activity that involves physical exertion**—Exposing your children to many forms of aerobic exercise and allowing them to choose what they would like to play, within safe and acceptable guidelines, increases their motivation to willingly do the activity. When given a choice, your child will be able to discover what they truly enjoy doing. The activity should be age-appropriate and suitable for your child's attention span, motor skills, and emotional maturity.
- **Be a role model for good health**—Participate in fun, heart-pumping activities with your child and keep it non-competitive, at least to start, so that they want to continue with the activity. Plan healthy activities where the whole family can participate. Examples include after-dinner walks, weekend hikes, bicycle rides, swimming, and skiing with your children. It is recommended that your child get at least 60 minutes a day of some form of moderate- to vigorous-intensity aerobic activity to maintain a high metabolism.[19]

- **Encourage "*activity*" over "*exercise*"**—Keeping it fun and allowing your child to choose the special activity is more exciting than "having to exercise." Encourage more physical activity by doing something fun like playing an outdoor game, running around with the family pet, or taking it for a walk.
- **Limit the amount of time that your child spends doing sedentary activities**—School-aged children should not be inactive for periods lasting more than two hours; younger children should not have an inactivity period for more than one hour. Encourage safe outdoor play with siblings and/or friends, if possible.
- **Establish a regular schedule for your child to participate in physical activities**—Encourage your child to participate in extracurricular activities after school. This is a great opportunity for your child to engage in a variety of fun-filled activities and experience positive group interactions.
- **Schedule daily active chores for your child to accomplish**—Choose age-appropriate chores that involve active movement such as vacuuming, collecting household trash, collecting dirty clothes and bringing them to the laundry room, taking the garbage to and from the curb, raking the leaves, weeding the garden, cutting the lawn, and shoveling snow.
- **Help create an activity program for your child**—If the community or school system does not support or is unable to afford athletic programs, you can initiate an activity into action by choosing one that your child and their peers would like to do. From there, you and other parents can locate a play area and schedule a day or two a week that best works for everyone to share in supervising an activity. This would help prompt children of all abilities and interests to get involved in a fun, physical activity. Start with noncompetitive games or activities in which everybody is involved and is a winner. Examples include nature hikes, bicycle rides on trails, scavenger hunts, or active noncompetitive games.
- **Sign your child up for a favorite sport**—If team sports are not his or her favorite, try karate, tennis, or yoga. Dance, gymnastics, golf, and even bowling can be a great way to get more physical exercise.

Refer to the chart showing the recommended daily caloric intake for children based on their age, gender, and physical activity levels.[20]

Daily Caloric Intake Recommendations for Children by Age, Gender, and Physical Activity

	Age (years)	Sedentary (calories)	Moderately Active (calories)	Very Active (calories)
Child	2–3	1,000	1,000–1,400	1,000–1,400
Female	4–8	1,200	1,400–1,600	1,400–1,800
	9–13	1,600	1,600–2,000	1,800–2,200
	14–18	1,800	2,000	2,400
Male	4–8	1,400	1,400–1,600	1,600–2,000
	9–13	1,800	1,800–2,200	2,000–2,600
	14–18	2,200	2,400–2,800	2,800–3,200

To get a better picture of how well you are setting your child up for healthy lifestyle habits, here are some questions to ask yourself:

- What foods do you have in your home?
- What foods do you eat daily?
- What messages do you tell your child about food?
- Do you encourage your child to engage in regular physical activity?
- How much physical activity do you get on a daily basis?
- What limits do you impose for cell phone/computer/video game/ television usage?
- Are you and your child's other parent on the same page with regards to eating and exercising practices?
- Do you ask your child for their input about healthy foods that they would enjoy eating regularly?
- Do you support a daily routine for your child so they can develop good eating and exercise habits?

It has been clearly demonstrated that a well-balanced diet and sufficient exercise help children grow and develop properly. Providing your children with a variety of healthy food choices and getting them involved in physical activities early in life better ensures their healthy development and long-term healthy lifestyle throughout adulthood.

———◦———

Instill healthy eating habits and an active lifestyle in your child early on to reduce the risk of health-related problems later in life.

———◦———

Conclusion

Creating a Positive Foundation
for Unleashing Your Child's Unlimited Potential

"We are unlimited in what we can achieve."

—Douglas Haddad, Ph.D. (author and educator)

Children today are doing some incredible things across the world. We see kids in movies and on television as child actors, on reality shows showcasing their talents and competing against adults, coming up with inventions for early cancer detection and helping people with different diseases, starting businesses worth millions of dollars, publishing books, designing and writing code for their own animations, and creating video games.

Also, many kids are volunteering their time to help others, getting involved in raising money for different causes, giving their own savings to help others in need, donating their hair to make wigs for people with cancer, and supporting causes that are close to their heart. Children are achieving at all kinds of levels academically, athletically, and as young leaders in their communities, making a difference through their talents, actions, and examples set forth.

Just about every parent wants the best for their children. They want to see their child grow up to be successful in all areas of their life and reach their full potential. However, it is also important to notice when the pressure and expectations can be too much on a child and result in negative effects.

Many of today's teens and tweens are being pressured and pulled in so many directions and lose their sense of self, become anxious, angry, emotionally drained, and lose intrinsic motivation and desire to achieve different things in life. This type of intense pressure around school, friends, athletics, and overall performance can lead to social, emotional, and physical stress.

After applying the "Child Unlimited Principles" that you have read throughout this book, you will have the necessary tools to apply optimal

209

support to help your child stay organized and on track academically, socially, emotionally, athletically, and throughout all avenues of their life to unlock their full potential and achieve the three S's: be *smart*, be *successful*, and be *self-disciplined*.

WHAT DOES "SMART" LOOK LIKE IN YOUR CHILD?

Intelligence has been defined in many different ways and varies from person to person.

Unfortunately, many kids who do not get good grades in school feel "stupid" or "dumb." This can have a lasting effect on a young person's psyche, diminish their self-esteem, and hinder future activities. However, "being smart" comes in a variety of forms.

Some children can correctly answer math problems in a short time frame. Other children create original stories or poems. Some kids can fix or build things with their hands, while others have a knack at drawing, acting, dancing, helping people in need, catching a football, playing the piano, creating and editing videos, or telling stories to others.

Teens and tweens who struggle for identity may find a sense of purpose or accomplishment in a certain sport or activity that is different from their siblings or peers.

Children cannot excel at every facet of "smart" and when the focus of "being smart" is centered on only one aspect—academic, athletic, creative, or social—that can significantly limit a child's self-discovery of their innate and unique talents out of a false belief system about their overall intelligence.

One of the jobs of raising a "smart" child is to provide opportunities for them to discover their own interests and talents while you continue to foster their passion and encourage them to be their best self.

WHAT DOES "SUCCESSFUL" LOOK LIKE IN YOUR CHILD?

People have their own definitions of "success" and equate it with things like money, prestige, power, the level of education obtained, mastering a particular skill, or accomplishing any result you set forth to achieve. No matter what view of success you may have, the "feeling of success" by your child is what counts.

Oftentimes, a parent's high expectations and critical evaluation of a child's achievement have been linked with a child's development of *fear of failure* and *feelings of shame and guilt* when not meeting parental expectations.[1] Raising successful children goes beyond the realm of achievements and status, and is rooted in a child's level of happiness.

Marci Shimoff, *New York Times* bestselling author of *Happy for No Reason*, said that success doesn't bring you happiness, but rather being happy brings you success.[2] Being happy is doing what you love to do in fulfilling your soul's purpose. A goal of raising a successful child is to help identify and guide a child's unique purpose and allow them to fulfill it through whatever means are necessary.

In education, the focus is typically on teaching a child skills that are necessary to succeed in the workforce, such as reading, writing, math, and problem-solving skills, and then choosing a career that fulfills a specific need in the world. Howard Thurman, author, educator, and civil rights leader spoke on what people should consider when faced with making decisions about what they should be doing with their lives. He said, "Don't ask what the world needs. Ask what makes you come alive, and go do it. Because what the world needs is people who have come alive."[3]

As your children go to school, play sports, read books, and engage in extracurricular activities, find out if they are experiencing joy, excitement, enthusiasm, passion, and meaning in what they are doing. If they are, that sense of aliveness is your child's built-in feedback system, telling them that they are on course to fulfill their purpose and what they should be doing in this world.

WHAT DOES "SELF-DISCIPLINED" LOOK LIKE IN YOUR CHILD?

Self-discipline is one of the most important qualities a child can develop. There is no formula for teaching children to become self-disciplined overnight. A child's social, mental, emotional, and physical well-being requires self-discipline. When children are taught self-control and how to respond in different social situations with a positive attitude and how to handle different pressures, they feel empowered and have the necessary tools to make good decisions. Children develop self-confidence and self-worth if they are able to self-manage and make decisions for themselves.

Knowing how to listen, speak in turn, say thank you and please, delay gratification, control impulses, and channel negative emotions appropriately all take practice. By modeling these behaviors and providing positive reinforcement, children will be able to carry out these important skills throughout their lives.

Getting your child involved in sports, music, and daily routines such as studying and doing homework at a set time, going to bed the same time each night, doing chores around the house, taking care of a pet, and doing other family-related activities provide a child with opportunities to learn responsibility, set goals, and build their self-discipline.

Some parents try to give their child a comfortable life by taking away responsibilities, making excuses and justifying their child's behavior, and failing to hold them accountable for their actions. Setting rules and expectations and following through with them is hard work as a parent, but it is the key ingredient toward developing your child's self-discipline.

MAKING A CONSCIOUS EFFORT TO FOCUS ON THE POSITIVE IN ALL THINGS

In a world filled with images, messages, and pressures that can sway a child away from achieving the three S's, it is important to realize that feelings of happiness don't come about by chance; they are the result of daily thought patterns, choices made, and actions taken. Your child will not always make the right decisions, but they can benefit from making their own decisions and learn life lessons along the way.

FOCUS POINTS FOR DEVELOPING THE THREE S'S IN YOUR CHILD SO THEY BECOME *UNLIMITED* IN THEIR POTENTIAL

- Put *love* and *acceptance* as top priorities with your child.
- Remain patient and calm with your child through difficult times. How you react in different situations models much of your child's behavior, including the ways they handle adversity.
- Allow your child to experience just being a kid. Refrain from adding intense pressure to succeed or imparting your personal stresses onto your child.
- Pay attention to your child and actively listen to what they are saying. Allow them to regularly communicate their feelings openly and honestly, without judgment, about a variety of topics from a young age.
- Allow your child to make decisions and hold them accountable for their actions.
- Get your child into daily routines and help them set goals.

- Applaud effort and encourage a child to persevere when they fall short of their goals.
- Get to know your child's friends and teachers.
- Draw boundaries and say "no" to your child when it comes to things that are unsafe or unreasonable.
- Spend quality family time together with your child.
- If possible, enjoy a family dinner together, free of electronic devices.
- Get your child involved in regular physical activity, healthy eating, and healthy sleeping patterns.
- Seek treatment early for any mental or physical disorder.

Children grow up quickly and they learn core principles of life from their parents. If a child has been waited on, not allowed to contribute to the household, hasn't given of their time, money, and service to others, and had parents pick up the pieces when things went bad, they will have a difficult transition and trouble adapting when they venture into life in the real world.

Through the years, you have an opportunity to leave an unforgettable impression on a young person's life like no one else. The time will come when your children will no longer be getting ready for school, doing their homework, and performing chores around the house. You will no longer be there to hold your child's hand and make them accountable for their actions.

By incorporating the *child unlimited* tools for nurturing the three S's in your adolescent starting today, your child will develop a strong sense of self and become *unlimited* in whatever road they choose to take along their life path. I leave you with the words of renowned advice columnist Ann Landers who wisely stated,

"It is not what you do for your children, but what you have taught them to do for themselves, that will make them successful human beings."[4]

Notes

INTRODUCTION

1. Dan Kelly, "Experts Testify That Truant Parents Should Not Be Jailed," *Reading Eagle*, September 23, 2014. Accessed October 11, 2015. http://readingeagle.com/news/article/experts-testify-that-truant-parents-should-not-be-jailed&template=mobileart.

2. Michael Males, "For Adults, Today's Youth Are Always the Worst," *Los Angeles Times*, November 21, 1999.

3. Michael Males, "For Adults, Today's Youth Are Always the Worst," *Los Angeles Times*, November 21, 1999.

4. Everytown for Gun Safety Support Fund. "173 School Shootings in America Since 2013." Accessed October 10, 2015. http://everytownresearch.org/school-shootings/.

CHAPTER 1

1. Foster Cline and Jim Fay, *Parenting with Love and Logic* (Colorado Springs, CO: NavPress Publishing, 2011).

CHAPTER 2

1. Kenneth Ginsburg, "The Importance of Play in Promoting Healthy Child Development and Maintaining Strong Parent–Child Bonds," *Pediatrics* 119 (2007): 182–91.

CHAPTER 3

1. AZ Quotes. "Sara Lawrence-Lightfoot Quotes." Accessed March 13, 2016. http://www.azquotes.com/quote/1264794.

2. Brainy Quote. "Hulk Hogan Quotes." Accessed November 1, 2015. http://www.brainyquote.com/quotes/authors/h/hulk_hogan.html.

3. N. Benokraitis, *Marriages and Families: Changes, Choices, and Constraints* (Englewood Cliffs, NJ: Pearson Prentice Hall, 2008).

4. CNN, "How to Make Your Kid Hate Sports without Really Trying." Accessed January 21, 2016, http://www.safekids.org/.

5. HSLDA, "Homeschool Progress Report 2009." Accessed January 20, 2013, http://www.hslda.org/docs/study/ray2009/2009_Ray_StudyFINAL.pdf.

6. NHERI, "Research Facts on Homeschooling." Accessed March 23, 2016, http://www.nheri.org/research/research-facts-on-homeschooling.html.

7. NHERI, "Research Facts on Homeschooling." Accessed March 23, 2016, http://www.nheri.org/research/research-facts-on-homeschooling.html.

8. United States Census Bureau, "America's Families and Living Arrangements: 2013: Children." Accessed October 20, 2015, https://www.census.gov/hhes/families/data/cps2013C.html.

9. Joe Peters, *Cry Silent Tears* (New York: Harper Element, 2008).

10. Psychology, "Emotional Development—Early Infancy (Birth–Six Months), Later Infancy Months (7–12)." Accessed October 21, 2015, http://psychology.jrank.org/pages/212/Emotional-Development.html.

11. Office of the Surgeon General (U.S.); National Center for Injury Prevention and Control (U.S.); National Institute of Mental Health (U.S.); Center for Mental Health Services (U.S.). Rockville (MD): Office of the Surgeon General (U.S.). *Youth Violence: A Report of the Surgeon General*. 2001.

CHAPTER 4

1. Charlotte Kasl, *If the Buddha Had Kids: Raising Children to Create a More Peaceful World* (New York: Penguin, 2012). Used by permission.

2. Frank Lawlis, *Mending the Broken Bond* (New York: Viking, 2007).

3. Encyclopedia of Children's Health, "Cognitive Development." Accessed March 13, 2016, http://www.healthofchildren.com/C/Cognitive-Development.html.

CHAPTER 5

1. J. Banks, "Childhood Discipline: Challenges for Clinicians and Parents," *American Family Physician* 66(8) (2002):1447–53.

2. Global Issues, "Children as Consumers." Accessed January 11, 2013, http://www.globalissues.org/print/article/237.

3. Kim Payne and Lisa Ross, *Simplicity Parenting: Using the Extraordinary Power of Less to Raise Calmer, Happier, and More Secure Kids* (New York: Ballantine Books, 2010).

4. Alfie Kohn, "Five Reasons to Stop Saying 'Good Job!'" Accessed June 21, 2016, http://www.alfiekohn.org/article/five-reasons-stop-saying-good-job/.

5. Jerry Adams, *Discipline without Anger: A Parent's Guide to Teaching Children Responsible Behavior* (Bloomington, IN: AuthorHouse, 2008).

CHAPTER 6

1. Isabel Myers and Peter Myers, *Gifts Differing: Understanding Personality Type* (Palo Alto, CA: Davies-Black Publishing, 1995).

2. Laurie Sargent, *Delight in Your Child's Design* (Wheaton, IL: Tyndale House Publishers, 2005).

3. M. Kimmel, "Masculinity as Homophobia Fear, Shame, and Silence in the Construction of Gender Identity," in *Theorizing Masculinities*, eds. Harry Brod and Michael Kaufman (Thousand Oaks, CA: SAGE, 1994): 227–41, doi: 10.4135/9781452243627.n7.

4. Albert Bandura, *Social Learning and Personality Development* (New York: International Thomson Publishing, 1963).

5. L. H. Weiss and J.C. Schwarz, "The Relationship between Parenting Types and Older Adolescents' Personality, Academic Achievement, Adjustment, and Substance Use," *Child Development*, 67(5) (1996): 2101–14.

6. Kevin Leman, *The Birth Order Book: Why You Are the Way You Are* (Grand Rapids, MI: Revell, 2004).

CHAPTER 7

1. BBC News, "Child Watch: The Apps That Let Parents 'Spy' on Their Kids." Accessed November 3, 2015, http://www.bbc.com/news/technology-30930512.

2. Bernie Siegel, *Peace, Love and Healing* (New York: HarperCollins Publishers, 1989).

CHAPTER 8

1. Haim Ginott, *Between Parent and Teenager* (New York: Scribner, 1969).

2. Quotes, "Famous Quotes and Sayings." Accessed November 13, 2015, http://www.quotes.net/quote/1931.

3. Howard Gardner. *Leading Minds: An Anatomy Of Leadership*. (New York: The Perseus Books Group, 1995).

4. Catherine Moreton, "10 Qualities That Made Abraham Lincoln a Great Leader." Accessed February 4, 2013, https://hr.blr.com/whitepapers/Staffing-Training/Leadership/10-Qualities-that-Made-Abraham-Lincoln-a-Great-Lea.

5. Listverse, "10 Great Philanthropists Who Are Kids." Accessed February 6, 2013, http://listverse.com/2011/01/27/10-great-philanthropists-who-are-kids/.

CHAPTER 9

1. Brainy Quotes. "Tony Robbins Quotes." March 14, 2016, http://www.brainyquote.com/quotes/quotes/t/tonyrobbin147771.html.

2. G. Brown, "India Must Ban Child Labor," December 21, 2012. Accessed November 14, 2015, http://www.huffingtonpost.com/gordon-brown/india-child-labor-laws_b_2345756.html.

3. L. Smith, "World Day against Child Labour 2015: Facts and Figures about Children in Forced Labour," June 12, 2015. Accessed November 16, 2015, http://www.ibtimes.co.uk/world-day-against-child-labour-2015-facts-figures-about-children-forced-labour-1505675.

4. The Office of the UN Special Envoy for Global Education, July 20, 2013, http://educationenvoy.org

5. D. Goslin, *Engaging Minds: Motivation and Learning in America's Schools*, (Lanham, MD: Scarecrow Press, 2003).

6. J. Twenge and W. Campbell, *The Narcissism Epidemic: Living in the Age of Entitlement* (New York: Free Press, 2010).

7. E. Kolbert, "Spoiled Rotten: Why Do Kids Rule the Roost?" July 2, 2012. Accessed February 3, 2013, http://www.newyorker.com/arts/critics/books/2012/07/02/120702crbo_books_kolbert.

8. NASP Resources: Helping children achieve their best. In school. At home. In life. 2013. Accessed February 13, 2013, http://www.nasponline.org/resources/home_school/earlychildmotiv_ho.aspx.

9. The Positivity Blog, "Zig Ziglar's Timeless Guide to Motivation." Accessed March 14, 2016, http://www.positivityblog.com/index.php/2012/12/06/zig-ziglar.

10. John Demartini, *The Values Factor: The Secret to Creating an Inspired and Fulfilling Life* (New York: Berkley Books, 2013).

11. Mojdeh Bayat, "Clarifying Issues Regarding the Use of Praise with Young Children," *Topics in Special Education* 31(2) (2011): 121–28.

CHAPTER 10

1. Good Reads. "Robert H. Schuller Quotes." Accessed February 2, 2016, http://www.goodreads.com/quotes/938611-goals-are-not-only-absolutely-necessary-to-motivate-us-they.

2. Cynthia Kersey, *Unstoppable: 45 Powerful Stories of Perseverance and Triumph from People Just Like You* (Naperville, IL: Sourcebooks, Inc., 1998).

3. Free the Children. "Our Mission and Our Model." Accessed November 10, 2015, http://www.freethechildren.com/about-us/our-model/.

4. Good Reads. "Anthony Robbins Quotes." Accessed March 14, 2016, http://www.goodreads.com/quotes/33903-people-who-fail-focus-on-what-they-will-have-to.

5. Michael Phelps and Brian Cazeneuve, *Beneath the Surface: My Story* (New York: Sports Publishing, 2012).

6. Gary Blair, "The Goals Guy." Accessed on March 7, 2013, http://www.goals-guy.com/Events/k_overview.html

7. Jack Canfield, *The Success Principles* (New York: HarperCollins Publishing, 2014).

8. Michael Jeffreys, *Success Secrets of the Motivational Superstars* (Rocklin, CA: Prima Lifestyles, 1996).

9. Napoleon Hill, *Think and Grow Rich* (New York: The Random House Publishing Group, 1937).

CHAPTER 11

1. Jeff Dess, Tammy White, Elizabeth Jaffe, and Steven Jaffe, *Understanding Playful vs. Hurtful Teasing and Bullying Behavior* (2011). Accessed February 2, 2016, http://www.cobbk12.org/bully/MidHighCCSD.pdf.

2. Daily News, "WATCH: Maryland Teen Bullied While Taping News Segment about Bullying." Accessed October 12, 2012, http://www.nydailynews.com/news/national/watch-teen-bullied-news-piece-bullying-article-1.1179008.

3. National School Boards Association, "Bullying Definitions in State Anti-Bullying Statues." Accessed February 28, 2012, https://www.nsba.org/sites/default/files/reports/State_Anti-Bullying_Statutes_Definitions_02_2012.pdf.

4. S. Lereya, W. Copeland, E. Costello, and D. Wolke, "Adult Mental Health Consequences of Peer Bullying and Maltreatment in Childhood: Two Cohorts in Two Countries," *The Lancet Psychiatry* 2(6) (2015): 524–31.

5. True Crime Report, "Phoebe Prince, 15, Commits Suicide after Onslaught of Cyber-Bullying from Fellow Students." Accessed January 28, 2010, http://www.truecrimereport.com/2010/01/phoebe_prince_15_commits_suici.php.

CHAPTER 12

1. M. Lysiak, "Why Adam Lanza Did It," January 7, 2014. Accessed February 15, 2016, http://www.newsweek.com/why-adam-lanza-did-it-226565

2. E. Landau, "Rejection, Bullying Are Risk Factors among Shooters," December 19, 2012. Accessed February 15, 2016, http://www.cnn.com/2012/12/18/health/ct-shooting-mental-illness/.

3. E. Landau, "Rejection, Bullying Are Risk Factors among Shooters," December 19, 2012. Accessed February 15, 2016, http://www.cnn.com/2012/12/18/health/ct-shooting-mental-illness/.

4. J. Garbarino, "How a Boy Becomes a Killer," December 19, 2012. Accessed February 15, 2016, http://www.cnn.com/2012/12/19/opinion/garbarino-violence-boys/.

5. S. Mednick, *Biological Bases of Antisocial Behavior* (Norwell, MA: Kluwer, 1988).

6. A. Sameroff, R. Seifer, R. Barocas, M. Zax, and S. Greenspan, "Intelligence Quotient Scores of 4-Year-Old Children: Social-Environmental Risk Factors," *Pediatrics* 79 (1987): 343–50.

7. E. Landau, "Rejection, Bullying Are Risk Factors among Shooters," December 19, 2012. Accessed February 15, 2016, http://www.cnn.com/2012/12/18/health/ct-shooting-mental-illness/.

8. The Washington Times. "142 school shootings since Sandy Hook massacre in Newtown, Conn.," *Washington Times*, October 1, 2015. Accessed February 15, 2016, http://www.washingtontimes.com/news/2015/oct/1/142-school-shootings-sandy-hook-massacre-newtown-c/.

9. Mark Ames, "Virginia Tech: Is the Scene of the Crime the Cause of the Crime?" Alternet, April 19, 2007. Accessed February 15, 2016, http://www.alternet.org/story/50758/virginia_tech%3A_is_the_scene_of_the_crime_the_cause_of_the_crime.

10. "'You Forced Me into a Corner,' Cho Says," *Washington Post*, April 19, 2007. Accessed February 15, 2016, http://www.washingtonpost.com/wp-dyn/content/article/2007/04/18/AR2007041802789.html.

11. Religious Tolerance, "Shootings, Other Violence, and Bullying in American Schools." Accessed February 15, 2016, http://www.religioustolerance.org/sch_viol.htm.

12. Daily Mail.com, "How 'Ticking Time Bomb' Adam Lanza Went from 'Genius' Tech Geek Who Grew Up in a $1.6 Million Home to Heartless Killer." December 16, 2012. Accessed February 16, 2016, http://www.dailymail.co.uk/news/article-2248782/Adam-Lanza-How-classmates-remember-genius-turned-heartless-killer.html.

13. CDC.gov, "Youth Violence: Facts at a Glance." November 25, 2015. http://www.cdc.gov/violenceprevention/pdf/yv-datasheet-a.pdf.

14. James Gilligan, *Preventing Violence* (New York: Thames & Hudson, 2001).

15. James Gilligan, "Shame, Guilt, and Violence," *Social Research* 70(4) (2003): 1149.

16. M. Kimmel and M. Mahler, "Adolescent Masculinity, Homophobia, and Violence," *American Behavioral Scientist* 46 (10) (2003): 1439–58.

17. Frank Peretti, *No More Bullies: For Those Who Wound or Are Wounded* (Nashville, TN: W Publishing Group, 2000).

18. "American Psycho," *The Times.* Accessed February 15, 2016, http://www.timesonline.co.uk/tol/news/world/us_and_americas/article1686784.ece.

19. "In Quotes: Virginia Gunman's Message," BBC News, April 19, 2007. Accessed February 15, 2016, http://news.bbc.co.uk/2/hi/americas/6570369.stm.

20. Eugene V. Beresin, "The Impact of Media Violence on Children and Adolescents: Opportunities for Clinical Interventions," American Academy of Child and Adolescent Psychiatry. Accessed July 14, 2013, https://www.aacap.org/aacap/Medical_Students_and_Residents/Mentorship_Matters/DevelopMentor/The_Impact_of_Media_Violence_on_Children_and_Adolescents_Opportunities_for_Clinical_Interventions.aspx.

21. "Depression: What You Need to Know," National Institute of Mental Health. Accessed July 14, 2013, http://www.nimh.nih.gov/health/publications/depression/complete-index.shtml#pub3.

22. Dave Grossman and Gloria Dagaetano, *Stop Teaching Our Kids to Kill: A Call to Action against TV, Movie and Video Game Violence.* (New York: Crown Publishers, 1999).

23. The Henry J. Kaiser Family Foundation. "Generation M2: Media in the Lives of 8–18 Year Olds," January 1, 2010. Accessed July 15, 2013, http://kff.org/other/poll-finding/report-generation-m2-media-in-the-lives/.

24. Tiffany Hsu, "Wal-Mart Worker Dies after Stampede in N.Y," *Los Angeles Times*, November 29, 2008. Accessed November 29, 2008, http://articles.latimes.com/2008/nov/29/nation/na-walmart-death29.

25. Jaya Narain, "Coroner Warns of Video Game Danger after Boy, 14, Dies: 18-Rating Is There for a Reason He Tells Distraught Mother," MailOnline.com, September 5, 2012. Accessed July 15, 2013, http://www.dailymail.co.uk/news/article-2198549/Coroner-warns-Call-Duty-video-game-danger-boy-14-dies-18-rating-reason-tells-distraught-mother.html.

26. Jaya Narain, "Coroner Warns of Video Game Danger after Boy, 14, Dies: 18-Rating Is There for a Reason He Tells Distraught Mother," MailOnline.com, September 5, 2012. Accessed July 15, 2013, http://www.dailymail.co.uk/news/article-2198549/Coroner-warns-Call-Duty-video-game-danger-boy-14-dies-18-rating-reason-tells-distraught-mother.html.

CHAPTER 13

1. Successories, "Jon Kelly Quotes." Accessed February 16, 2016, http://www.successories.com/iquote/author/29830/jon-kelly-quotes/1.

2. D. Jacobs, "Youth Gambling in North America: Long-Term Trends and Future Prospects," in *Gambling Problems in Youth: Theoretical and Applied Perspectives*, ed. J. Derevensky and R. Gupta (New York: Kluwer Academic/Plenum Publishers, 2004).

3. Paula Lavigne, "Youth Coaches Face Gambling Charges," ESPN.com, October 30, 2012. Accessed February 16, 2016, http://espn.go.com/espn/otl/story/_/id/8568724/nine-south-florida-youth-football-coaches-face-gambling-charges.

4. Paula Lavigne, "Youth Coaches Face Gambling Charges," ESPN.com, October 30, 2012. Accessed February 16, 2016, http://espn.go.com/espn/otl/story/_/id/8568724/nine-south-florida-youth-football-coaches-face-gambling-charges.

5. ABC Local 10 News, "Youth football coaches charged in 'Operation Dirty Play," October 31, 2012. Accessed February 16, 2016, http://www.local10.com/news/youth-football-coaches-charged-in-operation-dirty-play.

6. CRC Health, "Teen Addiction to Online Gambling." Accessed June 22, 2016, http://www.crchealth.com/troubled-teenagers/teen-gambling/.

7. St. Joseph's Care Group, "Youth Addiction Programs." Accessed February 19, 2016, http://www.mha.sjcg.net/as/gambling/youth/.

8. Saskatchewan, "Problem Gambling and Youth," Accessed July 16, 2013, http://www.saskatchewan.ca/residents/health/accessing-health-care-services/mental-health-and-addictions-support-services/gambling-support/problem-gambling-resources#problem-gambling-and-youth.

9. Florida Council on Compulsive Gambling, "Lottery Tickets Aren't Kids Play," December 10, 2014. Accessed February 16, 2016, http://www.gamblinghelp.org/fccg/read_news/54.

10. Steve268, "Online Gambling Has Ruined My Life," Gambling Therapy, September 27, 2012. Accessed September 27, 2013, https://www.gamblingtherapy.org/online-gambling-has-ruined-my-life.

11. Steve268, "Online Gambling Has Ruined My Life," Gambling Therapy, September 27, 2012. Accessed September 27, 2013, https://www.gamblingtherapy.org/online-gambling-has-ruined-my-life.

12. National Council on Problem Gambling. "Screening Tools," National Endowment for Financial Education, 2000. Accessed February 16, 2016. http://www.ncpgambling.org/wp-content/uploads/2014/08/problem_gamblers_finances-a-guide-for-treatment-profs.pdf.

CHAPTER 14

1. Angelfire, "Quotes by Famous People." Accessed March 16, 2016, http://www.angelfire.com/tn/Quotes/famous.html.

2. CDC, "Vital Signs: Births to Teens Aged 15–17 Years – United States, 1991–2012," April 11, 2014. Accessed February 17, 2016, http://www.cdc.gov/mmwr/preview/mmwrhtml/mm6314a4.htm?s_cid=mm6314a4_w.

3. Mish Way, "Teen Mom: The Most Depressing Show on Earth," *Hearty Magazine*, December 10, 2009.

4. CDC, "National Survey of Family Growth," Accessed December 6, 2015, http://www.cdc.gov/nchs/nsfg.htm.

5. CDC, "April Is STD Awareness Month." Accessed July 18, 2013, http://www.cdc.gov/features/stdawareness/index.html#references.

6. Margaret J. Meeker, *Your Kids at Risk: How Teen Sex Threatens Our Sons and Daughters* (Washington, DC: Regnery Publishing Company, 2007).

7. Tamar Lewin, "Are These Parties for Real," *The New York Times*, August 27, 2009.

8. J. Mendle, J. Jerrero, S. Moore, and K. Harden, "Depression and Adolescent Sexual Activity in Romantic and Nonromantic Relational Contexts: A Genetically-Informative Sibling Comparison," *Journal of Abnormal Psychology* 122(1) (2013): 51–63.

9. R. E. Rector, K. A. Johnson, and L. R. Noyes, "Sexually Active Teenagers Are More Likely to Be Depressed and to Attempt Suicide," *Center for Data Analysis Report, #03-04* (2003).

10. D. Hallfors et al., "Which Comes First in Adolescence—Sex and Drugs or Depression?" *American Journal of Preventive Medicine* 29(3) (2005): 163–70.

11. Karen Powell, "Does Sexting Take the Place of Sex for Teenagers?" FYI, September 27, 2012. Accessed July 18, 2013, http://fulleryouthinstitute.org/blog/does-sexting-take-the-place-of-sex-for-teenagers.

12. Amanda Lenhart, "Teens, Social Media and Technology Overview 2015," Pew Research Center, April 9, 2015. Accessed February 20, 2016, http://www.pewinternet.org/2015/04/09/teens-social-media-technology-2015/.

13. John Ribeiro, "Social App Skout Suspends Teen Community after Rape Allegations," PC World, June 13, 2012. Accessed February 20, 2016, http://www.pcworld.com/article/257505/social_app_skout_suspends_teen_community_after_rape_allegations.html.

14. The Henry J. Kaiser Family Foundation and The National Center on Addiction and Substance Abuse at Columbia University, "Millions of Young People Mix Sex with Alcohol or Drugs—With Dangerous Consequences," January 30, 2002. Accessed February 20, 2016, http://kff.org/hivaids/fact-sheet/sexual-activity-and-substance-use-among-youth/.

15. National Conference of State Legislatures, "State Policies on Sex Education in Schools." Accessed February 20, 2016, http://www.ncsl.org/research/health/state-policies-on-sex-education-in-schools.aspx#1.

16. Resolute Treatment Center, "Causes and Symptoms of Sexually Maladaptive Behaviors." Accessed February 20, 2016, http://www.resolutetreatmentcenter.com/behavioral/sexually-maladaptive/symptoms-effects.

17. Desert Hills, "Causes and Symptoms of Impulse Control Disorder," http://www.deserthills-nm.com/behavioral/impulse-control/signs-symptoms-effects.

18. P. Orpinas, A. Home, X. Song, P. Reeves, and H. Hsieh, "Dating Trajectories from Middle to High School: Association with Academic Performance and Drug Use," *Journal of Research on Adolescence* 23(4) (2013): 772–84.

CHAPTER 15

1. Quotes-Messages. Accessed March 16, 2016, http://www.quotes-messages.com/search-list.

2. Christina Zdanowicz, "Teen Narrowly Escapes Death after Smoking Synthetic Marijuana," CNN.com, February 5, 2013. Accessed July 19, 2013, http://www.cnn.com/2013/02/04/health/synthetic-marijuana-irpt.

3. Donna Bush and David Woodwell, "Update: Drug-Related Emergency Department Visits Involving Synthetic Cannabinoids," *SAMHSA: The CBHSQ Report*, October 16, 2014, http://www.samhsa.gov/data/sites/default/files/SR-1378/SR-1378.pdf.

4. R. Law et al., "Notes from the Field: Increase in Reported Adverse Health Effects Related to Synthetic Cannabionoid Use—United States, January-May 2015," *Morbidity and Mortality Weekly Report* 64(22) (2015): 618–19.

5. Stephanie Pappas, "Latest Designer Drug Called 'Smiles' Linked to Teen Deaths," September 21, 2012. Accessed July 19, 2013, http://www.livescience.com/23388-designer-drug-smiles-teen-deaths.html.

6. CADCA, "2012 Monitoring the Future Survey Finds Marijuana Use Continuing to Rise among Youth." Accessed July 19, 2013, http://www.cadca.org/resources/detail/2012-monitoring-future-survey-finds-marijuana-use-continuing-rise-among-youth.

7. NIH, "Marijuana." Accessed December 12, 2015, http://www.drugabuse.gov/PDF/RRMarijuana.pdf.

8. Colorado Department of Revenue, "Colorado Marijuana Tax Data." Accessed December 12, 2015, https://www.colorado.gov/pacific/revenue/colorado-marijuana-tax-data.

9. Aaron Smith, "Marijuana Legalization Passes in Colorado, Washington," CNN.com, November 8, 2012. Accessed July 20, 2013, http://money.cnn.com/2012/11/07/news/economy/marijuana-legalization-washington-colorado/index.html.

10. American College of Pediatricians, "Report Confirms Marijuana is Dangerous," September 22, 2015. Accessed December 12, 2015, http://www.acpeds.org/report-confirms-marijuana-is-dangerous.

11. Bill Bumpas, "Colorado Youth Marijuana Use Highest since Legalization," OneNewsNow.com, September 29, 2015. Accessed February 22, 2016, http://www.onenewsnow.com/culture/2015/09/29/colorado-youth-marijuana-use-highest-since-legalization.

12. Partnership for Drug-Free Kids, "Prescription for Danger: A Report on the Troubling Trend of Prescription and Over-the-Counter Drug Abuse among the Nation's Teens." Accessed January 4, 2016, https://www.drugfreeactionalliance.org/files/downloadables/background-knowledge/B-Prescription-for-Danger.pdf.

13. The Partnership for Drug-Free Kids. "The Partnership Attitude Tracking Study: Teens and Parents 2013." Accessed June 23, 2016, http://www.drugfree.org/wp-content/uploads/2014/07/PATS-2013-FULL-REPORT.pdf.

14. R. Morgan Griffin. "Teen Abuse of Cough and Cold Medicine." Accessed June 23, 2016, http://www.webmd.com/parenting/teen-abuse-cough-medicine-9/teens-and-dxm-drug-abuse?page=1.

15. Donna Leinwand, "Prescription Drugs Find Place in Teen Culture," *USA Today*, January 13, 2006.

16. G. Krimsky and J. Peck, "Generation Rx Popping Pills," *Republican-American*, p. A1, June 12, 2005.

17. Hazelden Betty Ford Foundation, "Club Drugs Linked to Sexual Assaults, Serious Health Effects." Accessed July 20, 2013, http://www.hazelden.org/web/public/ade00131.page.

18. CDC.gov, "Vital Signs: Demographic and Substance Use Trends among Heroin Users—United States, 2002–2013," July 10, 2015. Accessed February 22, 2016, http://www.cdc.gov/mmwr/preview/mmwrhtml/mm6426a3.htm.

19. The Right Step, "Heroin: A Rising Teen Fad," January 13, 2014. Accessed February 22, 2016, https://www.rightstep.com/teen-drug-addiction/heroin-a-rising-teen-fad/.

20. Nora D. Volkow, "Marijuana: Facts Parents Need to Know," NIH. Accessed February 22, 2016, http://www.nida.nih.gov/MarijBroch/parentpg9-10N.html#Effects.

21. Jim Carroll, *The Basketball Diaries* (New York: Penguin Books, 1987).

22. Jim Carroll, *The Basketball Diaries* (New York: Penguin Books, 1987).

23. B. Morton, "Social Influences on Adolescent Substance Use," *American Journal of Health Behavior* 31 (6) (2007): 672–84.

24. Foundations for a Drug-Free World, "Real Life Stories: About Drug Abuse." Accessed July 20, 2013, http://www.drugfreeworld.org/real-life-stories.html.

25. Teen Rehab Center, "What Is Drug Rehab?" Accessed February 22, 2016, https://www.teenrehabcenter.org/rehab/.

26. SAMHSA, "Find a Facility in Your State." Accessed February 22, 2016, https://findtreatment.samhsa.gov/TreatmentLocator/faces/quickSearch.jspx.

CHAPTER 16

1. Good Reads, "Viktor Frankl Quotes." Accessed February 23, 2016, https://www.goodreads.com/author/quotes/2782.Viktor_E_Frankl.

2. Jessica Sidman, "A College Student's Death May Help Save Lives," USAToday.com, June 26, 2006. Accessed February 23, 2016, http://usatoday30.usatoday.com/news/health/2006-06-26-spady-binge-drinking_x.htm.

3. Brian Dakss, "Binge Drinking Turning Deadly," CBSNews.com, October 14, 2004. Accessed Februrary 23, 2016, http://www.cbsnews.com/stories/2004/10/14/earlyshow/living/parenting/main649375.shtml.

4. AlcoholPolicyMD.com, "Reducing Underage Drinking through Coalitions (RUDC) Youth and Adults United for Change." Accessed February 23, 2016, http://www.alcoholpolicymd.com/programs/rudc.htm.

5. Addiction Center. "Binge Drinking." Accessed June 23, 2016, https://www.addictioncenter.com/college/binge-drinking.

6. Brian Burrough, "Missing White Female," VanityFair.com, January 2006. Accessed July 21, 2013, http://www.vanityfair.com/culture/features/2006/01/natalee200601.

7. Daniel Schorn, "Natalie Holloway: New Clues," CBSNews.com, March 22, 2006. Accessed July 21, 2013, http://www.cbsnews.com/stories/2006/03/22/48hours/main1430644.shtml.

8. Snejana Farberov, "Popular College Freshman, 18, Falls to His Death from Fifth-Floor Balcony 'after Trying to Hide from Police during Drunken Party,'" September 4, 2012. Accessed July 21, 2013, http://www.dailymail.co.uk/news/article-2198376/Xavier-Somerville-Popular-college-freshman-18-falls-death-fifth-floor-balcony.html.

9. Jan Withers, "National Governors' Spouses Association Winter Meeting," MADD.org, February 28, 2012. Accessed July 21, 2013, http://www.madd.org/blog/2012/february/POP_Governorsspouse.html.

10. C. Jackson, S. Ennett, D. Dickinson, and J. Bowling, "Letting Children Sip: Understanding Why Parents Allow Alcohol Use by Elementary School-aged Children," *Archives of Pediatrics and Adolescent Medicine* 166(11) (2012): 1053–57.

11. MyHealthNewsDaily,"Most Kids Who Drink Get Alcohol from Family," NBCNews.com, February 17, 2011. Accessed July 22, 2013, http://www.nbcnews.com/id/41647460/ns/health-addictions/t/most-kids-who-drink-get-alcohol-family/#.V1rNJPkrKUk.

12. National Survey on Drug Use and Health, "About the Survey." Accessed March 16, 2016, https://nsduhweb.rti.org/respweb/project_description.html.

13. Jane St. Clair, Keystone Treatment Center, "Alcohol Consumption Increasing in Girls and Young Women," Keystone Treatment Center. Accessed March 16, 2016, http://www.keystonetreatment.com/addiction/articles/alcohol-consumption-young-women/.

14. D. Zeigler, et al., "The Neurocognitive Effects of Alcohol on Adolescents and College Students," *Preventive Medicine* 40 (2005): 23–32.

15. Foundations for a Drug-Free World, "Real People-Real Stories: The Truth about Alcohol." 2013. Accessed July 22, 2013, http://www.drugfreeworld.org/real-life-stories/alcohol.html.

16. HelpGuide.org, "Alcohol Abuse and Alcoholism." Accessed July 23, 2013, http://www.helpguide.org/articles/addiction/alcoholism-and-alcohol-abuse.htm.

17. Karen Kaplan, "About 88,000 U.S. deaths each year traced to alcohol use, study says," *Los Angeles Times*, March 13, 2014. Accessed January 13, 2016, http://www.latimes.com/science/sciencenow/la-sci-sn-alcohol-related-deaths-years-lost-sxsw-20140313-story.html.

18. B. A. Kitchener, A. F. Jorm, and C. M. Kelly, Orygen Youth Health Research Centre 2010, *Intellectual Disability Mental Health First Aid Manual, 2nd Edition*, adapted by Ruth Pappas and Matt Frize, Office of the Senior Practitioner, NSW Department of Human Services, and Ageing Disability and Homecare. Accessed February 24, 2016, https://www.adhc.nsw.gov.au/__data/assets/file/0008/338813/Intellectual_Disability_Mental_Health_First_Aid_Manual_2nd_ed.pdf.

19. Too Smart to Start, "Signs of Underage Alcohol Use." Accessed February 24, 2016, http://toosmarttostart.samhsa.gov/educators/signs/default.aspx.

20. Too Smart to Start. "Signs of Underage Alcohol Use." Accessed February 24, 2016, http://toosmarttostart.samhsa.gov/educators/signs/default.aspx.

21. U.S. Department of Health and Human Services, *The Surgeon General's Call to Action to Prevent and Reduce Underage Drinking 2007*. Accessed February 24, 2016, http://www.camy.org/_docs/resources/fact-sheets/Call_To_Action.pdf.

22. College Drinking, "Make a Difference: Talk to Your Child about Alcohol." Accessed February 25, 2016, http://www.collegedrinkingprevention.gov/OtherAlcoholInformation/makeDifference.aspx.

23. M. Hallgren, T. Sjoland, H. Kallmen, and S. Andreasson, "Modifying Alcohol Consumption among High School Students: An Efficacy Trial of an Alcohol Risk Reduction Program (PRIME for Life)." *Health Education*, 111 (3) (2011): 216–29.

24. SAMHSA, "Find a Facility in Your State." Accessed February 22, 2016. https://findtreatment.samhsa.gov/TreatmentLocator/faces/quickSearch.jspx.

CHAPTER 17

1. Brainy Quotes, "Mehmet Oz Quotes." Accessed February 28, 2016, http://www.brainyquote.com/quotes/quotes/m/mehmetoz433775.html.

2. Science Daily, "Children Whose Parents Smoked Are Twice as Likely to Begin Smoking Between 13 and 21," September 29, 2005. Accessed February 28, 2016, http://www.sciencedaily.com/releases/2005/09/050929082408.htm.

3. Science Daily, "Children Whose Parents Smoked Are Twice as Likely to Begin Smoking Between 13 and 21," September 29, 2005. Accessed February 28, 2016, www.sciencedaily.com/releases/2005/09/050929082408.htm.

4. L. Snegireff and O. Lombard, "Survey of Smoking Habits of Massachusetts Physicians," *New England Journal of Medicine* 250 (24) (1954): 1042–45.

5. HemOnc Today, "Cigarettes Were Once 'Physician' Tested, Approved: From the 1930s to the 1950s, 'Doctors' Once Lit Up the Pages of Cigarette Advertisements," Helio.com, March 10, 2009. Accessed February 28, 2016, http://www.healio.com/hematology-oncology/news/print/hemonc-today/%7B241d62a7-fe6e-4c5b-9fed-a33cc6e4bd7c%7D/cigarettes-were-once-physician-tested-approved.

6. FDA.gov, "Tobacco Control Act." Accessed February 28, 2016, http://www.fda.gov/TobaccoProducts/GuidanceComplianceRegulatoryInformation/ucm246129.htm.

7. CDC.gov, "Smoking and Tobacco Use." Accessed February 28, 2016, http://www.cdc.gov/tobacco/data_statistics/fact_sheets/youth_data/tobacco_use/.

8. CDC.gov, "Youth and Tobacco Use." Accessed June 23, 2016. http://www.cdc.gov/tobacco/data_statistics/fact_sheets/youth_data/tobacco_use/.

9. World Health Organization, "Tobacco." Accessed July 6, 2015, http://www.who.int/mediacentre/factsheets.

10. CDC.gov, "Smoking and Tobacco Use." Accessed July 22, 2013, http://www.cdc.gov/tobacco/data_statistics/fact_sheets/fast_facts/index.htm#toll.

11. EPA.gov, "Asthma Triggers: Gain Control." Accessed July 22, 2013, http://www.epa.gov/asthma/shs.html.

12. KidsHealth.org, "Kids and Smoking." Accessed July 22, 2013, http://kidshealth.org/parent/positive/talk/smoking.html.

13. FDA.gov, "Tobacco Products." Accessed July 22, 2013, http://www.fda.gov/tobaccoproducts/guidancecomplianceregulatoryinformation/ucm246129.htm.

14. V. Maralani,"Understanding the Links between Education and Smoking," *Social Science Research* 48 (2014): 20–34.

15. K. Lasser et al., "Smoking and Mental Illness: A Population Based Prevalence Study," *Journal of the American Medical Association* 284 (2000): 2606–10.

16. National Fire Protection Association, "Home Structure Fires." September 2015, http://www.nfpa.org.

17. ScienceDaily, "Talking and Treating Erectile Dysfunction," February 14, 2009. Accessed February 14, 2009, http://www.sciencedaily.com/releases/2009/02/090204172216.htm.

18. U.S. National Library of Medicine, "Chronic Obstructive Pulmonary Disease." Accessed March 7, 2016, https://www.nlm.nih.gov/medlineplus/ency/article/000091.htm.

19. Mayo Clinic, "Healthy Lifestyle: Tween and Teen Health." Accessed March 7, 2016, http://www.mayoclinic.org/healthy-lifestyle/tween-and-teen-health/indepth/teen-smoking/art-20046474?pg=2.

20. CDC.gov, "A Report of the Surgeon General: Preventing Tobacco Use among Youth and Young Adults." Accessed March 7, 2016, http://www.cdc.gov/tobacco/data_statistics/sgr/2012/consumer_booklet/pdfs/consumer.pdf.

21. CDC.gov, "A Report of the Surgeon General: Preventing Tobacco Use among Youth and Young Adults." Accessed March 7, 2016, http://www.cdc.gov/tobacco/data_statistics/sgr/2012/consumer_booklet/pdfs/consumer.pdf.

CHAPTER 18

1. Elizabeth Wurtzel, *Prozac Nation: Young and Depressed in America* (New York: Houghton Mifflin Company, 1994).

2. S. Burcusa and W. Iacono, "Risk for Recurrence in Depression," *Clinical Psychology Review* 27(8) (2007): 959–85.

3. SAMHSA, "Behavioral Health Trends in the United States: Results from the 2014 National Survey on Drug Use and Health." Accessed March 6, 2016, http://www.samhsa.gov/data/sites/default/files/NSDUH-FRR1-2014/NSDUH-FRR1-2014.pdf.

4. WebMD, "Causes of Depression." Accessed January 14, 2016, http://www.webmd.com/depression/guide/causes-depression.

5. M. Teesson, T. Slade, and K. Mills, "Comorbidity in Australia: Findings of the 2007 National Survey of Mental Health and Wellbeing," *Australian and New Zealand Journal of Psychiatry* 43 (2009): 606–14.

6. National Institute of Mental Health, "Depression: What You Need to Know." Accessed March 6, 2016, http://www.nimh.nih.gov/health/publications/depression/complete-index.shtml#pub3.

7. National Institute of Mental Health, "What Are the Signs and Symptoms of Depression?" Accessed March 6, 2016, http://www.nimh.nih.gov/health/publications/depression/what-are-the-signs-and-symptoms-of-depress.shtml.

8. C. Jacobson and M. Gould, "The Epidemiology and Phenomenology of Non-Suicidal Self Injurious Behavior among Adolescents: A Critical Review of the Literature," *Archives of Suicide Research* 11 (2007): 129–47.

9. New Mexico State University, "Teens and Self-Cutting (Self-Harm): Information for Parents Guide I-104." Accessed March 9, 2016, http://aces.nmsu.edu/pubs/_i/I104/.

10. J. Klein, R. Jacobs, and M. Reinecke, "Cognitive Behavioral Therapy for Adolescent Depression: A Meta Analytic Investigation of Changes in Effect-Size Estimates," *Journal of the American Academy of Child and Adolescent Psychiatry* 46 (2007): 1403–13.

11. G. Keitner, R. Archambault, C. Ryan, and I. Miller, "Family Therapy and Chronic Depression," *Journal of Clinical Psychology* 59(8) (2003): 873–84.

12. Child Welfare Information Gateway, "Trauma-Focused Cognitive Behavioral Therapy for Children Affected by Sexual Abuse or Trauma," 2012. Accessed March 6, 2016. https://www.childwelfare.gov/pubs/trauma/.

13. J. Mark et al., "Mindfulness-Based Cognitive Therapy for Preventing Relapse in Recurrent Depression: A Randomized Dismantling Trial," *Journal of Consulting and Clinical Psychology* 82(2) (2014): 275–86.

14. M. Weissman, "Recent Non-Medication Trials of Interpersonal Psychotherapy for Depression," *International Journal of Neuropsychopharmacology* 10 (2006): 117–22.

15. New World Encyclopedia, "Suicide." March 6, 2016, http://www.newworldencyclopedia.org/entry/Suicide.

16. S. Russell and K. Joyner, "Adolescent Sexual Orientation and Suicide Risk: Evidence from a National Study," *American Journal of Public Health* 91 (2001): 1276–81.

17. CDC.gov, "Web-based Injury Statistics Query and Reporting System (WISQARS)." Accessed March 9, 2016, http://www.cdc.gov/injury/wisqars/.

18. AllAboutDepression.com, "Suicide and Depression." Accessed March 9, 2016, http://www.allaboutdepression.com/gen_04.html.

19. James Gilligan, *Preventing Violence* (New York: Thames and Hudson, 2001).

20. Helen Lewis, *Shame and Guilt in Neurosis* (New York: International University, 1971).

21. Merle Fossum and Marilyn Mason, *Facing Shame: Families in Recovery* (New York: W.W. Norton & Company, 1986).

22. Teen Suicide, "Teen Suicide Warning Signs." Accessed March 10, 2016, http://www.teensuicide.us/articles2.html.

23. National Institute of Mental Health, "Depression in Young and Teenage Boys." Accessed January 14, 2016, http://www.medicinenet.com/script/main/art.asp?articlekey=23376.

24. Helpguide.org, "Suicide Prevention." Accessed March 6, 2016, http://www.helpguide.org/articles/suicide-prevention/suicide-prevention-helping-someone-who-is-suicidal.htm.

25. Suicide.org, "Suicide Hotlines." Accessed March 6, 2016, http://www.suicide.org/.

CHAPTER 19

1. Dodai Stewart, "'Bulimia and Anorexia Since I Was 15': Lady Gaga Responds to 'Fat' Headlines with Half-Naked Pics and a Confession," September 25, 2012. Accessed July 24, 2013, http://jezebel.com/5946233/?post=52965115.

2. MSN.com. "Celebrities Speak about Eating Disorders," February 23, 2015. Accessed March 8, 2016, http://www.msn.com/en-gb/health/mindandbody/celebrities-speak-about-eating-disorders/ss-BBhSJu8#image=1.

3. Laura Belekeviciute, *Anorexia Nervosa in Sociological Perspective: The Factors for the Emergence of Illness and Patients' Personal Experiences*, Bachelor's Paper, 2007.

4. Chris Shilling, *The Body and Social Theory* (London: SAGE, 2003).

5. T. Wade, A. Keski-Rahkonen, and J. Hudson, "Epidemiology of Eating Disorders," in *Textbook in Psychiatric Epidemiology* (3rd ed.), ed. M. Tsuang and M. Tohens (New York: Wiley, 2011), 343–60.

6. Casa Palmera, "Teens and Eating Disorders: Get the Facts," August 19, 2009. Accessed March 8, 2016, https://casapalmera.com/teens-and-eating-disorders-get-the-facts/.

7. B. Engel, N. Staats-Reiss, and M. Dombeck, "Causes of Eating Disorders—Family Influences." Accessed January 18, 2016, https://www.mentalhelp.net/articles/causes-of-eating-disorders-family-influences/.

8. J. Dyl, J. Kittler, K. Phillips, and J. Hunt, "Body Dysmorphic Disorder and Other Clinically Significant Body Image Concerns in Adolescent Psychiatric Inpatients: Prevalence and Clinical Characteristics," *Child Psychiatry and Human Development* 36(4) (2006): 369–82.

9. K. Phillips and W. Menard, "Suicidality in Body Dysmorphic Disorder: A Prospective Study," *Journal of Marriage and Family*, 163 (2006): 1280–82.

10. Simona Giordano, *Understanding Eating Disorders* (New York: Oxford University Press, 2005).

11. American Psychiatric Association, "Treatment of Patients with Eating Disorders," *American Journal of Psychiatry* 163(7 Suppl) (2007): 4–54.

12. Susan Donaldson James, "Anorexia Can Strike and Kill as Early as Kindergarten," ABCNews.com, February 25, 2012. Accessed July 25, 2013, http://abcnews.go.com/Health/anorexia-nervosa-strike-kill-early-kindergarten/story?id=18581747.

13. N. Berkman, K. Lohr , and C. Bulik, "Outcomes of Eating Disorders: A Systematic Review of the Literature," *International Journal of Eating Disorders* 40(4) (2007): 293–309.

14. T. Wade, A. Keski-Rahkonen, and J. Hudson, "Epidemiology of Eating Disorders," in *Textbook in Psychiatric Epidemiology* (3rd ed.), ed. M. Tsuang and M. Tohen (New York: Wiley, 2011), 343–60.

15. Mandy Morgan, "Toddlers and Tears: The Sexualization of Young Girls," *Deseret News*, November 17, 2012. Accessed July 25, 2013, http://www.deseretnews. com/article/865567072/Toddlers-and-Tears-The-sexualization-of-young-girls. html?pg=all.

16. Girl Scouts. "Girls and Reality TV." Accessed July 26, 2013, http://www. girlscouts.org/research/pdf/real_to_me_factsheet.pdf.

17. Carolyn Coker Ross, "Why Do Women Hate Their Bodies?" Psych Central. Accessed July 26, 2013, http://psychcentral.com/blog/archives/2012/06/02/why-do-women-hate-their-bodies/.

18. NEDA, "Anorexia Nervosa." Accessed January 18, 2016, http://www.nation-aleatingdisorders.org/anorexia-nervosa.

19. NEDA, "Health Consequences of Eating Disorders." Accessed January 18, 2016, https://www.nationaleatingdisorders.org/health-consequences-eating-disor-ders.

20. *Psychology Today*, "Bulimia Nervosa." Accessed March 8, 2016, https://www. psychologytoday.com/conditions/bulimia-nervosa.

21. Shaye Boddington, "The 2 Most Significant Causes of Bulimia," YouTube. com. Accessed July 26, 2011, http://www.youtube.com/watch?v=OvdPqMu5Vmg&l ist=UULoKEyCzx_lKv0O1SGVy-1A&index=20.

22. Douglas Haddad (journalist), discussion with Shaye Boddington, June 3, 2013. http://www.your-bulimia-recovery.com.

23. G. Gidwani and E. Rome, "Eating Disorders," *Clinical Obstetrics and Gynecology* 40(3) (1997): 601–15.

24. NEDA, "Bulimia Nervosa." Accessed January 18, 2016, https://www.nation-aleatingdisorders.org/bulimia-nervosa.

25. NEDA, "Bulimia Nervosa." Accessed January 18, 2016, https://www.nation-aleatingdisorders.org/bulimia-nervosa.

26. J. Hudson, E. Hiripi, H. Pope, and R. Kessler. "The Prevalence and Corre-lates of Eating Disorders in the National Comorbidity Survey Replication," *Biological Psychiatry* 61 (2007): 348–58.

27. PBS.org, "Binge Eating Disorder." Accessed January 18, 2016, http://www. pbs.org/perfectillusions/eatingdisorders/bingeeating.html.

28. NEDA, "Binge Eating Disorder." Accessed January 18, 2016, https://www. nationaleatingdisorders.org/binge-eating-disorder.

29. FoxNews.com, "Survey: Binging Most Common Eating Disorder in Amer-ica," February 1, 2007. Accessed January 18, 2016, http://www.foxnews.com/ story/0,2933,249481,00.html?sPage=fnc/health/mentalhealth.

30. Douglas Haddad (journalist), discussion with Ruth Striegel-Moore, Wesleyan University, May 2005.

31. Cindy Maynard, "Body Image." Accessed January 18, 2016, http://www.edre-ferral.com/body_image.htm.

32. National Institute of Mental Health, "Eating Disorders: About More Than Food." Accessed January 18, 2016, https://www.nimh.nih.gov/health/publications/ eating-disorders-new-trifold/index.shtml.

33. G. Wilson, C. Grilo, and K. Vitousek, "Psychological Treatment of Eating Disorders," *American Psychologist* 62 (2007): 199–216.

34. NEDA, "Find Help and Support." Accessed January 18, 2016, https://www.nationaleatingdisorders.org/find-help-support.

CHAPTER 20

1. Brainy Quote, "Sasha Cohen Quotes." Accessed March 8, 2016, http://www.brainyquote.com/quotes/quotes/s/sashacohen243162.html.

2. American Psychological Association, "The Impact of Food Advertising on Childhood Obesity." Accessed July 27, 2013, http://www.apa.org/topics/kids-media/food.aspx.

3. Paul Bentley, "Healthiest Children Are Those Who Eat the Same as Their Parents," DailyMail.com, May 5, 2013." Accessed July 31, 2013, http://www.daily-mail.co.uk/news/article-2319770/Healthiest-children-eat-parents.html.

4. Organic Consumers Association, "Scientists Report 80% of Cancer Cases Caused by Environmental and Food Carcinogens," June 28, 2004. Accessed March 8, 2016, http://www.organicconsumers.org/foodsafety/cancer070104.cfm.

5. EPA, "Reduce Your Child's Chances of Pesticide Poisoning," https://www.epa.gov/safepestcontrol/reduce-your-childs-chances-pesticide-poisoning.

6. Whfoods.org, "What Does GMO Mean?" Accessed July 28, 2013, http://whfoods.org/genpage.php?tname=dailytip&dbid=345.

7. AllergicChild, "Possible Causes of Food Allergies." Accessed December 16, 2015, http://www.allergicchild.com/causes_food_allergy.html.

8. Rebecca Harrington, "Does Artificial Food Coloring Contribute to ADHD in Children?: The FDA Maintains Dyes Are Safe, but Some Studies Have Linked Them to Hyperactivity in Children," *Scientific American*, April 27, 2015. Accessed April 27, 2015, http://www.scientificamerican.com/article/does-artificial-food-coloring-contribute-to-adhd-in-children/.

9. W. Kiess et al., "Type 2 Diabetes Mellitus in Children and Adolescents," *Hormone Research* 59 (Suppl. 1) (2003): 77–84.

10. Erika Gebel, "More Kids Than Ever Have Type 2 Diabetes: Doctors Seek to Establish a Gold Standard for Their Care," Diabetes Forecast, November 2012. Accessed January 11, 2016, http://www.diabetesforecast.org/2012/nov/more-kids-than-ever-have-type-2-diabetes.html.

11. American Heart Association, "Dietary Recommendations for Healthy Children." Accessed July 28, 2013, http://www.heart.org/HEARTORG/GettingHealthy/Dietary-Recommendations-for-Healthy-Children_UCM_303886_Article.jsp.

12. World Health Organization, "Obesity and Overweight," January 2015. Accessed June 24, 2016, http://www.who.int/mediacentre/factsheets/fs311/en/.

13. W. James, "The Challenge of Childhood Obesity," *International Journal of Pediatric Obesity* 1 (2006): 7–10.

14. *Herald Sun*, "Casey Heynes Appearance on TV Won't Fix Issue Says Dr. Michael Carr-Gregg." Accessed July 30, 2013, http://www.heraldsun.com.au/news/special-reports/bully-victim-casey-haynes-faces-more-torment-after-tv-interview/story-fn85r9s4-1226024850202.

15. L. Jonides, V. Buschbacher, and S. Barlow, "Management of Child and Adolescent Obesity: Psychological, Emotional, and Behavioral Assessment," *Pediatrics* 110 (1) (2002): 215–21.

16. John Ratey, *Spark: The Revolutionary New Science of Exercise and the Brain* (New York: Hatchett Book Group, 2008).

17. W. Dietz, "Relationship of Childhood Obesity to Coronary Heart Disease Risk Factors in Adulthood: The Bogalusa Heart Study," *Pediatrics* 108(3) (2001): 712–19.

18. Dietz, W. "Critical periods in childhood for the development of obesity." *American Journal of Clinical Nutrition*, 59 (1994): 955–59.

19. WHO, "Physical Activity and Young People." Accessed June 24, 2016, http://www.who.int/dietphysicalactivity/factsheet_young_people/en/.

20. USDA, "Recommended Daily Caloric Intake." Accessed December 29, 2015, https://www.getfit.tn.gov/fitnesstracker/calorie_levels.pdf.

CONCLUSION

1. S. Sugar and J. Stoeber, "Perfectionism, Fear of Failure, and Affective Responses to Success and Failure: The Central Role of Fear of Experiencing Shame and Embarrassment," *Journal of Sport & Exercise Psychology* 31 (5) (2009): 602–27.

2. Marci Shimoff, *Happy for No Reason: 7 Steps to Being Happy from the Inside Out* (New York: Atria Books, 2009).

3. Good Reads, "Howard Thurman Quotes." Accessed March 26, 2016, https://www.goodreads.com/author/quotes/56230.Howard_Thurman.

4. Daily Parent, "25 Powerful Parenting Quotes." Accessed March 26, 2016, http://dailyparent.com/articles/25-powerful-parenting-quotes/.

Bibliography

ABC Local 10 News. "Youth Football Coaches Charged in 'Operation Dirty Play.'" October 31, 2012. Accessed February 16, 2016. http://www.local10.com/news/youth-football-coaches-charged-in-operation-dirty-play.

Adams, Jerry. *Discipline without Anger: A Parent's Guide to Teaching Children Responsible Behavior.* Bloomington, IN: AuthorHouse, 2008.

Addiction Center. "Binge Drinking." Accessed June 23, 2016. https://www.addiction center.com/college/binge-drinking.

AlcoholPolicyMD.com. "Reducing Underage Drinking through Coalitions (RUDC) Youth and Adults United for Change." Accessed February 23, 2016. http://www.alcoholpolicymd.com/programs/rudc.htm.

AllAboutDepression.com. "Suicide and Depression." Accessed March 9, 2016. http://www.allaboutdepression.com/gen_04.html.

AllergicChild. "Possible Causes of Food Allergies." Accessed December 16, 2015. http://www.allergicchild.com/causes_food_allergy.html.

American College of Pediatricians. "Report Confirms Marijuana Is Dangerous." September 22, 2015. Accessed December 12, 2015. http://www.acpeds.org/report-confirms-marijuana-is-dangerous.

American Heart Association. "Dietary Recommendations for Healthy Children." May 14, 2015. Accessed July 28, 2013. http://www.heart.org/HEARTORG/GettingHealthy/Dietary-Recommendations-for-Healthy-Children_UCM_303886_Article.jsp.

American Psychiatric Association. "Treatment of Patients with Eating Disorders." *American Journal of Psychiatry* 163(7 Suppl) (2007): 4–54.

American Psychological Association. "The Impact of Food Advertising on Childhood Obesity." Accessed July 27, 2013. http://www.apa.org/topics/kids-media/food.aspx.

Ames, Mark. "Virginia Tech: Is the Scene of the Crime the Cause of the Crime?" Alternet, April 19, 2007. Accessed February 15, 2016. http://www.alternet.org/

story/50758/virginia_tech%3A_is_the_scene_of_the_crime_the_cause_of_the_crime.

Angelfire. "Quotes by Famous People." Accessed March 16, 2016. http://www.angelfire.com/tn/Quotes/famous.html.

AZ Quotes. "Sara Lawrence-Lightfoot Quotes." Accessed March 13, 2016. http://www.azquotes.com/quote/1264794.

Bandura Albert. *Social Learning and Personality Development.* New York: International Thomson Publishing, 1963.

Banks, J. "Childhood Discipline: Challenges for Clinicians and Parents." *American Family Physician* 66(8) (2002):1447–53.

Bartkewicz, Anthony. "WATCH: Maryland Teen Bullied While Taping News Segment about Bullying." *Daily News*, October 10, 2012. Accessed October 12, 2012. http://www.nydailynews.com/news/national/watch-teen-bullied-news-piece-bullying-article-1.1179008.

Bayat, Mojdeh. "Clarifying Issues Regarding the Use of Praise with Young Children." *Topics in Special Education* 31(2) (2011): 121–28.

BBC News. "In Quotes: Virginia Gunman's Message." April 19, 2007. Accessed February 15, 2016. http://news.bbc.co.uk/2/hi/americas/6570369.stm.

Belekeviciute, Laura. Bachelor's Paper – *Anorexia Nervosa in Sociological Perspective: The Factors for the Emergence of Illness and Patients' Personal Experiences*, 2007.

Benokraitis, N. *Marriages and Families: Changes, Choices, and Constraints.* Englewood Cliffs, NJ: Pearson Prentice Hall, 2008.

Bentley, Paul. "Healthiest children Are Those Who Eat the Same as Their Parents." DailyMail.com, May 6, 2013. Accessed July 31, 2013. http://www.dailymail.co.uk/news/article-2319770/Healthiest-children-eat-parents.html.

Beresin, Eugene V. "The Impact of Media Violence on Children and Adolescents: Opportunities for Clinical Interventions." American Academy of Child and Adolescent Psychiatry. Accessed July 14, 2013. https://www.aacap.org/aacap/Medical_Students_and_Residents/Mentorship_Matters/DevelopMentor/The_Impact_of_Media_Violence_on_Children_and_Adolescents_Opportunities_for_Clinical_Interventions.aspx.

Berkman, N., K. Lohr, and C. Bulik. "Outcomes of Eating Disorders: A Systematic Review of the Literature." *International Journal of Eating Disorders* 40(4) (2007): 293–309.

Blair, Gary. "The Goals Guy." Accessed on March 7, 2013. http://www.goalsguy.com/Events/k_overview.html.

Boddington, Shaye. "The 2 Most Significant Causes of Bulimia." YouTube.com. Accessed July 26, 2011. http://www.youtube.com/watch?v=OvdPqMu5Vmg&list=UULoKEyCzx_lKv0O1SGVy-1A&index=20.

Brainy Quote. "Hulk Hogan Quotes." Accessed November 1, 2015. http://www.brainyquote.com/quotes/authors/h/hulk_hogan.html.

Brainy Quote. "Mehmet Oz Quotes." Accessed February 28, 2016. http://www.brainyquote.com/quotes/quotes/m/mehmetoz433775.html.

Brainy Quote. "Sasha Cohen Quotes." Accessed March 8, 2016. http://www.brainyquote.com/quotes/quotes/s/sashacohen243162.html.

Brainy Quote. "Tony Robbins Quotes." March 14, 2016, http://www.brainyquote .com/quotes/quotes/t/tonyrobbin147771.html.

Brown, G. "India Must Ban Child Labor." December 21, 2012. Accessed November 14, 2015. http://www.huffingtonpost.com/gordon-brown/india-childlabor-laws _b_2345756.html.

Bumpas, Bill. "Colorado Youth Marijuana Use Highest since Legalization." One News Now, September 29, 2015. Accessed February 22, 2016. http://www.one-newsnow.com/culture/2015/09/29/colorado-youth-marijuana-use-highest-since -legalization.

Burcusa, S., and W. Iacono. "Risk for Recurrence in Depression." *Clinical Psychology Review* 27(8) (2007): 959–85.

Burrough, Bryan. "Missing White Female." VanityFair.com, January 2006. Accessed July 21, 2013. http://www.vanityfair.com/culture/features/2006/01/natalee200601.

Bush, Donna, and David Woodwell. "Update: Drug-Related Emergency Department Visits Involving Synthetic Cannabinoids." *SAMHSA: The CBHSQ Report*. October 16, 2014. http://www.samhsa.gov/data/sites/default/files/SR-1378/SR-1378.pdf.

CADCA. "2012 Monitoring the Future Survey Finds Marijuana Use Continuing to Rise among Youth." Accessed July 19, 2013. http://www.cadca.org/ resources/detail/2012-monitoring-future-survey-finds-marijuana-use-continuing -rise-among-youth.

Canfield, Jack. *The Success Principles*. New York: HarperCollins, 2014.

Carroll, Jim. *The Basketball Diaries*. New York: Penguin, 1987.

Casa Palmera. "Teens and Eating Disorders: Get the Facts." August 19, 2009. Accessed March 8, 2016. https://casapalmera.com/teens-and-eating-disorders-get -the-facts/.

CDC. "April Is STD Awareness Month." Accessed July 18, 2013. http://www.cdc .gov/features/stdawareness/index.html#references.

CDC. "National Survey of Family Growth." Accessed December 6, 2015. http:// www.cdc.gov/nchs/nsfg.htm.

CDC. "Smoking and Tobacco Use." Accessed February 28, 2016. http://www.cdc .gov/tobacco/data_statistics/fact_sheets/youth_data/tobacco_use/.

CDC. "Smoking and Tobacco Use." Accessed July 22, 2013. http://www.cdc.gov/ tobacco/data_statistics/fact_sheets/fast_facts/index.htm#toll.

CDC. "Vital Signs: Births to Teens Aged 15–17 Years—United States, 1991–2012." April 11, 2014. Accessed February 17, 2016. http://www.cdc.gov/mmwr/preview/ mmwrhtml/mm6314a4.htm?s_cid=mm6314a4_w.

CDC.gov. "A Report of the Surgeon General: Preventing Tobacco Use among Youth and Young Adults." Accessed March 7, 2016. http://www.cdc.gov/tobacco/ data_statistics/sgr/2012/consumer_booklet/pdfs/consumer.pdf.

CDC.gov. "I'm Ready to Quit!" Accessed March 7, 2016. http://www.cdc.gov/ tobacco/campaign/tips/quit-smoking/?gclid=CPPAuuTrr8sCFYKQHwodMqE MUA.

CDC.gov. "Web-Based Injury Statistics Query and Reporting System (WISQARS)." Accessed March 9, 2016. http://www.cdc.gov/injury/wisqars/.

CDC.gov. "Youth and Tobacco Use." Accessed June 23, 2016. http://www.cdc.gov/tobacco/data_statistics/fact_sheets/youth_data/tobacco_use/.

CDC.gov. "Youth Violence: Facts at a Glance." November 25, 2015. http://www.cdc.gov/violenceprevention/pdf/yv-datasheet-a.pdf.

Centers for Disease Control and Prevention. "Vital Signs: Demographic and Substance Use Trends Among Heroin Users—United States, 2002–2013." July 10, 2015. Accessed February 22, 2016. http://www.cdc.gov/mmwr/preview/mmwrhtml/mm6426a3.htm.

Child Welfare Information Gateway. "Trauma-Focused Cognitive Behavioral Therapy for Children Affected by Sexual Abuse or Trauma." Accessed March 6, 2016. https://www.childwelfare.gov/pubs/trauma/.

Cline, Foster, and Jim Fay. *Parenting with Love and Logic.* Colorado Springs, CO: NavPress Publishing, 2011.

Coker Ross, Carolyn. "Why Do Women Hate Their Bodies?" Psych Central. Accessed July 26, 2013. http://psychcentral.com/blog/archives/2012/06/02/why-do-women-hate-their-bodies/.

College Drinking. "Make a Difference: Talk to Your Child about Alcohol." Accessed February 25, 2016. http://www.collegedrinkingprevention.gov/OtherAlcoholInformation/makeDifference.aspx.

Colorado Department of Revenue. "Colorado Marijuana Tax Data." Accessed December 12, 2015. https://www.colorado.gov/pacific/revenue/colorado-marijuana-tax-data.

CRC Health. "Teen Addiction to Online Gambling." Accessed June 22, 2016. http://www.crchealth.com/troubled-teenagers/teen-gambling.

Daily Parent. "25 Powerful Parenting Quotes." Accessed March 26, 2016. http://dailyparent.com/articles/25-powerful-parenting-quotes/.

Dakss, Brian. "Binge Drinking Turning Deadly." CBSNews.com, October 14, 2004. Accessed February 23, 2016. http://www.cbsnews.com/stories/2004/10/14/early show/living/parenting/main649375.shtml.

Demartini, John. *The Values Factor: The Secret to Creating an Inspired and Fulfilling Life.* New York: Berkley Books, 2013.

Desert Hills. "Causes and Symptoms of Impulse Control Disorder." http://www.deserthills-nm.com/behavioral/impulse-control/signs-symptoms-effects.

Dess, Jeff, Tammy White, Elizabeth Jaffe, and Steven Jaffe. *Understanding Playful vs. Hurtful Teasing and Bullying Behavior.* 2011. Accessed February 2, 2016. http://www.cobbk12.org/bully/MidHighCCSD.pdf.

Dietz, W. "Critical Periods in Childhood for the Development of Obesity." *American Journal of Clinical Nutrition* 59 (1994): 955–59.

Dietz, W. "Relationship of Childhood Obesity to Coronary Heart Disease Risk Factors in "Adulthood: The Bogalusa Heart Study." *Pediatrics* 108(3) (2001): 712–19.

Donaldson James, Susan. "Anorexia Can Strike and Kill as Early as Kindergarten." ABCNews.com, February 25, 2012. Accessed July 25, 2013. http://abcnews.go.com/Health/anorexia-nervosa-strike-kill-early-kindergarten/story?id=18581747.

Douglas Haddad (journalist), discussion with Ruth Striegel-Moore, Wesleyan University, May 2005.

Douglas Haddad (journalist), discussion with Shaye Boddington, June 3, 2013. http://www.your-bulimia-recovery.com.

Dyl, J., J. Kittler, K. Phillips , and J. Hunt. "Body Dysmorphic Disorder and Other Clinically Significant Body Image Concerns in Adolescent Psychiatric Inpatients: Prevalence and Clinical Characteristics." *Child Psychiatry and Human Development* 36(4) (2006): 369–82.

Edberg, Henrik. "Zig Ziglar's Timeless Guide to Motivation." Positivity Blog. Accessed March 14 2016. http://www.positivityblog.com/index.php/2012/12/06/zig-ziglar.

Encyclopedia of Children's Health. "Cognitive Development." Accessed March 13,2016. http://www.healthofchildren.com/C/Cognitive-Development.html.

Engel, B., N. Staats-Reiss, and M. Dombeck. "Causes of Eating Disorders—Family Influences." February 2, 2007. Accessed January 18, 2016. https://www.mentalhelp.net/articles/causes-of-eating-disorders-family-influences/.

EPA. "Asthma Triggers: Gain Control." Accessed July 22, 2013. http://www.epa.gov/asthma/shs.html.

EPA. "Reduce Your Child's Chances of Pesticide Poisoning." https://www.epa.gov/safepestcontrol/reduce-your-childs-chances-pesticide-poisoning.

Everytown for Gun Safety Support Fund. "173 School Shootings in America Since 2013." Accessed October 10, 2015. http://everytownresearch.org/school-shootings/.

Farberov, Snejana. "Popular College Freshman, 18, Falls to His Death from Fifth-Floor Balcony 'after Trying to Hide from Police during Drunken Party.'" DailyMail.com, September 4, 2012. Accessed July 21, 2013. http://www.dailymail.co.uk/news/article-2198376/Xavier-Somerville-Popular-college-freshman-18-falls-death-fifth-floor-balcony.html.

FDA.gov. "Tobacco Control Act." Accessed February 28, 2016. http://www.fda.gov/TobaccoProducts/GuidanceComplianceRegulatoryInformation/ucm246129.htm.

FDA.gov. "Tobacco Products." Accessed July 22, 2013. http://www.fda.gov/tobacproducts/guidancecomplianceregulatoryinformation/ucm246129.htm.

Ferrales, Diane, and Sonja Koukel. "Teens and Self-Cutting (Self-Harm): Information for Parents." Guide I-104. New Mexico State University. Accessed March 9, 2016. http://aces.nmsu.edu/pubs/_i/I104/.

Florida Council on Compulsive Gambling. "Lottery Tickets Aren't Kids Play." Accessed February 16, 2016. http://www.gamblinghelp.org/fccg/read_news/54.

Fossum, Merle, and Marilyn Mason. *Facing Shame: Families in Recovery.* New York: W.W. Norton & Company, 1986.

Foundation for a Drug-Free World. "Real Life Stories: About Drug Abuse." Accessed July 20, 2013. http://www.drugfreeworld.org/real-life-stories.html.

Foundation for a Drug-Free World. "Real People-Real Stories: The Truth about Alcohol." 2013. Accessed July 22, 2013. http://www.drugfreeworld.org/real-life-stories/alcohol.html.

FoxNews.com. "Survey: Binging Most Common Eating Disorder in America." Associated Press, February 1, 2007. Accessed January 18, 2016. http://www.foxnews.com/story/0,2933,249481,00.html?sPage=fnc/health/mentalhealth.

Free the Children. "Our Mission and Our Model." Accessed November 10, 2015. http://www.freethechildren.com/about-us/our-model/.

Garbarino, J. "How a Boy Becomes a Killer." CNN, December 19, 2012. Accessed February 15, 2016. http://www.cnn.com/2012/12/19/opinion/garbarino-violence -boys/.

Gardner, Howard. *Leading Minds: An Anatomy of Leadership.* New York: Perseus, 1995.

Gebel, Erika. "More Kids Than Ever Have Type 2 Diabetes: Doctors Seek to Establish a Gold Standard for Their Care." Diabetes Forecast., November 2012. Accessed January 11, 2016. http://www.diabetesforecast.org/2012/nov/more-kids -than-ever-have-type-2-diabetes.html.

Gidwani, G., and E. Rome. "Eating Disorders." *Clinical Obstetrics and Gynecology* 40(3) (1997): 601–15.

Gilligan, James. *Preventing Violence.* New York: Thames & Hudson, 2001.

Gilligan, James. "Shame, Guilt, and Violence." *Social Research* 70(4) (2003): 1149.

Ginott, Haim. *Between Parent and Teenager.* New York: Scribner, 1969.

Ginsburg, Kenneth. "The Importance of Play in Promoting Healthy Child Development and Maintaining Strong Parent-Child Bonds." *Pediatrics* 119 (2007): 182–91.

Giordano, Simona. *Understanding Eating Disorders.* New York: Oxford University Press, 2005.

Girl Scouts. "Girls and Reality TV." Accessed July 26, 2013. http://www.girlscouts.org/ content/dam/girlscouts-gsusa/forms-and-documents/about-girl-scouts/research /real_to_me_factsheet.pdf.

Good Reads. "Anthony Robbins Quotes." Accessed March 14, 2016. http://www .goodreads.com/quotes/33903-people-who-fail-focus-on-what-they-will-have-to.

Good Reads. "Howard Thurman Quotes." Accessed March 26, 2016. https://www .goodreads.com/author/quotes/56230.Howard_Thurman.

Good Reads. "Robert H. Schuller Quotes." Accessed February 2, 2016. http:// www.goodreads.com/quotes/938611-goals-are-not-only-absolutely-necessary-to -motivate-us-they.

Good Reads. "Viktor Frankl Quotes." Accessed February 23, 2016. https://www .goodreads.com/author/quotes/2782.Viktor_E_Frankl.

Goslin, D. *Engaging Minds: Motivation and Learning in America's Public Schools.* Lanham, MD: Scarecrow Press, 2003.

Griffin, R. Morgan. "Teen Abuse of Cough and Cold Medicine." Accessed June 23, 2016 http://www.webmd.com/parenting/teen-abuse-cough-medicine-9/teens- and-dxm-drug-abuse?page=1.

Grossman, Dave, and Gloria Dagaetano. *Stop Teaching Our Kids to Kill: A Call to Action against TV, Movie and Video Game Violence.* New York: Crown Publishers, 1999.

Hallfors, D., et al. "Which Comes First in Adolescence—Sex and Drugs or Depression?" *American Journal of Preventive Medicine* 29(3) (2005): 163–70.

Hallgren, M., T. Sjoland, H. Kallmen, and S. Andreasson. "Modifying Alcohol Consumption among High School Students: An Efficacy Trial of an Alcohol Risk Reduction Program (PRIME for Life)." *Health Education* 111 (3) (2011): 216–29.

Harrington, Rebecca. "Does Artificial Food Coloring Contribute to ADHD in Children?: The FDA Maintains Dyes Are Safe, But Some Studies Have Linked Them to Hyperactivity in Children." *Scientific American*, April 27, 2015. Accessed April 27, 2015. http://www.scientificamerican.com/article/does-artificial-food-coloring-contribute-to-adhd-in-children/.

Hazelden Betty Ford Foundation. "Club Drugs Linked to Sexual Assaults, Serious Health Effects." Accessed July 20, 2013. http://www.hazelden.org/web/public/ade00131.page.

Healio. "Cigarettes Were Once 'Physician' Tested, Approved: From the 1930s to the 1950s, 'Doctors' Once Lit Up the Pages of Cigarette Advertisement." March 10, 2009. Accessed February 28, 2016. http://www.healio.com/hematology-oncology/news/print/hemonc-today/%7B241d62a7-fe6e-4c5b-9fed-a33cc6e4bd7c%7D/cigarettes-were-once-physician-tested-approved.

HelpGuide.org. "Alcohol Abuse and Alcoholism." Accessed July 23, 2013. http://www.helpguide.org/mental/alcohol_abuse_alcoholism_signs_effects_treatment.htm.

HelpGuide.org. "Suicide Prevention." Accessed March 6, 2016. http://www.helpguide.org/articles/suicide-prevention/suicide-prevention-helping-someone-who-is-suicidal.htm.

Henry J. Kaiser Family Foundation and the National Center on Addiction and Substance Abuse at Columbia University. "Millions of Young People Mix Sex with Alcohol or Drugs—With Dangerous Consequences." January 30, 2002. Accessed February 20, 2016. http://kff.org/hivaids/fact-sheet/sexual-activity-and-substance-use-among-youth/.

Henry J. Kaiser Family Foundation. "Generation M2: Media in the Lives of 8- to 18-Year Olds." January 1, 2010. Accessed July 15, 2013. http://kff.org/other/poll-finding/report-generation-m2-media-in-the-lives/.

Herald Sun. "Casey Heynes Appearance on TV Won't Fix Issue Says Dr. Michael Carr-Gregg." Accessed July 30, 2013. http://www.heraldsun.com.au/news/special-reports/bully-victim-casey-haynes-faces-more-torment-after-tv-interview/story-fn85r9s4-1226024850202.

Hill, Napoleon. *Think and Grow Rich*. New York: Random House, 1937.

HSLDA. "Homeschool Progress Report 2009." Accessed January 20, 2013. http://www.hslda.org/docs/study/ray2009/2009_Ray_StudyFINAL.pdf.

Hsu, Tiffany. "Wal-Mart Worker Dies after Stampede in N.Y." *Los Angeles Times*, November 29, 2008. Accessed November 29, 2008. http://articles.latimes.com/2008/nov/29/nation/na-walmart-death29.

Hudson J., E. Hiripi, H. Pope, and R. Kessler. "The Prevalence and Correlates of Eating Disorders in the National Comorbidity Survey Replication." *Biological Psychiatry* 61 (2007): 348–58.

Jackson, C., S. Ennett, D. Dickinson, and J. Bowling. (2012). "Letting Children Sip: Understanding Why Parents Allow Alcohol Use by Elementary School-aged Children." *Archives of Pediatrics and Adolescent Medicine* 166(11) (2012): 1053–57.

Jacobs, D. "Youth Gambling in North America: Long-Term Trends and Future Prospects." In *Gambling Problems in Youth: Theoretical and Applied Perspectives*, edited by J. Derevensky and R. Gupta, 1–24. New York: Kluwer Academic/Plenum Publishers, 2004.

Jacobson, C., and M. Gould. "The Epidemiology and Phenomenology of Non-Suicidal Self Injurious Behavior among Adolescents: A Critical Review of the Literature." *Archives of Suicide Research* 11 (2007): 129–47.

James, W. "The Challenge of Childhood Obesity. *International Journal of Pediatric Obesity* 1 (2006): 7–10.

Jeffreys, Michael. *Success Secrets of the Motivational Superstars.* Rocklin, CA: Prima Lifestyles, 1996.

Jonides, L., V. Buschbacher, and S. Barlow. "Management of Child and Adolescent Obesity: Psychological, Emotional, and Behavioral Assessment." *Pediatrics* 110 (1) (2002): 215–21.

Kaplan, Karen. "About 88,000 U.S. Deaths Each Year Traced to Alcohol Use, Study Says." *Los Angeles Times*, March 13, 2014. Accessed January 13, 2016. http://www.latimes.com/science/sciencenow/la-sci-sn-alcohol-related-deaths-years-lost-sxsw-20140313-story.html.

Karlson, Jay. "10 Great Philanthropists Who Are Kids." Listverse, January 27, 2011. Accessed February 6, 2013. http://listverse.com/2011/01/27/10-great-philanthropists-who-are-kids/.

Kasl, Charlotte. *If the Buddha Had Kids: Raising Children to Create a More Peaceful World.* New York: Penguin, 2012. Used by permission.

Keitner, G., R. Archambault, C. Ryan, and I. Miller. "Family Therapy and Chronic Depression. *Journal of Clinical Psychology* 59(8) (2003): 873–84.

Kelly, Dan. "Experts Testify That Truant Parents Should Not Be Jailed." *Reading Eagle*, September 23, 2014. Accessed October 11, 2015. http://readingeagle.com/news/article/experts-testify-that-truant-parents-should-not-be-jailed&template=mobileart.

Kersey, Cynthia. *Unstoppable: 45 Powerful Stories of Perseverance and Triumph from People Just Like You.* Naperville, IL: Sourcebooks, 1998.

Keystone Treatment Center. "Alcohol Consumption Increasing in Girls and Young Women." Accessed March 16, 2016. http://www.keystonetreatment.com/addiction/articles/alcohol-consumption-young-women/.

KidsHealth.org. "Kids and Smoking." Accessed July 22, 2013. http://kidshealth.org/parent/positive/talk/smoking.html.

Kiess, W., et al. "Type 2 Diabetes Mellitus in Children and Adolescents." *Hormone Research* 59 (Suppl. 1) (2003): 77–84.

Kimmel, M. "Masculinity as Homophobia Fear, Shame, and Silence in the Construction of Gender Identity." In *Theorizing Masculinities*, edited by Harry Brod and Michael Kaufman, 227–41. Thousand Oaks, CA: SAGE, 1994. doi: 10.4135/9781452243627.n7.

Kimmel, M., and M. Mahler. "Adolescent Masculinity, Homophobia, and Violence." *American Behavioral Scientist* 46(10) (2003): 1439–58.

Klein, J., R. Jacobs, and M. Reinecke. "Cognitive Behavioral Therapy for Adolescent Depression: A Meta Analytic Investigation of Changes in Effect-Size Estimates."

Journal of the American Academy of Child and Adolescent Psychiatry 46 (2007): 1403–13.

Kohn, Alfie. *Punished by Rewards*. New York: Mariner Books, 1999.

Kolbert, E. "Spoiled Rotten: Why Do Kids Rule the Roost?" July 2, 2012. Accessed February 3, 2013, http://www.newyorker.com/arts/critics/books/2012/07/02/120702crbo_books_kolbert.

Kotz, Pete. "Phoebe Prince, 15, Commits Suicide after Onslaught of Cyber-Bullying from Fellow Students." True Crime Report, January 28, 2010. Accessed January 28, 2010. http://www.truecrimereport.com/2010/01/phoebe_prince_15_commits_suici.php.

Krimsky, G., and J. Peck. "Generation Rx Popping Pills." *Republican-American*, p. A1. June 12, 2005.

Landau, E. "Rejection, Bullying Are Risk Factors among Shooters." CNN, December 19, 2012. Accessed February 15, 2016. http://www.cnn.com/2012/12/18/health/ct-shooting-mental-illness/.

Lasser, K., et al., "Smoking and Mental Illness: A Population Based Prevalence Study." *Journal of the American Medical Association* 284 (2000): 2606–10.

Lavigne, Paula. "Youth Coaches Face Gambling Charges." ESPN.com, October 30, 2012. Accessed February 16, 2016. http://espn.go.com/espn/otl/story/_/id/8568724/nine-south-florida-youth-football-coaches-face-gambling-charges.

Law, R., et al. "Notes from the Field: Increase in Reported Adverse Health Effects Related to Synthetic Cannabionoid Use—United States, January–May 2015." *Morbidity and Mortality Weekly Report* 64(22): 618–19.

Lawlis, Frank. *Mending the Broken Bond*. New York: Penguin, 2007.

Leinwand, Donna. "Prescription Drugs Find Place in Teen Culture." *USA Today*. January 13, 2006.

Leman, Kevin. *The Birth Order Book: Why You Are the Way You Are*. Grand Rapids, MI: Revell, 2004.

Lenhart, Amanda. "Teens, Social Media and Technology Overview 2015." Pew Research Center, April 9, 2015. Accessed February 20, 2016. http://www.pewinternet.org/2015/04/09/teens-social-media-technology-2015/.

Lereya, S., W. Copeland, E. Costello, and D. Wolke. "Adult Mental Health Consequences of Peer Bullying and Maltreatment in Childhood: Two Cohorts in Two Countries." *The Lancet Psychiatry* 2(6) (2015): 524–31.

Lewin, Tamar. "Are These Parties for Real." *New York Times*, August 27, 2009.

Lewis, Helen. *Shame and Guilt in Neurosis*. New York: International University, 1971.

Lysiak, M. "Why Adam Lanza Did It." *Newsweek*, January 17, 2014. Accessed February 15, 2016. http://www.newsweek.com/why-adam-lanza-did-it-226565.

Males, Michael. "For Adults, Today's Youth Are Always the Worst." *Los Angeles Times*, November 21, 1999.

Maralani, V. "Understanding the Links between Education and Smoking." *Social Science Research* 48 (2014): 20–34.

Mark, J., et al. "Mindfulness-Based Cognitive Therapy for Preventing Relapse in Recurrent Depression: A Randomized Dismantling Trial." *Journal of Consulting and Clinical Psychology* 82(2) (2014): 275–86.

Maynard, Cindy. "Body Image." Accessed January 18, 2016. http://www.edreferral. com/body_image.htm.

Mayo Clinic. "Healthy Lifestyle: Tween and Teen Health." Accessed March 7, 2016. http://www.mayoclinic.org/healthy-lifestyle/tween-and-teen-health/in-depth/ teen-smoking/art-20046474?pg=2.

Mednick S. *Biological Bases of Antisocial Behavior*. Norwell: Kluwer, 1988.

Meeker, Margaret J. *Your Kids at Risk: How Teen Sex Threatens Our Sons and Daughters*. Washington, DC: Regnery, 2007.

Mendle, J., J. Jerrero, S. Moore, and K. Harden. "Depression and Adolescent Sexual Activity in Romantic and Nonromantic Relational Contexts: A Genetically-Informative Sibling Comparison." *Journal of Abnormal Psychology* 122(1) (2013): 51–63.

Moreton, Catherine. "10 Qualities That Made Abraham Lincoln a Great Leader." HR.BLR.com, June 25, 2008. Accessed February 4, 2013. https://hr.blr.com/ whitepapers/Staffing-Training/Leadership/10-Qualities-that-Made-Abraham-Lincoln-a-Great-Lea.

Morgan, Mandy. "Toddlers and Tears: The Sexualization of Young Girls." Deseret News, November 17, 2012. Accessed July 25, 2013. http://www.deseretnews. com/article/865567072/Toddlers-and-Tears-The-sexualization-of-young-girls. html?pg=all.

Morris, Regan. "Child Watch: The Apps That Let Parents 'Spy' on Their Kids." BBC News, January 2015. Accessed November 3, 2015. http://www.bbc.com/ news/technology-30930512.

Morton, B. "Social Influences on Adolescent Substance Use." *American Journal of Health Behavior* 31 (6) (2007): 672–84.

MSN.com. "Celebrities Speak about Eating Disorders." February 23, 2015. Accessed March 8, 2016. http://www.msn.com/en-gb/health/mindandbody/celebrities-speak-about-eating-disorders/ss-BBhSJu8#image=1.

Myers, Isabel, and Peter Myers. *Gifts Differing: Understanding Personality Type*. Mountain View, CA: Davies-Black, 1995.

Narain, Jaya. "Coroner Warns of Video Game Danger after Boy, 14, Dies: 18-Rating Is There for a Reason He Tells Distraught Mother." DailyMail.com, September 5, 2012. Accessed July 15, 2013. http://www.dailymail.co.uk/news/article-2198549/ coroner-warns-call-duty-video-game-danger-boy-14-dies-18-rating-reason-tells-distraught-mother.html.

NASP Resources: Helping children achieve their best. In school. At home. In life. 2013. Accessed February 13, 2013. http://www.nasponline.org/resources/home_ school/earlychildmotiv_ho.aspx.

National Conference of State Legislatures. "State Policies on Sex Education in Schools." Accessed February 20, 2016. http://www.ncsl.org/research/health/state-policies-on-sex-education-in-schools.aspx#1.

National Council on Problem Gambling. "Screening Tools." Accessed February 16, 2016. http://www.ncpgambling.org/wp-content/uploads/2014/08/problem_gam-blers_finances-a-guide-for-treatment-profs.pdf.

National Fire Protection Association. "Home Structure Fires." September 2015. http://www.nfpa.org.

National Institute of Mental Health. "Depression in Young and Teenage Boys." Accessed January 14, 2016. http://www.medicinenet.com/script/main/art. asp?articlekey=23376.

National Institute of Mental Health. "Depression: What You Need to Know." Accessed July 14, 2013. http://www.nimh.nih.gov/health/publications/depression/ complete-index.shtml#pub3.

National Institute of Mental Health. "Eating Disorders: About More Than Food." Accessed January 18, 2016. https://www.nimh.nih.gov/health/publications/eating-disorders-new-trifold/index.shtml.

National Institute of Mental Health. "What Are the Signs and Symptoms of Depression?" Accessed March 6, 2016. http://www.nimh.nih.gov/health/publications/ depression/what-are-the-signs-and-symptoms-of-depress.shtml.

National School Boards Association. "Bullying Definitions in State Anti-Bullying Statutes." Accessed February 28, 2012. https://www.nsba.org/sites/default/files/ reports/State_Anti-Bullying_Statutes_Definitions_02_2012.pdf.

National Survey on Drug Use and Health. "About the Survey." Accessed March 16, 2016. https://nsduhweb.rti.org/respweb/project_description.html.

NBCNews.com. "My Health News Daily: Most Kids Who Drink Get Alcohol from Family." February 17, 2011. Accessed July 22, 2013. http://www.nbcnews.com/ id/41647460/ns/health-addictions/t/most-kids-who-drink-get-alcohol-family/#. V2F5K_krKUk.

NEDA. "Anorexia Nervosa." Accessed January 18, 2016. http://www.nationaleating-disorders.org/anorexia-nervosa.

NEDA. "Binge Eating Disorder." Accessed January 18, 2016. https://www.nation-aleatingdisorders.org/binge-eating-disorder.

NEDA. "Bulimia Nervosa." Accessed January 18, 2016. https://www.nationaleating-disorders.org/bulimia-nervosa.

NEDA. "Find Help and Support." Accessed January 18, 2016. https://www.nation-aleatingdisorders.org/find-help-support.

NEDA. "Health Consequences of Eating Disorders." Accessed January 18, 2016. https://www.nationaleatingdisorders.org/health-consequences-eating-disorders.

New World Encyclopedia. "Suicide." March 6, 2016. http://www.newworldencyclo-pedia.org/entry/Suicide.

NIH. "Marijuana." Accessed December 12, 2015. http://www.drugabuse.gov/PDF/ RRMarijuana.pdf.

NIH. "Marijuana: Facts Parents Need to Know." Accessed February 22, 2016. http:// www.nida.nih.gov/MarijBroch/parentpg9-10N.html#Effects.

Office of the Surgeon General (U.S.); National Center for Injury Prevention and Control (U.S.); National Institute of Mental Health (U.S.); Center for Mental Health Services (U.S.). *Youth Violence: A Report of the Surgeon General.* 2001. Rockville, MD: Office of the Surgeon General (U.S.).

Office of the UN Special Envoy for Global Education, July 20, 2013, http://educa-tionenvoy.org.

Organic Consumers Association. "Scientists Report 80% of Cancer Cases Caused by Environmental and Food Carcinogens." June 28, 2004. Accessed March 8, 2016. http://www.organicconsumers.org/foodsafety/cancer070104.cfm.

Orpinas, P., A. Home, X. Song, P. Reeves, and H. Hsieh. "Dating Trajectories from Middle to High School: Association with Academic Performance and Drug Use." *Journal of Research on Adolescence* 23(4) (2013): 772–84.

Orygen Youth Health Research Centre. *Intellectual Disability Mental Health First Aid Manual. 2nd Edition*. University of Melbourne. Accessed February 24, 2016. https://www.adhc.nsw.gov.au/__data/assets/file/0008/338813/Intellectual_Disability_Mental_Health_First_Aid_Manual_2nd_ed.pdf.

Pappas, Stephanie. "2C-I or 'Smiles': The New Killer Drug Every Parent Should Know About." LiveScience.com, September 21, 2012. Accessed July 19, 2013. http://www.livescience.com/23388-designer-drug-smiles-teen-deaths.html.

Partnership for Drug-Free Kids. "Prescription for Danger: A Report on the Troubling Trend of Prescription and Over-the-Counter Drug Abuse among the Nation's Teens." Accessed January 4, 2016. https://www.drugfreeactionalliance.org/files/downloadables/background-knowledge/B-Prescription-for-Danger.pdf.

Partnership for Drug-Free Kids. "The Partnership Attitude Tracking Study: Teens and Parents 2013." Accessed June 23, 2016. http://www.drugfree.org/wp-content/uploads/2014/07/PATS-2013-FULL-REPORT.pdf.

Payne, Kim, and Lisa Ross. *Simplicity Parenting: Using the Extraordinary Power of Less to Raise Calmer, Happier, and More Secure Kids*. New York: Ballantine Books, 2010.

PBS.org. "Binge Eating Disorder." Accessed January 18, 2016. http://www.pbs.org/perfectillusions/eatingdisorders/bingeeating.html.

Peretti, Frank. *No More Bullies: For Those Who Wound or Are Wounded*. Nashville, TN: W Publishing Group, 2000.

Peters, Joe. *Cry Silent Tears*. New York: Harper Element, 2008.

Phelps, Michael, and Brian Cazeneuve. *Beneath the Surface: My Story*. New York: Sports Publishing, 2012.

Phillips, K., and W. Menard. "Suicidality in Body Dysmorphic Disorder: A Prospective Study. *Journal of Marriage and Family* 163 (2006): 1280–82.

Powell, Kara. "Does Sexting Take the Place of Sex for Teenagers?" FYI, September 27, 2012. Accessed July 18, 2013. http://fulleryouthinstitute.org/blog/does-sexting-take-the-place-of-sex-for-teenagers.

Psychology. "Emotional Development – Early infancy (birth–six months), Later infancy months (7–12). Accessed October 21, 2015. http://psychology.jrank.org/pages/212/Emotional-Development.html.

Psychology Today. "Bulimia Nervosa." Accessed March 8, 2016. https://www.psychologytoday.com/conditions/bulimia-nervosa.

Quigley, Rachel, Thomas Durante, Hayley Peterson, and Michael Zennie. "How 'Ticking Time Bomb' Adam Lanza Went from 'Genius' Tech Geek Who Grew Up in a $1.6 Million Home to Heartless Killer." DailyMail.com, December 16, 2012. Accessed February 16, 2016. http://www.dailymail.co.uk/news/article-2248782/Adam-Lanza-How-classmates-remember-genius-turned-heartless-killer.html.

Quotes. "Famous Quotes and Sayings." Accessed November 13, 2015. http://www.quotes.net/quote/1931.

Quotes-Messages. Accessed March 16, 2016. http://www.quotes-messages.com/search-list.

Ratey, John. *Spark: The Revolutionary New Science of Exercise and the Brain*. New York: Hatchett, 2008.

Ray, Brian D. "Research Facts on Homeschooling." NHERI, March 23, 2016. Accessed March 23, 2016. http://www.nheri.org/research/research-facts-on-homeschooling.html.

Rector, R. E., K. A. Johnson, and L. R. Noyes. "Sexually Active Teenagers Are More Likely to Be Depressed and to Attempt Suicide." *Center for Data Analysis Report*, *#03-04* (2003).

Religious Tolerance. "Shootings, Other Violence, and Bullying in American Schools." Accessed February 15, 2016. http://www.religioustolerance.org/sch_viol.htm.

Resolute Treatment Center. "Causes and Symptoms of Sexually Maladaptive Behaviors." Accessed February 20, 2016. http://www.resolutetreatmentcenter.com/behavioral/sexually-maladaptive/symptoms-effects.

Ribeiro, John. "Social App Skout Suspends Teen Community after Rape Allegations." *PC World*, June 13, 2012. Accessed February 20, 2016. http://www.pcworld.com/article/257505/social_app_skout_suspends_teen_community_after_rape_allegations.html.

Right Step. "Heroin: A Rising Teen Fad." January 13, 2004. Accessed February 22, 2016. https://www.rightstep.com/teen-drug-addiction/heroin-a-rising-teen-fad/.

Russell, S., and K. Joyner. "Adolescent Sexual Orientation and Suicide Risk: Evidence from a National Study." *American Journal of Public Health* 91 (2001): 1276–81.

Sameroff, A., R. Seifer, R. Barocas, M. Zax, and S. Greenspan. "Intelligence Quotient Scores of 4-Year-Old Children: Social-Environmental Risk Factors." *Pediatrics* 79 (1987): 343–50.

SAMHSA. "Behavioral Health Trends in the United States: Results from the 2014 National Survey on Drug Use and Health." Accessed March 6, 2016. http://www.samhsa.gov/data/sites/default/files/NSDUH-FRR1-2014/NSDUH-FRR1-2014.pdf.

SAMHSA. "Find a Facility in Your State." Accessed February 22, 2016. https://findtreatment.samhsa.gov/TreatmentLocator/faces/quickSearch.jspx.

Sargent, Laurie. *Delight in Your Child's Design*. Carol Stream, IL: Tyndale House Publishers, 2005.

Saskatchewan. "Problem Gambling and Youth." Accessed July 16, 2013. https://www.saskatchewan.ca/residents/health/accessing-health-care-services/mental-health-and-addictions-support-services/gambling-support/problem-gambling-resources#problem-gambling-and-youth.

Schorn, Daniel. "Natalie Holloway: New Clues." CBSNews.com, March 22, 2006. Accessed July 21, 2013. http://www.cbsnews.com/stories/2006/03/22/48hours/main1430644.shtml.

Science Daily. "Children Whose Parents Smoked Are Twice as Likely to Begin Smoking between 13 And 21." Accessed February 28, 2016. http://www.sciencedaily.com/releases/2005/09/050929082408.htm.

Science Daily. "Talking and Treating Erectile Dysfunction." February 14, 2009. Accessed February 14, 2009. http://www.sciencedaily.com/releases/2009/02/090204172216. htm.

Shah, Anup. "Children as Consumers." Global Issues, November 21, 2010. Accessed January 11, 2013. http://www.globalissues.org/print/article/237.

Shilling, Chris. *The Body and Social Theory.* London: SAGE, 2003.

Shimoff, Marci. *Happy for No Reason: 7 Steps to Being Happy from the Inside Out.* New York: Atria, 2009.

Sidman, Jessica. "A College Student's Death May Help Save Lives." USAToday. com, June 26, 2006. Accessed February 23, 2016. http://usatoday30.usatoday.com/ news/health/2006-06-26-spady-binge-drinking_x.htm.

Siegel, Bernie. *Peace, Love and Healing.* New York: HarperCollins Publishers, 1989.

Smith, Aaron. "Marijuana Legalization Passes in Colorado, Washington." CNN.com, November 8, 2012. Accessed July 20, 2013. http://money.cnn.com/2012/11/07/ news/economy/marijuana-legalization-washington-colorado/index.html.

Smith, L. "World Day against Child Labour 2015: Facts and Figures about Children in Forced Labour," June 12, 2015. Accessed November 16, 2015. http://www. ibtimes.co.uk/world-day-against-child-labour-2015-facts-figures-aboutchildren-forced-labour-1505675.

Snegireff, L., and O. Lombard. "Survey of Smoking Habits of Massachusetts Physicians." *New England Journal of Medicine* 250 (24) (1954): 1042–45.

St. Joseph's Care Group. "Youth Addiction Program." Accessed February 19, 2016. http://www.mha.sjcg.net/as/gambling/youth/.

Steve268. "Online Gambling Has Ruined My Life." Gambling Therapy, September 27, 2012. Accessed September 27, 2013. https://www.gamblingtherapy.org/ online-gambling-has-ruined-my-life.

Stewart, Dodai. "'Bulimia and Anorexia since I Was 15': Lady Gaga Responds to 'Fat' Headlines with Half-Naked Pics and a Confession." Jezebel.com, September 25, 2012. Accessed July 24, 2013. http://jezebel.com/5946233/?post=52965115.

Successories. "Jon Kelly Quotes." Accessed February 16, 2016. http://www.successories.com/iquote/author/29830/jon-kelly-quotes/1.

Sugar, S., and J. Stoeber. "Perfectionism, Fear of Failure, and Affective Responses to Success and Failure: The Central Role of Fear of Experiencing Shame and Embarrassment." *Journal of Sport & Exercise Psychology* 31 (5) (2009): 602–27.

Suicide.org. "Suicide Hotlines." Accessed March 6, 2016. http://www.suicide.org/.

Teen Rehab Center. "What Is Drug Rehab?" Accessed February 22, 2016. https:// www.teenrehabcenter.org/rehab/.

Teen Suicide. "Teen Suicide Warning Signs." Accessed March 10, 2016. http://www. teensuicide.us/articles2.html.

Teesson, M., T. Slade, and K. Mills. "Comorbidity in Australia: Findings of the 2007 National Survey of Mental Health and Wellbeing." *Australian and New Zealand Journal of Psychiatry* 43 (2009): 606–14.

Times. "American Psycho." Accessed February 15, 2016. http://www.timesonline. co.uk/tol/news/world/us_and_americas/article1686784.ece.

Too Smart to Start. "Signs of Underage Alcohol Use." Accessed February 24, 2016. http://toosmarttostart.samhsa.gov/educators/signs/default.aspx.

Twenge, J., and W. Campbell. *The Narcissism Epidemic: Living in the Age of Entitlement.* New York: Free Press, 2010.

United States Census Bureau. "America's Families and Living Arrangements: 2013: Children." Accessed October 20, 2015. https://www.census.gov/hhes/families/data/cps2013C.html.

U.S. Department of Health and Human Services. *The Surgeon General's Call to Action to Prevent and Reduce Underage Drinking 2007.* Accessed February 24, 2016. http://www.camy.org/_docs/resources/fact-sheets/call_to_action.pdf.

U.S. National Library of Medicine. "Chronic Obstructive Pulmonary Disease." Accessed March 7, 2016. https://www.nlm.nih.gov/medlineplus/ency/article/000091.htm.

USDA. "Recommended Daily Caloric Intake." Accessed December 29, 2015. https://www.getfit.tn.gov/fitnesstracker/calorie_levels.pdf.

Wade, T., A. Keski-Rahkonen, and J. Hudson. "Epidemiology of Eating Disorders." In *Textbook in Psychiatric Epidemiology* (3rd ed.), edited by M. Tsuang and M. Tohen, 343–60. New York: Wiley, 2011.

Wallace, Kelly. "How to Make Your Kid Hate Sports without Really Trying." CNN.com, January 21, 2016. http://http://www.cnn.com/2016/01/21/health/kids-youth-sports-parents/.

Washington Post. "'You Forced Me into a Corner,' Cho Says." April 19, 2007. Accessed February 15, 2016. http://www.washingtonpost.com/wp-dyn/content/article/2007/04/18/AR2007041802789.html.

Washington Times. "142 School Shootings since Sandy Hook Massacre in Newtown, Conn." October 1, 2015. Accessed February 15, 2016. http://www.washingtontimes.com/news/2015/oct/1/142-school-shootings-sandy-hook-massacre-newtown-c/.

Way, Mish. "Teen Mom: The Most Depressing Show on Earth." *Hearty Magazine,* December 10, 2009.

WebMD.com. "Causes of Depression." Accessed January 14, 2016. http://www.webmd.com/depression/guide/causes-depression.

WebMD.com, "Slideshow: Surprising Ways Smoking Affects Your Looks and Life." Accessed June 23, 2016. http://www.webmd.com/smoking-cessation/ss/slideshow-ways-smoking-affects-looks.

Weiss, L. H., and J. C. Schwarz. "The Relationship between Parenting Types and Older Adolescents' Personality, Academic Achievement, Adjustment, and Substance Use." *Child Development* 67(5) (1996): 2101–14.

Weissman, M. "Recent Non-Medication Trials of Interpersonal Psychotherapy for Depression." *International Journal of Neuropsychopharmacology* 10 (2006): 117–22.

Whfoods.org. "What does GMO mean?" Accessed July 28, 2013. http://whfoods.org/genpage.php?tname=dailytip&dbid=345.

Wilson, G., C. Grilo, and K. Vitousek. "Psychological Treatment of Eating Disorders." *American Psychologist* 62 (2007): 199–216.

Withers, Ian. "National Governors' Spouses Association Winter Meeting." MADD. org, February 28, 2012. Accessed July 21, 2013. http://www.madd.org/blog/2012/february/POP_Governorsspouse.html.

World Health Organization. "Obesity and Overweight." January 2015. Accessed July 29, 2013. http://www.who.int/mediacentre/factsheets/fs311/en/.

World Health Organization. "Physical Activity and Young People." Accessed June 24, 2016. http://www.who.int/dietphysicalactivity/factsheet_young_people/en/.

World Health Organization. "Tobacco." Accessed July 6, 2015. http://www.who.int/mediacentre/factsheets/fs339/en/.

Wurtzel, Elizabeth. *Prozac Nation: Young and Depressed in America*. Boston: Houghton Mifflin, 1994.

Zdanowicz, Christina. "Teen Narrowly Escapes Death after Smoking Synthetic Marijuana." CNN.com, February 5, 2013. Accessed July 19, 2013. http://www.cnn.com/2013/02/04/health/synthetic-marijuana-irpt.

Zeigler, D., et al. "The Neurocognitive Effects of Alcohol on Adolescents and College Students." *Preventive Medicine* 40 (2005): 23–32.

Index

About the Author

Douglas Haddad, PhD, has worked as a middle school teacher, coach, mentor, nutritionist, and inspirational speaker. Dr. Haddad was awarded the 2016–2017 Teacher of the Year by the Simsbury School District and named a 2017 Teacher-Ambassador in Public Education for the State of Connecticut. He has spoken with hundreds of parents and has worked with them to better understand and communicate with their children in a loving way. Through his innovative teaching styles and educational games, music, and videos he has originally created for children, Dr. Doug has helped different learners become motivated, set goals, self-manage, learn how to make good choices, become self-reliant and stable-minded, achieve healthy lifestyle habits, and navigate through peer pressures to overcome the many challenges they are faced with each day. Dr. Doug has written for and been featured in many national magazines and popular online websites and is a regular guest expert on television discussing topics related to parenting, education, and health and wellness.

For more information on empowering you and your child, check out Dr. Doug's official website: www.douglashaddad.com.